JUAN LANDAETA

LIFE IN A TEST-TUBE

MEDICAL AND ETHICAL ISSUES FACING SOCIETY TODAY

DR DANIEL CH. OVERDUIN
FR JOHN I. FLEMING

National Library of Australia
Cataloguing-in-Publication data

Overduin, Daniel Ch. (Daniel Christiaan).
Life in a test-tube.

Includes bibliographical references and index.
ISBN 0 85910 203 3.

1. Medical ethics. 2. Life. 3. Christian ethics.
I. Fleming, John I., 1943- . II. Title.

174'.2

First printing August 1982
Second printing December 1982
Third printing July 1983

Printed and published by
Lutheran Publishing House,
205 Halifax Street, Adelaide, South Australia

Cover designed by Wolfgang Rogge.

I will neither give a deadly drug to anybody if asked for it, nor will I make a suggestion to this effect. Similarly I will not give to a woman an abortive remedy. In purity and holiness I will guard my life and my art.

The Oath of Hippocrates, sixth century BC

I will maintain the utmost respect for human life from the time of conception; even under threat, I will not use my medical knowledge contrary to the laws of humanity.

The Declaration of Geneva,
World Medical Association, 1948

In research on man, the interest of science and society should never take precedence over considerations related to the well-being of the subject.

The Declaration of Helsinki,
World Medical Association, 1964, 1975

Inspire me with love for my art and for Thy creatures. Do not allow thirst for profit, ambition for renown and admiration, to interfere with my profession, for these are the enemies of truth and of love for mankind and they can lead astray in the great task of attending to the welfare of Thy creatures.

Daily Prayer of a Physician,
Moses Maimonides, twelfth century

Sometimes success is in the doctors' hands, since they in turn will beseech the Lord to grant them the grace to relieve and to heal, that life may be saved.

Ecclesiasticus 38:13,14

ACKNOWLEDGMENTS

The book is the result of several years of continuing research, lecturing, and writing at home and abroad.

Our interest in biomedical, socio-legal, and medical-moral issues stems from our social consciousness.

It is written because of a deep-felt concern about what is happening in hospitals, in research laboratories, and in society-at-large.

The bioethical dimensions of personal morality, professional ethics, and community standards are discussed in relation to sixteen medical-moral issues pertaining to human life and death.

We are indebted to Meredith Kidd who typed the final manuscript, and to Annelie Brixius who read and checked the manuscript.

We gratefully acknowledge both the valuable research and writings of others which we have used, and the encouragement of our loved ones and friends.

Last but not least, we thank the editor and staff of the Lutheran Publishing House for their advice and for publishing this book in an attractive and useful format.

The Authors

FOREWORD

The last 30 years have seen wondrous advances in science. Never before has man had such power. He has the capability to manipulate and control the environment. He can already manipulate human reproduction, and is even confronting the challenge of human replication. He can now bring about destruction on a global scale in a few moments.

The same 30 years have seen a major revolution in social behaviour, affecting virtually every aspect of our lives. Many factors have been involved in this process. Important among these are such things as the effects of urbanization, the immense power (for good or ill) of the media of mass communication, and the progressive growth of bureaucracy. Thus, gradually, pressures have developed which threaten our sense of individualness and our apparent capacity to make decisions governing our personal lives.

In response to these pressures, there has been a growing demand for personal freedom and a concentration upon the rights of the individual at the expense of (and often with rejection of the notion of) communal responsibility. In Western society, there has been a concurrent growth of economic power, extending into a larger proportion of the population. When combined, these factors have resulted in the growth of the cult of materialism, and a progressive widening of the gap in the community between the poor or underprivileged minority and the well-to-do majority.

It would be surprising if traditional teachings and authority structures had survived unchallenged through all this. Indeed, it is widely acknowledged that they have not. In recent years, the Church, at one time our accepted guide in moral and ethical matters, has been seen to be more and more irrelevant by more and more people. Nor has any alternative source of ethical guidance developed.

So we have moved into a situation where our power grows greater at a time when the rules for the use of power and the sense of public responsibility are progressively less and less compelling. Put another way, the development of scientific technology has far outpaced the growth of ethical understanding in our society.

One senses, however, a disquiet with the way things are moving. This is particularly true of younger people and of students. Symptomatic of this concern is a dialogue I have had in recent years with medical students regarding the understanding of ethical factors in medical decision-making. This has resulted in a 'pilot course' in Medical Ethics (in the real meaning of the word), organized in 1981 by students at the University of Adelaide, and its further extension in 1982.

I was encouraged in pursuing my discussions with the medical students by my long-standing friendship with Dr Overduin. Frequently over the years, we have had vigorous discussions on questions of ethics. It was not by accident that I turned to him, as a professional ethicist, to help us plan and undertake our course on medical ethics.

My friendship with Father Fleming spans an almost equal period of time. I have always recognized him to be an astute observer and a keen student of society, but especially I admire his skills with the English language — in both its spoken and written forms. He is what we call today a 'good communicator'.

So it was with considerable enthusiasm and expectation that I undertook my first reading of this book. That accomplished, it is with the same enthusiasm and much pleasure that I approach the writing of this foreword to their combined work.

Here is a treatise, based on sound research and scholarship, which considers the ethical aspects of a range of major issues confronting our society today. The approach is different from any other I have seen in this field. The writers have reviewed for each topic the development of ethical ideas in the Judean tradition, in the orthodox Christian religions, in the fundamental Christian view (where this is available), and finally from the secular humanistic viewpoint. Only a real expert who is genuinely familiar with his subject material could reduce this task to manageable proportions. This they have done, and they have presented their condensation in a pleasantly readable and easily understood form.

The authors do not stop at a mere compendium. Rather, they raise lots of questions, and they move easily to the task of providing the reader with clear guidance as to how they consider the *mores* of modern society should be encouraged to evolve. They seek to bring this about in such a way that we maintain continuity with our heritage while developing an accommodation with our changed circumstances and our vastly-increased power. Constraints of space have meant that the logic involved in reaching these conclusions is sometimes frugally documented. I am sure they will be criticized for this; but to have attempted to meet this objection would have expanded the book to unwieldy proportions and would have completely changed its objectives and general interest.

As it is, for readers with no particular religious affiliation and for Christians alike, this book represents an important opportunity to be informed about many of the major ethical issues of our day. It provides a review of the historical development of ideas relevant to these problems.

Ultimately, it must be in public discussion and debate of these issues that our ethic will be formulated. Concerned citizens who would wish to promote an ethic which has as its objective the genuine well-being of all members of our society in a responsible and longer-term view, will welcome this volume as an important and timely contribution. I certainly do. I congratulate the authors on their achievement, and I commend this volume to you.

Dr E.G. Cleary, M.D., B.S., F.R.A.C.P.
Reader in Pathology, Medical School,
University of Adelaide, South Australia.

CONTENTS

INTRODUCTION

Religious and Moral Traditions in Health Care
The Revolution in Medical Science
The Social Implications
The Moral Imperative

Religious and Moral Traditions in Health Care

Everyone wants to be healthy and active. To be sick, infirm, disabled, or hospitalized is unattractive, something to be avoided. No wonder, then, that the quality of health care is one of society's most important human concerns. Indeed, most societies strive to provide excellence in both private and public health care.

The importance to us of good health has meant that the healing profession has been seen as a very 'honourable' profession, especially in the Jewish and Christian traditions.

The concept of health care enshrined in those great religious traditions is not simply a 'caring for one's body' in a limited physical sense. There was such a deep understanding of the spiritual and psychological aspects of health care that the roles of both priest and physician were often combined in the work of one and the same person.

For an understanding of health care in the Jewish tradition, the Old Testament, especially the teachings of the *Torah*, together with the *Talmud* and *Halakah*, are indispensable sources. (The *Torah* is the Law; the *Talmud* the two commentaries on the *Mishnah* [AD 375 and 500], the revealed 'instruction' on the meaning of Jewish scripture; and the *Halakah* contains 'the body of legal decisions not directly enacted in the *Torah*'.)

The Christian tradition of health care owes much to the medical ethics of Judaism. However, Christian theologians in general, and those of the Reformation tradition in particular, have shown far less interest in medical science and its moral imperatives than Jewish rabbinic scholars.

The concern for people's health is nowhere more evident in the Jewish (and Christian) tradition than in the *Torah* which is part of the Old Testament of the Christian's Bible. This concern for health is deeply connected with the spiritual and psycho-social health of the people. For example, the Hebrew word *shalēm*, healthy or whole, has the same origin as *shalōm*, peace. And the ancient Hebrews were alert to the close interrelationship of godliness and health.

> If you will diligently hearken to the voice of the LORD your God, and do that which is right in his eyes, and give heed to his commandments and keep all his statutes, I will put none of the diseases upon you which I put upon the Egyptians; for I am the LORD, your healer (Exodus 15:26).

The primary emphasis of the *Torah* is on the prevention of illness.

> Because of this unique therapeutic emphasis, Moses may well be spoken of as the father of preventive medicine. In the medical enactments of the Pentateuch (the Five Books of Moses), social hygiene was elevated to the level of science, and the precepts of the Mosaic era survive to the present as a model of sanitary and hygienic insight. The medical code received its most comprehensive expression in Leviticus. This is, in effect, a priestly handbook (R.K. Harrison).

The basic necessities for good health in the *Torah* may be summarized as rest, good food, circumcision, sexual hygiene, sexual relationships, cleanliness, and sanitation.

Rest: The provisions of the Sabbath law in Exodus 31:13–17 and 23:12 may just as easily be viewed as health regulations. Man is required to work for six days, but on the seventh day he must rest. This mandatory 'rest' is applied even to the land itself to ensure the continued fertility of the soil; this 'sabbath of the land' is described in Leviticus 25:2-7.

Diet: Dietary rules, set out in Leviticus 11 and Deuteronomy 14, were designed for the individual and communal health of the ancient people of Israel.

Circumcision: Circumcision of males had a deep religious significance according to Genesis 17:9-14. It was the only form of physical mutilation which the law sanctioned. It had, and still has, in certain environmental and social circumstances, positive hygienic value of a preventive kind.

Male circumcision should not be confused, as an issue, with the abhorrent practice of 'female circumcision', genital and sexual mutilation to which millions of girls and women in Africa and the Middle East are forced to subject themselves (cf 'Hosken Report', published by *WIN News*, 1979).

Sexual Hygiene: The regulations in Leviticus 15 relating to sexual hygiene, and the prohibition in Leviticus 20:18 of the deliberate practice of intercourse during the woman's catamenia (menstruation), were designed for the maintenance of physical health and the psychological health of the women.

Sexual Relationships: The laws on sexual relationships in Leviticus 18 were designed to safeguard the moral, sociological, and biological 'health' of the nation.

Cleanliness and Sanitation: Great emphasis was given to the need to wash one's body and one's clothes. This is clear from a reading of the purification rituals in Leviticus 14 and the purpose of the bronze laver in Exodus 30:17-21. As well, Deuteronomy 23:10-14 lays down carefully-regulated sanitary procedures.

Of course, the Old Testament is not a medical text-book. It does not provide us with the facts of medical science or with *materia medica* (remedial substances used in the practice of medicine) in the technical sense of the term. But it is important to remember that Israel was called to look to God for healing: 'For I am the LORD your healer' (Exodus 15:26 RSV). Some Jewish commentators maintained that these words demand a total rejection of medicine and physicians — a view also found in some extreme Christian sects.

Healing is, in the best tradition of both Judaism and Christendom, an activity of both the intellect and faith. The New Testament, which describes the activities of Christ and his apostles, places due emphasis on their 'healing ministry'.

Jesus healed 'every disease' (Matthew 4:23; 9:35; Mark 1:34; Luke 4:40; 6:17,18; 7:21) and gave authority to heal to his twelve disciples (Matthew 10:1; Mark 3:15; Luke 9:1). Healing 'miracles' as part of Christ's ministry are frequently mentioned (Matthew 11:4-6; Mark 1:29-31, 40-45; Luke 5:17).

After Pentecost, the apostles of Christ continued their work of healing (Acts 5:16; 19:11,12); and among the 'gifts of the Holy Spirit' healing is also mentioned (1 Corinthians 12:9,28,30). St James exhorts the sick to call upon the 'elders of the church' to 'save' them through the anointing with oil and with prayer (James 5:14-16).

Christ, on the other hand, clearly stated that the sick are in need of a physician (Matthew 9:12; Mark 2:17). And in Ecclesiasticus 38:1-15, Ben Sira has written beautifully of both the art of a physician and the responsibility of the sick person:

> Honour the doctor with the honour that is his due in return for his services; for he too has been created by the Lord. Healing itself comes from the Most High, like a gift from a king. The doctor's learning keeps his head high, he is regarded with awe by potentates. The Lord has brought medicines into existence from the earth, and the sensible man will not despise them. Did not a piece of wood once sweeten the water, thus giving proof of its virtue? He has also given men learning so that they may glory in his mighty works. He uses them to heal and to relieve pain, the chemist makes up a mixture from them. Thus there is no end to his activities, and through him health extends across the world. My son, when you are ill, do not be depressed, but pray to the Lord and he will heal you. Renounce your faults, keep your hands unsoiled, and cleanse your heart from all sin. Offer incense and a memorial of fine flour, and make as rich an offering as you can afford. Then let the doctor take over — the Lord created him too — and do not let him leave you, for you need him. Sometimes success is in their hands, since they in turn will beseech the Lord to grant them the grace to relieve and to heal, that life may be saved. A man sins in the eyes of his Maker if he defies the doctor (*Jerusalem Bible*. Note: the last sentence is the footnote translation).

In the context of health care, the Judaic and Christian traditions both emphasize the profound respect we ought to have for the life and welfare of the patient. The Sacred Scriptures of Judaism and Christianity contain fundamental principles on which several *Codes for the Practice of Medicine* have been based; but those writings do not themselves contain explicit codes for the practice of medicine.

In our consideration of moral perspectives in health care, it is important, therefore, to briefly refer to a number of 'General Codes' some of which are based on the Jewish and Christian traditions, and some of which are not.

A very early and important summary of medical ethics is the Oath of Hippocrates (sixth century BC). This contains the basic 'creed' to which all doctors should subscribe. It says in part:

> I will keep them (the patients) from harm and injustice. I will neither give a deadly drug to anybody if asked for it, nor will I make a suggestion to this effect. Similarly I will not give to a woman an abortive remedy. In purity and holiness I will guard my life and my art.

The Indian physician Caraka wrote the ancient Indian oath for medical students around the first century AD. It is different from the Hippocratic oath, but it contains some significant and controversial moral imperatives.

> Thou shalt behave and act without arrogance, with care and attention and with undistracted mind, humility, constant reflection and ungrudging obedience (to your teacher) ... Day and night, however thou mayest be engaged, thou shalt endeavour for the relief of patients with all thy heart and soul. Thou shalt not desert or injure thy patients for the sake of thy life or thy living ... Those who are extremely abnormal, wicked, and of miserable character and conduct, those who have not vindicated their honour, those who are on the point of death, and similarly women who are unattended by their husbands or guardians shall not receive treatment.

The oldest Hebrew medical text was written by a Hebrew physician, Asaph Judaeus, in the sixth century AD. The Oath of Asaph contains the following warnings:

> Take heed that ye kill not any man with the sap of a root; and ye shall not dispense a potion to a woman with child by adultery to cause her to miscarry ... Put your trust in the Lord your God, the God of truth, the living God, for He doth kill and make alive, smite and heal ... Ye shall not cause the shedding of blood by any manner of medical treatment. Take heed that ye do not cause a malady to any man; and ye shall not cause any man injury by hastening to cut through flesh and blood with an iron instrument or by branding, but shall first observe twice and thrice and only then shall ye give your counsel.

In *Advice to a Physician* given by a Persian physician and ethicist, Haly Abbas, who died in 994 AD, we find:

> You are to prohibit the unsuited and undeserving from studying medicine. A physician is to prudently treat his patients with food and medicine out of good and spiritual motives, not for the sake of gain. He should never prescribe or use a harmful drug or abortifacient ... He must not drink alcohol because it injures the brain. He must study medical books constantly and never grow tired of research ... A medical student should be constantly present in the hospital so as to study disease processes and complications under the learned professor and proficient physicians.

In the Chinese statement on medical ethics called *Five Commandments and Ten Requirements* (1617), it is written:

> 1. Physicians should be ever ready to respond to any calls of patients, high or low, rich or poor. They should treat them equally and care not for financial reward ...
> 3. ... Patients should be instructed, if necessary, how to mix the prescriptions themselves in order to avoid suspicion ...
> 5. Prostitutes should be treated just like patients from a good family, and gratuitous services should be given to the poor ones.

Mohammed Hosin Aghili of Shiraz advises in his 1770 *A Physician's Ethical Duties* that a doctor

> must be energetic in studying diseases and drugs and earnest in the diagnosis and treatment of a patient or disease. If he is not successful in the treatment of a case or if he has found the patient did not have confidence in his work or that the patient would like to refer to another physician, it is better to offer an excuse and ask him to consult another physician. He must not be prejudiced against any method of treatment and never continue any wrong practice.

When the American Medical Association was founded in 1847, its first work was the formulation of a *Code of Ethics*. The Code relied heavily on the work of the Englishman Thomas Percival, and consists of three chapters containing a total of eleven articles. Chapter I, Article 1, deals with the 'Duties of Physicians to Their Patients':

> The physician should be the minister of hope and comfort to the sick . . . The life of a sick person can be shortened not only by the acts, but also by the words or the manner of a physician.

This rather lengthy document also provides interesting reading concerning 'Obligations of Patients to Their Physicians'; 'Professional Services of Physicians to Each Other'; 'Duties of the Profession to the Public', and other relevant subjects.

The well-known *Declaration of Geneva*, issued by the World Medical Association in 1948, states in part:

> I will maintain the utmost respect for human life from the time of conception; even under threat, I will not use my medical knowledge contrary to the laws of humanity.

The same Association in 1949 issued an *International Code of Medical Ethics*, which contains the sentence: 'A doctor must always bear in mind the obligation of preserving human life'. In the original draft, this sentence was expanded by the addition of the words: 'from conception. Therapeutic abortion may only be performed if the conscience of the doctors and the national laws permit.' However, these words were deleted from the final adopted version of the Code!

Reference could be made to the *Principles of Medical Ethics (1957) with Reports and Statements* (American Medical Association), the *Oath of Soviet Physicians* (1971), the *Ethical and Religious Directives for Catholic Health Facilities* (United States Catholic Conference, 1971) and *Medical Ethics, Statements of Policy Definitions and Rules*

(British Medical Association, 1974). However, because of the nature and length of this Introduction, the few quotations cited will give readers a sufficient basis for reflection as they take up this book dealing with a number of moral-medical issues.

Among the vital questions relating to the very essence and practice of health care, we have to consider:

1. Who is to determine the fundamental values by which we live and act?
2. What judgments should we pass on the current explosion of knowledge and its application in the fields of medicine, life sciences, biomedical engineering, and genetics?
3. How do we evaluate the activities of those working and experimenting in the areas of life sciences, medicine, and health care?
4. How can we arrive at an ethic advantageous to the common good of all (including doctors and their patients)?

These and other questions will be examined in this book. Our purpose is to arrive at a clearer understanding of 'the obligation of a moral nature which governs the practice of medicine' (cf G.R. Dunstan's 'Introduction' to the 1981 revised and enlarged edition of the *Dictionary of Medical Ethics*).

The Revolution in Medical Science

The closing decades of the twentieth century are being characterized by enormous advances in medical science. Socio-medical and bioethical issues have multiplied as modern medicine and related disciplines have revolutionized what is technologically real and possible in those fields. We read in the popular press about sex chips, test-tube babies, surrogate mothers (the 'rent-a-womb' business), frozen embryos, clones, and bodies-for-sale. Terms like **neomorts** (human bodies with the legal status of the dead, but having some qualities of the living, such as breathing) and **bioemporiums** (permanent hospital wards for storing such bodies) no longer refer only to ideas found in science-fiction, but to possible programs for the enlargement of the field of experimentation on human subjects. **Cryonics** (the very expensive practice of the freezing and storing of dead human bodies in cylinders filled with liquid nitrogen at -195°C), has its attraction for those who, in addition to being rich, hope that medical science will find a remedy for mortality so that frozen persons can then be brought back to life.

Aldous Huxley's *Brave New World*, written as long ago as 1932, addressed itself to the problems we now face. In the 1946 Foreword of this book, we were warned that 'the final and most searching revolution — this really revolutionary revolution — is to be achieved, not in the external world, but in the souls and flesh of human beings'.

Modern man is faced with a technological revolution in medicine which involves all kinds of experimentations on human subjects. And that revolution has begun without the consent of society, without due consideration of its moral and social implications, and without any established ethical guidelines which would make the medical scientists accountable to the community.

This revolution in medical science does involve human values and the common good of human society. Society must decide, through its appropriate institutions, what is ethically acceptable, particularly with respect to such life-issues as conception, artificial insemination, laboratory fertilization, contraception, abortion, infanticide, suicide, euthanasia, research on human subjects, genetic engineering, cloning, and so on.

Our approach to medical ethics, including bioethics (ethics of life), is crucial if we are to make morally sound decisions on such life-issues. For example, some people have argued that these decisions are best left to those directly involved: the members of the medical profession, and their 'patients'. Others, however, have argued against that view, and want the community to decide because the community generally will be affected by the developments in medical technology (for example, Ian Kennedy in his 1980 BBC Reith Lectures).

The most vital question, derived from the ones we posed previously, is: Which ethics will help us in arriving at a moral decision, both in health care and biomedical labours, which does not violate the laws and common good of humanity? We firmly believe that the answer to this question can be best formulated in this manner:

> A social ethics, including medical ethics, advantageous to the common good of all, should be based on the laws of humanity (or, natural law), and should not violate the laws of nature.

This obviously implies that society should promote and adhere to a *rule ethics* which should be clearly codified in legally-enforceable socio-medical codes.

Legally-enforceable socio-medical codes will ensure that the contemporary revolution in medical science will be permanently bound to the six fundamental concepts in all life-ethics, namely:

the sanctity of human life
the principle of double effect
the principle of totality
the distinction between ordinary and extraordinary treatment
the principle of justice
the necessary involvement of socio-moral policy-making institutions in society.

These fundamental concepts will be treated in Section VI of this book. They are mentioned already here because, in our appraisal of contemporary socio-medical and bioethical issues, these concepts will play a major role in determining our considerations, conclusions, and judgments.

We recognize that many people have abandoned the Judaic and Christian traditions with their emphasis on respect for human life. Modern secular humanism has declared war on these traditions, and instead fosters the human desire to be independent of nature and to control it completely. Secular humanists believe that we should live as autonomous human beings in a man-made Paradise in which there is no need for the help and intervention of God. The great moral revolution brought about by secular humanism forcefully manifested itself in the post-World-War-II decades in our human history. It has aided the revolution in medical science at the expense of the long-standing influence of a value-centred ethics upon which Christian Western civilization has grown and developed.

The promotion of a so-called 'value-free' ethics has also contributed to the moral vacuum which makes any rational ethical evaluation of modern technological achievements very difficult.

The Social Implications

The most fashionable morality among an influential and trend-setting group of people in our society is the one which has often been vulgarized by the slogans: 'Do your own thing', 'If it feels good, do it', and 'If it works, it must be OK'. This is a morality which is a radical revolt against all forms of authority — ranging from the authority of the Church to the authority of the State and its institutions. It is a revolt against the law and against rules in general.

This challenge to authority in the Western world, fomented in the academic institutions, and permeating every area of society, has represented a retreat from the pursuit of objective truth in favour of subjectivist 'self-awareness' programs. As far as ethics is concerned, most statements of a 'This is right' or 'This is wrong' kind are now qualified with a 'for me'. This means that no institution should say 'This is right'; only the individual can say what is right or wrong for himself — but not for others. Of course, there is great diversity and complexity in contemporary ethics, but a morality based on entirely-subjective considerations cannot meaningfully be discussed.

The rejection of 'rule ethics' (ethics based on objective criteria) in favour of 'act ethics' (ethics based on the subjective notion that if an act seems good to me it is good) has had enormous social implications. A morality which does not acknowledge the need for socio-moral rules, by which our behaviour and activities must be governed, will, if officially embraced, reduce an ordered human society to a state of chaos and lawlessness.

Since a civilized society cannot survive in the ways we have known if human beings are to be permitted to act without reference to the possible consequences of their actions for others, the social implications of an act-without-rule ethics are simply enormous.

It follows then that people such as the medical researcher, the technological expert, the laboratory scientist, the attending physician, and others involved in socio-medical decision-making and health care of human beings, ought not to be allowed to pursue their work without rules of conduct to govern their behaviour and activities.

The ethics of these professions are of concern not only to the members of the professions; they affect all members of society as potential patients, and as the providers of the financial means necessary for the experts to do their work and accomplish their hoped-for results.

Since there are enormous social implications from the possible uses of medical research and technologies, it is vital that people be informed not only of what is happening, but of the ethical justifications for it happening. Accurate information as to exactly what scientists are doing, and the ethical basis for their work, is not, in fact, readily available to the community. Further, legal and ethical authorities have expressed great concern about the inadequacy of legally-enforceable moral guidelines to determine the social limitations within which socio-medical research and technologies can and should be advanced.

The impact of modern biomedical achievements on the social fabric of our society should be considered very seriously before this revolution 'in the souls and flesh of human beings' (Huxley) becomes the embodiment of an irreversible dehumanization process. The issues with which this book deals concern us all. We should therefore examine them critically and honestly to the best of our ability.

The Moral Imperative

The moral imperative (what we as citizens ought to do in the light of what is actually happening in our hospitals and laboratories) follows from what we have said above. To begin with, we ought to consider and critically evaluate the moral legitimacy of current socio-medical practices. The assertions of those engaged in this work ought to be challenged from a bioethical standpoint, and not complacently accepted as the infallible pronouncements of 'experts'.

Bioethics is a discipline which

> studies the morality of human conduct in the area of the life (*bios* means life in Greek) sciences. Although ethics has been examining human conduct in this area for a long time, bioethics as a special ethical discipline has emerged only recently. The rapid growth of knowledge in the life sciences has created a great number of ethical problems that call for special study. Bioethics includes medical ethics, but it goes beyond the customary ethical problems of medicine because it also examines the various ethical problems of the life sciences which are not primarily medical (Andrew C. Varga).

This book is not meant to be an academic treatise on bioethics. The authors wish to bring to the notice of people from all walks of life a number of contemporary socio-medical and bioethical issues, to help them to make a critical evaluation of those issues in an ethical context.

In the Judaic and Christian traditions, life is seen as a gift from God, the Creator:

> God blessed them [the male and female human beings], and said unto them: 'Be fruitful, and multiply, and replenish the earth, and subdue it; and have dominion over the fish of the sea, and over the fowl of the air, and over every living thing that moves upon the earth' (Genesis 1:28).

Thus, the very first book of the Sacred Scriptures for both Jews and Christians clearly states that the gift of life is a blessing from God. The precise formulation of our moral imperative, therefore, begins with the recognition that human life is a good in itself because its origin lies in the creative activity of God.

There are some who would want us to ignore everything which belongs to the supernatural, to revelation, or to faith, if we are to give a credible, non-sectarian appraisal of bioethical and related issues. But this is a demand to which the authors cannot and will not accede. A belief in God is basic to most citizens in all Western societies. In the interests of truth, God simply cannot be ignored. We will, however, endeavour to avoid the danger of mixing the respective realms of the spiritual and the secular in our appraisal. In any case, it is our view that reason contradicts neither legitimate belief or faith, nor that which can be responsibly and scientifically established.

The moral imperative applies to Christians and non-Christians alike, and must be faced by all. The common basis for all ethics is to be found in the recognition that human beings are endowed with reason and conscience. Without reason, there can be no articulation of right and wrong; and without conscience, there can be no adherence to the laws of nature and of humanity which inspire and judge the behaviour and actions of man.

CHAPTER

THE BEGINNING OF HUMAN LIFE

Conception

Artificial Insemination by Husband (AIH)

Artificial Insemination by Donor (AID)

In Vitro Fertilization (IVF)

Surrogate Motherhood

Conception

In the Judaic and Christian traditions, the beginning of human life is to be seen in the context of human fertility. The Creator God confers the blessing of fertility on the first human couple which he made.

> And God created man in his own image, in the image of God created He him; male and female created He them. And God blessed them; and God said unto them: 'Be fruitful, and multiply, and replenish the earth, and subdue it; and have dominion over the fish of the sea, and over the fowl of the air, and over every living thing that creepeth upon the earth' (Genesis 1:27,28. Translation from *The Soncino Chumash* in *The Soncino Books of the Bible*, ed. A. Cohen, 14 vols. published by the Soncino Press, London, 1947).

This blessing of fertility given to man and woman in Genesis's Paradise (Garden of Eden) was reiterated to Noah and his sons after the Flood (Genesis 9:1,7), to Abraham and Sarah (Genesis 17:15,16), and to Jacob (Genesis 28:14). It was often included, as well, in the special blessings with which the fathers blessed their children and grandchildren (Genesis 24:60; 28:3; 48:16; 49:25, 'blessings of the breasts and of the womb').

It is clear from these ancient writings that the Creator's delight in his creatures, and the goodness which is associated with life itself, form the ultimate motivation for the blessing of fertility. According to various Jewish commentators, this blessing is also a 'commandment' for human beings.

> Commandments can be issued to man alone. Other creatures procreate instinctively. Man can organize and discipline his procreative activity. He can consciously limit it; he can destroy it; he can use it indiscriminately, perversely, and self-destructively. Other creatures mate seasonally. For man, mating knows no limitations (David S. Shapiro).

The Jewish 'Oral Tradition' declares procreation to be 'a religious duty'. In spite of longstanding controversy as to whether the commandment to be fruitful applies to both men and women, orthodox Jews believe that procreation is 'the first of the commandments'.

Controversy arose in the Jewish tradition over the statement that

> a man is not permitted to live without a wife, but a woman may live without a husband; a man is not allowed to drink a root-drink for the purpose of rendering himself impotent; a woman may drink a root-drink to render herself sterile; a man may not marry a woman who is barren, old, or wombless, or one who is too young or incapable of bearing children; but a woman may marry even a eunuch; the castration of a male involves specific biblical penalties; the sterilization of a female does not involve specific biblical penalties.

This view of Maimonides, supported by various passages in the *Talmud*, is deeply embedded in religious Jewish ethics. But, even taking this view, that women have no obligation to bear children, it is still true that women are unavoidably involved in the commandment to be fruitful (the first *mitzvah* or commandment). Since a man needs a woman through whom he can fulfil his obligation to be fruitful, such involvement constitutes a primary religious duty for the woman as well. If we recognize the validity of the argument that the Jewish woman is not under the divine obligation of procreation, this remains an interesting point of discussion.

The above view is different from the Islamic view, in which 'a woman is not considered a woman unless she has had children'. In the Jewish tradition, the biblical injunction to man in Genesis 2:24 that he 'shall forsake his father and mother' (and cling to his wife) is never applied to the woman, thus liberating her from the pagan notion of viewing women as 'symbols of fertility'!

The question of the size of the family is often raised in this context. How many children should a couple have to fulfil the primary commandment of fertility? The two famous schools in Jewish religious thought (those of Shammai and Hillel) give the following answer:

> A man shall not abstain from the performance of the duty of the propagation of the race unless he already has children. As to the number, Bet Shammai ruled: two males, and Bet Hillel ruled: a male and a female, for it is stated in Scripture, 'Male and female created He them'.

Now, sometimes a man refuses to obey the command to procreate. Within the tradition that sees fertility as a blessing from God, Jewish scholars have seen such a deliberate refusal as a negation of the value of human life created as it is in the image of God. It is also a denial of that service which every man owes to his Creator: the service of procreation, as a continuing process of preparation for the coming of the Messianic age — when God's chosen King will bring to a glorious completion life as man presently knows it.

In the light of the above discussion, we should not be surprised to find that marriage and procreation occupy a special and significant place in the mystical literature of Judaism.

> The human family, consisting of father, mother, son, and daughter (according to the normative view of the House of Hillel), is thus the earthly embodiment of Supernal Man. The family together makes up a person. Where the family is incomplete, personality remains fragmented, and the Divine potencies, which are to find their expression in the life of man through human activity, remain unfulfilled. Man's failures thus turn into cosmic tragedies (David S. Shapiro).

It is true that we live in a social environment which is no longer very sympathetic to the great values inherited from a tradition of deep spiritual wisdom. But it is also true that the Christian churches of the East and West, still significant world-wide institutions, have inherited a great deal of this ancient wisdom.

However, the Christian tradition cannot simply be identified with a development of Judaic thinking. The Christian churches ascribe a particular authority to the teachings of Christ and his apostles (including their interpretation of the ancient Jewish writings embodied in the Old Testament). And they have also been open to other extra-Jewish influences of a philosophical and moral nature.

So there are distinct Jewish and Christian traditions, both claiming divine revelation as their basis. For Christians it would be as unthinkable to divorce their belief and practice from the teachings of the New Testament as it would be impossible for religious Jews to accept Christ and his apostles as authoritative interpreters of their sacred writings.

What, then, does the Christian tradition say about conception? The answer to this question may simply be stated as follows: The Christian church views conception as a divine blessing bestowed upon a human couple united in a life-long covenant of marriage. The church does not speak in favour of procreation outside of marriage. Since, in Christian thinking, conception cannot be divorced from a specific view of marriage both as an institution and a human relationship, it is important to look at some of the ways Christians have understood marriage.

The distinctiveness of the Christian doctrine of marriage can be seen, in part, in the tremendous social changes that occurred in ancient society following the birth of the Christian church and its subsequent missionary work.

St Paul, in his letters to congregations and their leaders, did not hesitate to attack the prevailing pagan attitudes toward marriage (especially the sexual aspect) which were marked by indifference, latitude, and inconsistency. He warned against sexual immorality (1 Corinthians 6:15-20) and divorce (1 Corinthians 7:10-16). The passages in the New Testament which deal with the husband-wife relationship (such as 1 Peter 3 and Ephesians 5) have had a great influence on the Christian view of the family.

Now, it is true that the Fathers of the early church and the theologians and pastors throughout the history of the Western church have not always been able to show clarity and precision in their pastoral admonitions and views on marriage. Furthermore, the negative tone frequently adopted in discussing sex probably indicated their antipathy to natural love. Even a man like St Augustine of Hippo (354-430) was never quite clear that the sexual aspect of the marriage relationship was part of God's work of creation. He often offended his flock because of his harsh criticism of the physical expression of natural love. Sexual desire in itself and for itself, even in marriage, was for St Augustine the result of sin, and even concupiscence (lust).

St Gregory the Great (c. 540-604), the fourth and last of the traditional Latin Doctors of the church, following the teachings of St Augustine, wrote in one of his 'Admonitions':

> The married must be admonished to bear in mind that they are united in wedlock for the purpose of procreation, and when they abandon themselves to immoderate intercourse, they transfer the occasion of procreation to the service of pleasure. Let them realize that though they

do not then pass beyond the bounds of wedlock, yet in wedlock they exceed its rights.

St Francis de Sales (1567-1622), Bishop of Geneva from 1602, was declared a 'Doctor of the Church' in 1877. In Chapter 39 of his famous work, *Introduction to the Devout Life*, he wrote:

> For inasmuch as the procreation of children is the first and principal end of marriage, it is never lawful to depart from the order established for this purpose, though for some accidental cause conception may not be possible, as happens when barrenness or pregnancy prevents procreation and generation; for in such cases the bodily intercourse does not cease to be capable of being just and holy, provided that the laws of generation be preserved, for no circumstances ever make it lawful to transgress the law which the principal end of marriage has imposed.

Despite the gap of nearly one thousand years between the two writers, St Francis de Sales closely followed St Augustine's views on the sexual aspect of marriage.

It is outside the scope of this chapter to scrutinize the development of Christian thought concerning marriage. It is, however, clear from all the marriage services at present in use in the churches that procreation is one of the principal purposes of marriage.

The Roman Catholic Church continues to maintain the essential positions of St Augustine, St Gregory the Great, and St Francis de Sales already outlined above. The present *Rite of Marriage*, used in the Roman Catholic Church since its revision in 1969, says in its Introduction:

> By their very nature, the institution of matrimony and wedded love are ordained for the procreation and education of children and find in them their ultimate crown. Therefore, married Christians, while not considering the other purposes of marriage of less account, should be steadfast and ready to co-operate with the love of the Creator and Saviour, who through them will constantly enrich and enlarge his own family.

The Lutheran tradition owes much to Martin Luther (1483-1546). A deep insight into his views on the marital relationship can be gained by reading his sermons on marriage and his polemics against the lasting validity of monastic vows. Some of his writings on the nature and purpose of marriage are controversial, especially when he gives approval to a woman having an extra-marital relationship for the purpose of conceiving a child in the case where her husband is impotent.

Luther wrote in 1523:

> We were all created to do as our parents have done, to beget and rear children. This is a duty which God has laid upon us, commanded, and implanted in us, as is proved by our bodily members, our daily emotions, and the example of all mankind.

The Lutheran Confessions, brought together in the *Book of Concord* (1580), teach and uphold that marriage was instituted by God, that it is pure and that it is sanctified by God's Word and prayer. These Confessions also state that marriage is a necessary estate, has God's command and promise, and is blessed and honoured of God. Marriage is founded on natural law, and its dissolution is against the Sacred Scriptures. The prohibition of marriage (as in the case of compulsory celibacy for religious orders and clergy) is condemned as a doctrine of demons, a mark of the Antichrist; marriage should be free, and the young are to be encouraged thereto. The Lutheran Confessions further maintain that virginity is an exalted gift; but, at the same time, they uphold 'that women are saved by conjugal intercourse, by bearing children, and the other duties, if they continue in faith'. Luther, who married on June 13, 1525, wrote his *Little Wedding Book* in 1529. The prayer in this booklet is significant:

> O God, who hast created man and woman and has ordained them for the married estate, has blessed them also with fruits of the womb, and has typified therein the sacramental union of thy dear Son, the Lord Jesus Christ, and the church, his bride: We beseech thy boundless goodness and mercy that thou wouldst not permit this thy creation, ordinance, and blessing to be disturbed or destroyed, but graciously preserve the same; through Jesus Christ our Lord. Amen.

The 'cross' which God has placed on marriage is, according to Luther, the word of God in Genesis 3:16: 'I will greatly multiply your pain in childbearing; in pain you shall bring forth children, yet your desire shall be for your husband, and he shall rule over you'. The blessing of fertility, of conception, pregnancy, and childbirth, is experienced in the context of 'pain'! This is not just pain in a 'physical' sense; Jewish interpreters have referred here to the pain of rearing children, of the loss of virginity, of menstruation, pregnancy, and of cohabitation 'in obedience'.

In the Anglican communion, 'The Form of Solemnization of Matrimony' in the *Book of Common Prayer* (1662) upholds the three-fold purpose of marriage:

> First, It was ordained for the procreation of children, to be brought up in the fear and nurture of the Lord, and to the praise of his holy name.

Secondly, It was ordained for a remedy against sin, and to avoid fornication; that such persons as have not the gift of continency might marry, and keep themselves undefiled members of Christ's body. Thirdly, It was ordained for the mutual society, help, and comfort that the one ought to have of the other, both in prosperity and adversity.

Subsequent revisions of the Marriage Service in the various national churches of the Anglican communion have sought to make two important modifications. First, the second purpose of marriage is now stated in a way that affirms the fundamental goodness and beauty of sex as against the negative tone of the 1662 original. Secondly, the order of the three reasons has generally been inverted so that the companionship aspect of marriage is presented as the first purpose of marriage.

Whether or not the order of the three purposes is important, the Anglican communion, through its various national churches, upholds the notion that procreation is essential to an understanding of marriage, and that marriage is the proper socio-moral context in which conception should take place.

The churches of the Reformed tradition (a tradition influenced by the famous French Reformer, John Calvin, 1509-64) also teach that the primary purpose of marriage is procreation. It is interesting to note that Calvin does not speak about marriage as a 'mutual companionship'. A study of the traditional Reformed confessional writings concerning marriage nevertheless confirms the view held by most Christians, namely, that marriage was ordained by God for life-long 'companionship, help, and comfort, which husband and wife ought to have of each other', 'for the continuance of the holy ordinance of family life', and 'for the welfare of human society'.

The social revolution of the twentieth century has brought tremendous changes to the lives of people inside and outside the church. These changes have, in turn, precipitated a critical reappraisal of traditional values, especially in the other disciplines which deal with human personality and inter-personal relationships. The institution most affected by the modern social revolution is marriage, a fact which carries all sorts of implications for the socio-moral context in which conception and procreation should take place.

What has happened to the institution of marriage?

In our contemporary situation, marriage has changed from an institution to a 'companionship arrangement'. The 'fixed roles' of husband and wife have become 'fluid roles'. The 'extended family' has become the 'nuclear family'. Marriage is no longer 'procreative-centred', but has become 'unitive-centred' with the main emphasis being placed on the celebration of the union between husband and wife. This has happened at a time when over-population has become a highly emotive issue.

In countries where good medical care is readily available, medical science has added years to the average life-span of people. One consequence of this is that married couples have longer to live with each other than ever before.

Modern marriage has also been deeply influenced by the reduced length of time in which couples are involved in their task of parenting. This has been brought about by smaller families, spacing of childbirth, and the devaluation of the maternal and homemaking role of married women.

The great changes in moral attitudes toward sex have been brought about by the influential advocates of sexual permissiveness. The age of sexual permissiveness is still in full swing, such that the traditional ethos relating to marriage and the family is claimed to be 'unworkable' (Alex Comfort).

We live in an ethically-pluralistic society which, according to David R. Mace, bears a resemblance to a 'three-layer cake':

> The bottom layer consists of those people who still accept the traditional Christian standard of sexual behaviour — premarital chastity, marital fidelity, and lifelong marriage. In the next layer are those who accept marriage as the proper, though not the exclusive, setting for sexual fulfilment; but they do not consider marriage as a permanent or binding obligation, and therefore regard themselves as free to divorce and remarry as often as they may wish to change partners. For some of these, the marriage bond is quite a loose tie, permitting them, whenever a romantic attachment runs out of steam, to end it and start on another — the Hollywood pattern, as we might call it. In the third or top layer of the cake are those persons who choose not to marry at all but to seek sexual experiences where they may be found, without accompanying interpersonal commitment of any kind and without family responsibilities. This threefold structure, which already constitutes our society, is the result of individual freedom, and seems likely to continue indefinitely (*The Christian Response to the Sexual Revolution*, 1971, 81).

Psychologists, social scientists, and others speak of the need for 'partnership revolutions' or 'relationship revolutions'. The literature on marriage and the family shows how deeply opinions are divided on the moral values associated with marriage and the family. Critics of traditional marriage commitments claim (sometimes with devastating socio-historical accuracy!) that, because Christian beliefs, traditions and lifestyles have not brought about a Utopia of marital bliss and family happiness, society would be better off with alternative models for marriage and the family.

In the last hundred years, the world has faced developments and changes that previous generations would never have imagined possible. The turmoil associated with world wars, local wars, revolutions, and with economic, social, and political upheavals, has dramatically altered the lifestyles of ordinary people. The progress in medical science has raised numerous socio-moral questions with which many of us cannot adequately cope. The arms race has caused deep anxiety among large numbers of people living in 'nuclear danger zones' both in the East and in the West.

For some, the future of the world today is one of hopelessness, anger, apathy, carelessness, corruption, and selfishness on the part of many people. The authors of this book believe, nevertheless, that there are also signs of hope, love, sympathy, care, honesty, and selflessness on the part of those who continue to speak and act for the common good of all.

In the midst of the confusion brought about by socio-moral revolution, the church continues to witness to the lasting values of life, love, and fidelity.

Pope Leo XIII's Encyclical Letter on Christian Marriage (February 10, 1880), Pope Pius XI's Encyclical Letter on the same subject (December 31, 1930), and Pope Paul VI's (controversial) Encyclical Letter on the Regulation of Birth (*Humanae Vitae*, July 25, 1968), are clear examples of the church's concern for the welfare of people.

Pope Paul VI began his Encyclical Letter on the Regulation of Birth with the words:

> The most serious duty of transmitting human life, for which married persons are the free and responsible collaborators of God the Creator, has always been a source of great joys to them, even if sometimes accompanied by not a few difficulties and by distress.

These words set the tone of the document which has been severely criticized both inside and outside of the Roman Catholic Church. After the paragraphs in the Letter dealing with 'conjugal love' (which he describes as fully human, total, faithful, exclusive and fecund), the Pope reminded his people (and the world) of what it means to exercise responsible parenthood:

> The responsible exercise of parenthood implies, therefore, that husband and wife recognize fully their own duties towards God, towards themselves, towards the family, and towards society, in a correct hierarchy of values. In the task of transmitting life, therefore, they are not free to proceed completely at will, as if they could determine in a wholly autonomous way the honest path to follow: but they must conform their activity to the creative intention of God, expressed in the very nature of marriage and of its acts, and manifested by the constant teaching of the Church.

It should be obvious to all Christians that the Pope places the marriage partners as individuals into their proper relational context: their faith in God, their esteem of self, their responsibility toward spouse, family, and the community-at-large.

The beginning of life, conception, should be viewed in that most important and wholesome context. If we accept the moral validity of looking at conception as being both divine gift and human responsibility, we will be even more able to appreciate the great scientific discoveries associated with the beginning of human life.

The ancient poet says:

> For thou didst form my inward parts,
> thou didst knit me together in my mother's womb.
> I praise thee, for thou art fearful and wonderful.
> Wonderful are thy works!
> Thou knowest me right well;
> my frame was not hidden from thee,
> when I was being made in secret,
> intricately wrought in the depths of the earth.
> Thy eyes beheld my unformed substance;
> in thy book were written, every one of them,
> the days that were formed for me,
> when as yet there was none of them (Psalm 139).

That human beings have indeed been 'intricately wrought', science has confirmed in no uncertain terms!

How Did We Begin and Develop before We Were Born?

We are human from the moment of conception (fertilization) — which is the result of the expression of the conjugal will of a man and a woman to parenthood. This expression of the conjugal will of a couple is commonly called sexual intercourse, the celebration of physical, mental, and spiritual intimacy.

Natural conception can occur only if the sexual organs of both man and woman are functional, and if both partners are fertile at the time of intercourse. After the ejaculation of semen, the sperm of the male must reach the egg (*ovum*) of the female which has been released from the woman's ovary during the time of her ovulation. A mature spermatozoon is 0.04 — 0.06mm long, and has a head, body, and tail. The oval head, which is about 0.003 — 0.005mm long, carries the genes responsible for hereditary characters of a newly-to-be-conceived human being. The body of the spermatozoon contains those elements necessary for forward movement, while the tail serves to move the cell actively. In other words, the spermatozoon can swim very fast toward its goal: the fertilizable egg, measuring about 0.1mm, situated in the woman's Fallopian tube.

After a few of the many millions of sperm cells ejaculated during sexual intercourse reach the ovum, they attempt to penetrate it. The penetration activity of the spermatozoa lasts for 20 to 30 hours, during which time the ovum is passive. Although a number of sperm cells may reach the nucleus (the inner essential part) of the egg, only the sperm which first reaches the nucleus unites with the ovum. At the moment of union, the two cells, sperm and egg, become a single living cell.

And so we began! Our size was 0.1mm, 'a pin prick, smaller than a grain of sand, smaller than a period typed at the end of a sentence'.

The union of the two nuclei of ovum and sperm bring together 23 chromosomes from the mother and 23 chromosomes from the father. These 46 chromosomes, the bodies within the cell nuclei, carry some 15,000 genes from each parent cell. The genes 'like letters of a divine alphabet, spell out the unique characteristics of the new individual'. The genetic coding determines, for instance, the colour of our eyes, hair, and skin, facial features, body type, and certain qualities of personality and intelligence. The number of chromosomes is the same in every human being: 23 pairs or 46 single ones. One of these pairs determines the sex of the human individual (i.e., the male has 44 somatic chromosomes and one pair of sex chromosomes *XY*; the female has also 44 somatic chromosomes and one pair of sex chromosomes *XX*. The single X or Y chromosome is carried in the father's sperm cell.).

At conception, a new human life 'with vast potential', weighing about 2mg, has begun. And after some 266 days, a new-born baby, weighing approximately 3.4 kilograms (7.5 lb), and containing millions upon millions of cells, 'changes his or her address'.

From the moment of our conception until the hour of our birth, our miraculous development takes place inside the body of our mother. We can recall this development with the help of a schematic outline of the events during a mother's pregnancy.

Schematic Outline of Our Development before Birth

In *Life* magazine, April 30, 1965, there appeared a beautiful photo-essay entitled, 'Drama of Life Before Birth'. It says in the introductory paragraphs (See *LIFE Educational Reprint 27*):

> In the Western world a person's life is reckoned from the day he comes out of the womb. But the Chinese, overestimating by three months, have traditionally counted a child one year old at birth in recognition of the unceasingly active life that has already taken place. In the 266 days from conception to birth, the single fertilized egg cell becomes a staggeringly complex organization of some 200 million cells, having increased the original weight a billionfold.

First Month:

During the first month after conception (fertilization, the beginning of pregnancy), the development of a new human life shows miraculous progress. Conception occurs approximately 24-26 hours after the sperm has penetrated the egg, and 12-14 hours after the formation of the nucleus within both the sperm and the egg. These nuclei contain the genetic information from the man and the woman (the father and the mother). The egg is about 90,000 times as large as the spermatozoon.

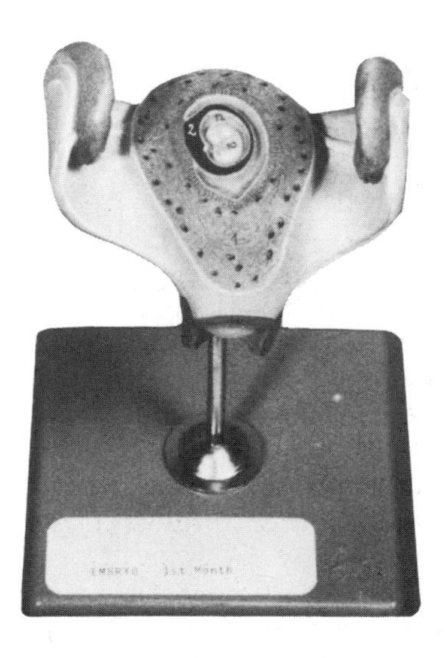

Shortly after the fusion of the two nuclei of sperm and ovum (4-6 hours), the newly-formed cell (*zygote*, from the Greek word for yoke) splits into two identical, smaller cells; 10-20 hours later, it has reached the four-cell stage. Two days after fertilization, the stage of 32 cells has arisen, and the tiny embryo looks like a mulberry (*morula*, from the Latin name for mulberry). Three days after conception it reaches the blastocyst stage (from the Greek *blastos*, germ, and *kystis*, bag). Implantation or embedding of the embryo in the mother's uterine wall mucosa, four to five days after conception, marks the end of the blastocyst stage ('wandering' in the Fallopian tube). Between conception and implantation, we count 120-140 hours, or five to six days.

During the remaining days of the first month after conception, the maturation stages of the embryo continue to follow all the genetic instructions contained in the very small nucleus of the fertilized ovum. In addition to its **growth manual**, the embryo, being a 'foreign body' in the mother's womb, also possesses from the moment of conception, a **protection manual**. This protection manual dictates the construction of 'the complex protective armamentarium — *amnion, umbilical cord, placenta* and all — that makes possible the embryo's existence in the womb'. The *amnion* is the thin, transparent, veil-like lining surrounding the embryonic human being, which contains its *amnios*, salt fluid which bathes the body's cells. The *umbilical cord*, the 'baby's pipeline to life', is connected with the *placenta*, popularly called the 'afterbirth' since it leaves the mother's body after the birth of the baby.

> The placenta is an extraordinary and multifunctional organ. It supplies the embryo with all its needs, carries off all its wastes, protects it in a variety of ways from harmful invaders. It does all this through the umbilical cord. Contrary to popular belief, there is no direct connection whatever between the mother's circulation and the baby's. In the placenta there are two separate sets of vessels. One set goes to and from the mother; the other goes to and from the embryo. They are side by side but are entirely closed off from one another. The blood vessel walls, however, are permeable. An exchange of ingredients — oxygen, dissolved food, waste matter, etc. — is constantly taking place through the walls. This may seem a peculiarly indirect and inefficient way of effecting the exchanges between mother and embryo. But it is the only way it can be done, for the baby is a parasite . . . The body, through its immunological system, always tries to reject foreign material . . . Yet the mother tolerates this entire foreign body in her system for nine whole months. She tolerates it only because of the placenta's unique ability to subvert her immunological defences (Albert Rosenfeld in *Life Before Birth*).

The unborn child is never 'part of a woman's body'. Yet, the baby depends on the loving care of a responsible woman who realizes that 'being with child' has made her a mother.

At the end of the first month, the human embryo measures 8mm 'from crown to rump'. By that time the embryo consists of outer, middle, and inner germinal layers. From the outer layer (*ectoderm*) develop the brain, spinal cord, nervous system, sense organs, skin and accessory organs such as hair, sweat glands, and nails. From the middle layer (*mesoderm*) develop the bones, tendons, ligaments and joints, blood vascular system, heart and blood, urinary and sex organs. From the inner layer (*endoderm*) develop organs of digestion and respiration with all their accessories: stomach, intestine, liver, pancreas, respiratory tract, lungs (K.H. Wrage).

The beginnings of the baby's organs are already there: eyes, spinal cord, nervous system, thyroid gland, lungs, stomach, liver, kidneys, and intestines. The primitive heart, which began beating on the 18th day, is 'now pumping more confidently'; in proportion to the body of the embryo, it is nine times as large as the heart of an adult. Limbs are appearing as buds; the arms a little earlier than the legs.

Second Month:

At the commencement of the second month, a very critical time begins for the tiny human embryo. From 28 to 42 days, deformities can be caused by drugs (for example, thalidomide, leading to the birth of 'thalidomide babies'), or by specific illnesses (such as the German measles virus).

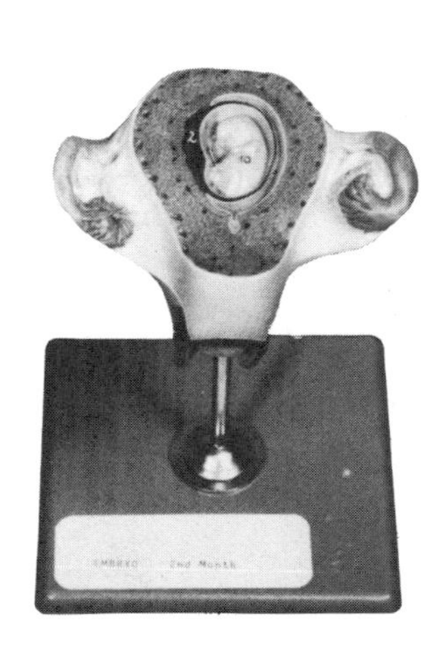

By the end of this month, the developing human being is no longer called *embryo* (a Greek word, meaning to swell), but *fetus* or *foetus* (a Latin word, meaning young or little one). It now measures 25mm and weighs a little more than 4 grams (by the time of birth the former will have multiplied by twenty times, and the latter by a thousand times!). Present are: eyes, upper and lower arms, rudimentary hands, elbows, knees, feet, fingers, and toes. The fetus moves in response to external stimuli (muscle and nerve responses).

Third Month:

At the 13th gestational week after conception, the fetus, enveloped by the blood-rich placenta, measures 9cm. 'It flows buoyantly in the amniotic fluid, along with the umbilical cord . . . though totally immersed, the fetus keeps inhaling and exhaling just enough to send the salty fluid into and out of its lungs. But it does not drown because it gets oxygen in the blood brought in by the umbilical cord, not from air. Bones, including the ribs, are now rapidly forming.' Eyebrows and the baby's first hair have appeared. It produces its first gastric juice and urine. In the mother's uterus (which is not entirely dark and rather noisy) the little one is alive, is growing, swallowing, and responding to light, noise, and pressure (a violent response occurs if the fetus is subjected to needle puncture or the injection of cold or concentrated solutions — Sir A. William Liley).

Fourth Month:

At the end of the fourth month, the preborn baby now measures 16cm. It starts to get crowded in the intra-uterine environment of the 'young one'. His or her sex organs are now distinguishable, and the mother can feel the movement of her child. The placenta is now too small to surround the amnion; it 'still hangs on to link the amnion with the wall of the uterus'. (See the magnificent colour photograph on pages 14, 15

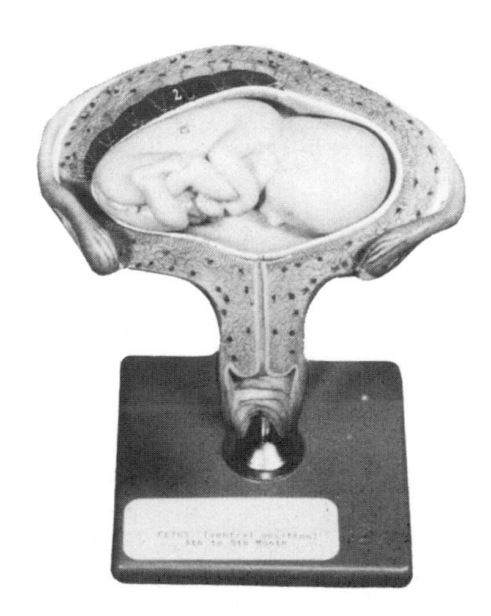

of 'Life Before Birth' in *LIFE Educational Reprint 27.*)

The eyes of the baby are still closed (for protection), but 'the nose, lips and ears finally look like nose, lips and ears'. Just over seventeen weeks have passed since conception. The unborn child has started to practise post-birth feeding by sucking its thumb. It is very active and 'energetic and does a lot of muscle-flexing. It can make an impressively hard fist, and the punches and kicks are plainly felt by the mother. It can go through the motions of crying, too. It is equipped with a complete set of vocal cords, but, without air, it cannot make a sound.'

From the Fifth Month to the Seventh Month:

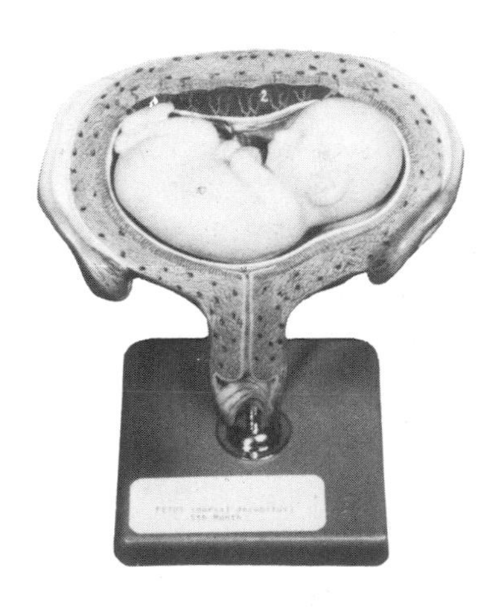

At the end of the fifth month, the baby measures 25cm; by the end of the sixth month 31cm. During this period of growth, the bone centres ossify (become bone). When the 28th gestational week has arrived, the baby weighs 1 kilogram (2.2 lb) and measures 35cm. The development of the fetus is almost completed. If prematurely born, the baby can survive if special medical care is available. From now on, the child in the mother's womb will receive added strength and health. The remaining time will serve the baby well because it acquires from its mother 'precious, though short term, immunity to a number of diseases'.

From the Seventh Month to Birth:

During the last two months of pregnancy, the baby simply grows. The miracle of life before birth is indeed a great miracle. We were 'knit together', 'intricately wrought' and 'formed' (Psalm 139) during the 266 days of our mother's pregnancy. From conception to birth — conceived, nurtured, and brought into the world by acts of love, care and joy, often accompanied by short-comings, discomfort, and pain! — we began and developed as human beings. In a society which tolerates — and even promotes — the destruction of prenatal human life (abortion), designates millions of children as being 'unwanted', and accepts the deliberate withdrawal of ordinary medical care from handicapped children (infanticide), it should be remembered that life is good in itself. One of the principal laws of humanity is: 'You shall not murder'. It is this law which is the basis of our obligation, as human beings, to protect human life. This is the reason why, in ancient and modern codes of medical ethics, physicians are called 'to maintain utmost respect for human life from the time of conception'. This 'utmost respect' should also be fostered among all members of our human society. Marriage and family laws, legislative provisions dealing with the protection of human life, are extremely important, and certainly reflect, facilitate, guide, and direct the moral attitudes of individuals, societies, and nations.

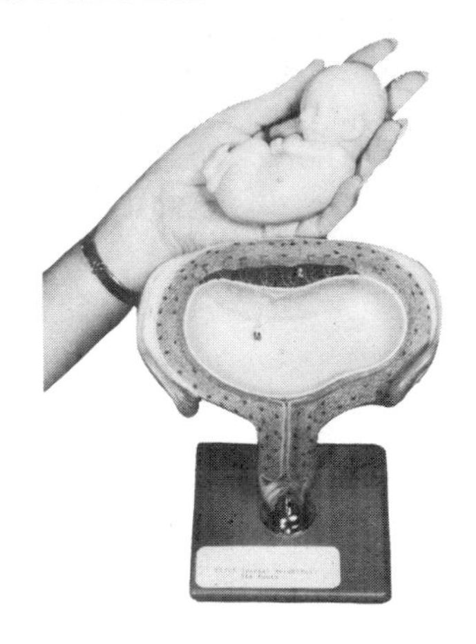

In the *U.N. Declaration of the Rights of the Child* (November 20, 1959), which has recently been under review, it is clearly stated in its *Preamble* that 'the child, by reason of his physical and mental immaturity, needs special safeguards and care, including appropriate legal protection, **before as well as after birth**' (*emphasis ours*). More than twenty years later, it seems that the reference in this Declaration to the unborn is no longer acceptable . . . We sincerely hope that the various proposed alterations

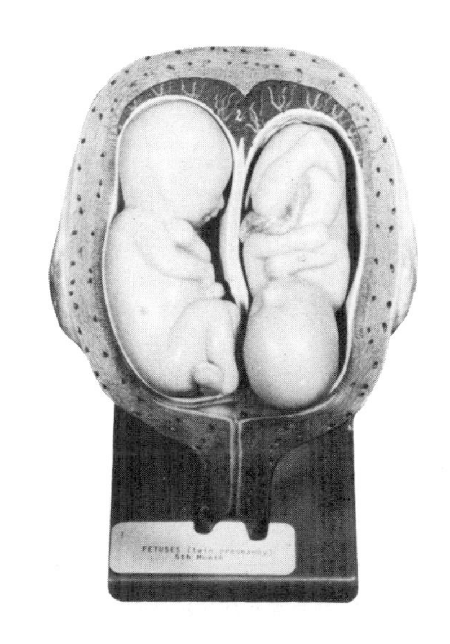

to the Declaration will not be accepted when this revision comes before the General Assembly of the United Nations. Conception is the beginning of human life. With every conception, something 'new' has begun: a human being has come into existence . . . a destiny is being shaped . . . new relationships are being formed . . . and, last but not least, the goodness of our Creator is again amply demonstrated.

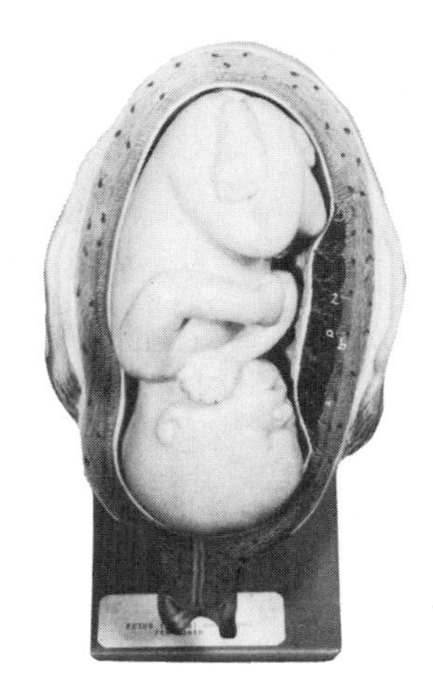

The eight photographs of the SOMSO models (distributed by Markham Publishing Corp., Stamford, Connecticut, USA), showing the uterus with embryo and fetus in various stages of pregnancy, were made available by courtesy of the Family Foundation (SA) Inc.

Artificial Insemination by Husband (AIH)

Artificial insemination is the instrumental placing of a man's semen (containing his sperm) in or near the cervix (neck) of a woman's womb. There are three methods of placing semen. The Royal College of Obstetricians and Gynaecologists (RCOG) in Britain found 'that of the three methods of placing semen, the most favoured was the "intracervical" used in 74 percent of cases, followed by placement in the vaginal vault in 18 percent, and inside the uterus in 8 percent' (Quoted in Russell Scott, *The Body as Property,* 1981, 200).

Some physicians prefer fresh semen, others frozen; and there are also doctors who use a mixture of both. The methods of collecting semen differ. Usually it is obtained by masturbation after a short period of abstinence from ejaculation (3 to 12 days). The reason for the recommended abstinence is that the quality of the semen (sperm concentration and semen volume) is improved by a short period of abstinence. However, ejaculation of semen after more than two weeks of abstinence may produce an aged, defective or less fertile sperm content.

It seems that the pioneers of artificial insemination were fourteenth-century Arab tribesmen. They used it 'as a device to alter the quality and purity of their enemies' horses. Their practice was to deposit secretly in the vaginas of enemy mares cloths soaked with the semen of inferior stallions' (R. Scott, 198).

The first successful human artificial insemination, using the husband's semen, was carried out by a Scottish anatomist and surgeon, John Hunter, in London in 1785. In the United States, J. Marion Sims is known to have carried out the first human artificial insemination in 1866.

The technique was first scientifically described by an Italian physiologist, Lazzaro Spallanzani, in 1784. He had succeeded in artificially inseminating a bitch. (Spallanzani was also the scientist who first thought of freezing human semen in 1776; after 120 years, others suggested 'frozen sperm banks'.) The regular practice of human artificial insemination began in the 1950s.

Artificial insemination by the husband (AIH) is usually sought when the wife, in spite of having regular sexual intercourse with her husband, does not conceive and the physician has diagnosed male infertility. Such infertility may be caused by impotence, anatomical defects of his urethra (the tube from the bladder conveying both urine and semen), 'some types of spinal injury', or commonly some defect in the quality of the sperm.

The technical difficulties in artificially raising the concentration of the infertile man's sperm have made the practice of AIH almost obsolete. Modern medical technologists prefer artificial insemination by donor (AID) in these cases because it is simpler and more successful in securing a woman's pregnancy.

Artificial insemination amounts to the generation of human life without sexual intercourse. This issue has been addressed both in Jewish and Christian moral traditions.

It seems that, in Jewish ethical thinking, artificial insemination by the husband is permissible

> if no other method is possible for the wife to become pregnant. However, certain qualifications exist. There must have been a reasonable period of waiting since marriage (2, 5, or 10 years, or until medical proof of the absolute necessity for AIH), and, according to many authorities, the insemination may not be performed during the wife's period of ritual impurity. It is permitted by most rabbis to obtain sperm from the husband both for analysis and for insemination, but difference of opinion exists as to the method to be used in the procurement of it. Masturbation should be avoided if at all possible, and coitus interruptus, retrieval of sperm from the vagina, or the use of a condom seem to be the preferred methods (Fred Rosner).

The reference to the ritually-unclean woman (*niddah*, Leviticus 12:2; 15:19-32) raises the question with regard to the time during which artificial insemination can be carried out. This is a specific problem for a woman who has a very short menstrual cycle, because her fertile period occurs during the seven days of her ritual uncleanliness. A typical Jewish ethical solution is the advice to abbreviate the unclean period to four days so that the insemination can take place after the woman's ritual immersion for purification (*tevilah*).

Fred Rosner's chapter on 'Artificial Insemination in Jewish Law' in *Jewish Bioethics* (1979) contains some very interesting comments on relevant passages from the Talmud. The opinions of Jewish scholars are divided on the issue. Some moral authorities state that AIH is permissible, while others permit this act 'only in extreme situations'. A curious argument is the one advanced by some rabbis who oppose artificial insemination on the ground that 'the physician might be tempted to add foreign semen to that of the husband in order to facilitate conception'. AIH is, from a moral point of view, a totally different issue from artificial insemination by a donor (AID). All Jewish counsellors, however, would recommend that married couples employ the services of a 'trustworthy physician' if artificial insemination is being contemplated.

In Roman Catholic moral teaching, AIH has been officially rejected.

Pope Pius XII in his Address to Midwives on October 29, 1951, stated:

> To consider unworthily the cohabitation of husband and wife, and the marital act, as a simple organic function for the transmission of seed, would be the same as to convert the domestic hearth, which is the family sanctuary, into a mere biological laboratory. For this reason, in Our address of September 29, 1949, made to the International Congress of Catholic Doctors, We formally rejected artificial insemination in marriage. The marital act, in its natural setting, is a personal action. It is the simultaneous and direct cooperation of husband and wife which, by the very nature of the agents and the propriety of the act, is the expression of the mutual giving which, in the words of Scripture, results in the union 'in one flesh'.

The argument used by the Pope is based on the hidden assumption that 'the child must always be conceived of an act of itself'. This becomes even clearer if we read the sentences following the quoted passage:

> There is much more than the union of two life-germs, which can be brought about even artificially, that is, without the cooperation of the husband and wife. The marital act, in the order of, and by nature's

design, consists of a personal cooperation which the husband and wife exchange as a right when they marry.

There is difference of opinion among Roman Catholic moral theologians with regard to the permissibility of AIH. However, a careful study of the Address of Pope Pius XII to a Group of Catholic Obstetricians and Gynaecologists on January 8, 1956, must lead to the conclusion that papal teaching does not allow the practice of AIH. The Pope said in his Address:

> Artificial fecundation exceeds the limits of the right which spouses have acquired by the matrimonial contract, namely, that of fully exercising their natural sexual capacity in the natural accomplishment of the marital act. The contract in question does not confer on them a right to artificial fecundation, for such a right is not in any way expressed in the right to the natural conjugal act and cannot be deduced from it. Still less can one derive it from the right to the 'child', the primary 'end' of marriage. The matrimonial contract does not give this right, because it has for its object not the 'child', but the 'natural acts' which are capable of engendering a new life and are destined to this end. It must likewise be said that artificial fecundation violates the natural law and is contrary to justice and morality.

This passage forbids not only AIH, but all artificial means by which conception may be achieved (for example, test-tube conception). If one still has doubts about the papal view after reading this passage, then consideration should also be given to what Pope Pius XII said in Rome during the 7th International Hematological Congress on September 12, 1958:

> We condemn(ed) once again all types of artificial insemination, on the ground that this practice is not included among the rights of married couples and because it is contrary to the natural law and Catholic morals. As for artificial insemination between unmarried persons, We declared in 1949 that this practice violates the principle of the natural law that new life may be procreated only in a valid marriage.

It seems to be very clear that those Roman Catholics who follow the moral teachings of their church cannot turn to artificial insemination as a means of achieving pregnancy.

In Anglican, Lutheran, and Protestant churches, we generally find a more tolerant attitude toward AIH. This is true even in the writings of those ethicists who strongly oppose AID (such as Paul Ramsey, Helmut Thielicke, Lindsay Dewar, and others).

Non-Roman Catholic arguments in favour of AIH place the emphasis on the context of the biological event of conception, namely, the 'more broadly human function — a man and a wife accepting responsibility for caring for and rearing a child'. Against this position, however, another Christian conviction argues that 'the same sexual love that generates ought to become in principle the parental love that nurtures' (McCormick, 1969). Parents 'do not love their children simply because the children are there and need love. They ought to love them because they have loved each other, and because the children are the visible fruit and extension of that love.'

Helmut Thielicke, a Lutheran theologian, deals with artificial insemination in his *Theological Ethics* (Vol. 3 — 'Sex'). Speaking of AIH in terms of "homologous insemination", he says:

> Artificial insemination threatens to remove the biological process of procreation from the psychophysical totality of the marital fellowship.

Following that statement, Thielicke deals in more detail with homologous insemination, which he defines 'as the artificial transmission of semen from a husband to a wife':

> It is employed as an expedient when for (certain) reasons a normal emplacement of the semen is impossible. In this case it is a matter of medical aid to fertilization, to which serious objections can hardly be raised if all medical efforts to make the normal act of procreation possible have been without result. For in a marriage thus handicapped it is entirely possible that there can be a personal and sexual fellowship which is in accord with the meaning and purpose of marriage. The sole handicap — and I choose the word deliberately — consists only in the fact that a particular physical particle or a psychic condition is missing and that this blocks the way to the fulfillment of the marriage in having a child (Thielicke, *Theological Ethics*, 3, 252).

Helmut Thielicke also deals with some serious objections, namely, that childlessness in a marriage may come from a 'deeper' disorder, such as an 'unerotic' marital relationship. AIH in such a case is not an aid to procreation, but a substitute for intercourse.

An 'unimportant' objection, in Thielicke's view, is one used in opposing the conclusions of the committee appointed by the Archbishop of Canterbury. The report of that committee, 'Artificial Human Insemination' (1948), came up with conclusions which amounted to 'being unconditionally in favour of homologous insemination'. Objectors to the report challenged the necessity of masturbation, seeing it as 'contrary to Christian moral law' even in the case of a husband providing semen for artificial insemination.

A fundamental question yet to be resolved relates to the distinction between what is 'natural' and what is 'unnatural'. Is AIH as a medical procedure a legitimate 'aid to the natural', or is it an illegitimate and 'unnatural' violation of nature and the natural process of procreation?

There are, of course, moral limits to medical intervention. In the case of AIH, there is a moral responsibility on the shoulders of the married couple as well as the attending physician. The arguments raised against this practice are serious arguments and ought to be considered by those Christians and non-Christians who, on the face of it, can see no objections to AIH. These arguments have been advanced for the sake of the moral and spiritual health of men and women. Health care involves much more than care of the body. The totality of human personhood must also be taken into account. This is especially so when we are dealing with such a fundamental human issue as conception being contrived outside of the immediate context of the loving union of husband and wife.

These ethical objections to AIH remain, despite the fact that, for pragmatic reasons, physicians increasingly prefer to use AID. With AIH now being used only rarely, it is over AID that the current ethical debate is most vigorously conducted.

Artificial Insemination by Donor (AID)

Artificial insemination by donor (AID) 'involves the replacement of the natural father by a biological father in order to satisfy the parental needs of infertile couples' (Carl Wood).

More than a decade ago, the noted American ethicist, Paul Ramsey, wrote:

> Aldous Huxley's fertilizing and decanting rooms in the Central London Hatchery (*Brave New World*) will become a possibility within the next fifteen to fifty years. I have no doubt they will become actualities — at least as a minority practice in our society. One reason this will come to pass is that philosophers, theologians and moralists, churches and synagogues, do not have the persuasive power to prevent the widespread social acceptance of morally objectionable technological 'achievements' if they occur. Philosophers whose business it is to transmit wisdom which begins in fear of the Lord, while criticizing, reshaping, and enlivening these wisdoms, have collectively abandoned understanding, and their voices ('Parenthood and the Future of Man by Artificial Donor Insemination' in *Fabricated Man*, 1970, 104).

Ramsey's statement certainly holds true today. Medical, biochemical, and related research, carried out by modern scientists, seem to have been cut loose from serious ethical thinking and moral considerations. It is as if scientific knowledge can be applied to human situations without ethical accountability, as if scientific achievements somehow justify themselves as 'progress' which dare not be questioned.

But, when conception of a new life as the fruit of the expression of marital love is being replaced by fertilization as a result of manipulative laboratory techniques, it is time that serious questions were asked about the moral legitimacy of such (scientific) activities.

To be conceived, born, and nurtured within a human family consisting of husband, wife, and children (and if necessary, other relatives) is essential for our human identity, growth, and welfare. To be fabricated, selected, and assigned to other human beings, for raising in an abnormal household structure of the latter's choice (perhaps lesbian, or unmarried single parent, etc.), constitutes a serious social disturbance which could well lead to the ultimate loss of our biological, moral, and socio-legal identity.

In Jewish ethical thinking, AID is not a morally acceptable practice. It is considered 'by most rabbinic opinion to be an abomination and strictly prohibited for a variety of reasons'. The Jewish ethicist, I. Jakobovits, says that artificial insemination (*Hazra's Melakhutit*) in the case of a donor's semen being used, should be condemned as 'an act of hideousness', or 'an abomination', or 'human stud farming'.

Some of the questions which have been asked and discussed in Jewish literature are:

> Is the woman prohibited to her husband following an artificial insemination? Is it considered an act of adultery? What is the status of the child? Is the child a *mamzer* (illegitimate)? Does the donor fulfil the commandment of procreation? Is the offspring considered the child of the donor? Is the woman considered to be the pregnant or nursing wife of another, and prohibited to marry again for a certain interval if her husband should die or divorce her? (Fred Rosner).

These questions may appear to be too speculative or philosophical. Yet, we should realize that in real-life situations such questions can and will arise. And there are even more serious socio-moral and legal issues related to AID which will be taken up later in the chapter.

In Roman Catholic moral teaching, AID is strictly forbidden (see references in the previous section on AIH). Pope Pius XII said in his Address to Delegates at the Fourth International Congress of Catholic Doctors (September 29, 1949):

> Artificial insemination in matrimony, but produced by means of the active element of a third person, is (equally) immoral, and as such is to be condemned without right of appeal. Only the husband and wife have the reciprocal right on the body of the other for the purpose of

> generating new life: an exclusive, inalienable, incommunicable right. And that is as it should be, also for the sake of the child.
> To whoever gives life to the tiny creature, nature imposes, in virtue of that very bond, the duty of protecting and educating the child. But when the child is the fruit of the active element of a third person — even granting the husband's consent — between the legitimate husband and the child there is no such bond of origin, nor the moral and juridical bond of conjugal procreation.

Anglican, Lutheran, and Protestant ethicists differ in their stances on AID. Joseph Fletcher, the well-known and influential proponent of situation-ethics, argues in favour of AID because he does not acknowledge any violation of the marriage bond if both husband and wife have consented to the procedure. He further maintains that the donor's relationship to the wife is 'completely impersonal'.

However, Canon Lindsay Dewar, in his influential book *An Outline of Anglican Moral Theology* (1968), expressed the view that AID 'would be condemned by the majority of Anglican moral theologians, but not by all'. Dewar gave four reasons why AID would be condemned in the Church of England:

1. In Great Britain it is illegal, and regarded as adulterous (see *Russell v Russell*, House of Lords 1924). Furthermore, in law the registration of a child begotten by AID as the child of the husband, would be a contravention of the Perjury Act 1911.
2. Even if it were legal, it would involve a large measure of deception, the facts being known only to the couple concerned and their medical adviser; but there are some advocates of AID who maintain that strict secrecy need not be observed.
3. The psychological danger both to the 'parents' and to any child so born are so grave as to make the action unwarranted.
4. The strong desire of a wife to bear a child may well be inordinate and pathological and one to be resisted for the ultimate good of the woman herself.

At the 1958 Lambeth Conference, the Bishops of the Anglican communion agreed that 'artificial insemination by anyone other than the husband raises problems of such gravity that the Committee cannot see any possibility of its acceptance by Christian people'. These views were reaffirmed by the 1968 Lambeth Conference.

Paul Ramsey (quoted above) and Helmut Thielicke both reject AID. Thielicke deals with 'heterologous insemination' from the standpoint of the persons in marriage and their possible motives and situations, of the person of the donor (the 'spermator'), and finally of the doctrine that 'everything can be made' (*Machbarkeit aller Dinge*).

The argument that AID is an act of adultery is, however, difficult to sustain. It is certainly true that we can speak of AID as an act of interference by a third person 'even though it is only his sperm that "represents" (?) him'. Adultery, however, is a **personal act of infidelity**, an entering into another relationship. Christians believe that adultery begins with 'lust' (Matthew 5:28) and that infidelity proceeds from the 'heart' (our 'personal centre').

AID normally takes place if both husband and wife consent to it (except in recent cases of 'do-it-yourself artificial insemination'). Since an 'AID-child' has at least a biological tie with the mother, some couples choose artificial insemination by donor rather than adoption as a means of achieving parenthood. In the case of an AID pregnancy, the parenthood of the father is social, and that of the mother social and biological. If a married couple adopts a child, they are parents in the social sense only. That, of course, does not mean that there are necessarily any psychological or other deficiencies in the relationship between the adopting parents and the adopted child.

If couples have children by means of AID, the missing factors in the relationship with their children are specifically related to their biological origins. Such children have not been conceived within the 'psychophysical totality of a marital relationship'. This also applies to couples who adopt children. However, there is no 'intruder' in the marital fellowship in the case of the adoption of a child or children. Adoption is not an immoral act on the part of married couples. There are positive ethical incentives for adoption, but there are serious moral objections to the practice of AID.

It is claimed in many reports written by physicians involved in AID that the practice is 'beneficial' for couples who want to have children, but who are not able to have a family because of the husband's 'fertility problem'. These physicians claim that there are no psychological problems associated with AID, and that this practice is 'harmless'.

The fact that problems are not recognized — or worse, ignored — would mean that we face serious difficulties. The loss of moral sensitivity, clarity, and discernment is certainly not a 'gain' when the common good of society is concerned.

The Practice of AID and Its Associated Problems

The practice of AID now seems to be widespread, but 'the actual number of human artificial inseminations performed from nation to nation is unknown. To some extent, this is because of the uncertain legal status of the procedure; but mainly our ignorance is the result of an absence of regulation and control, which means that it is impossible to ascertain how many people and organizations are carrying out artificial insemination, let alone its total incidence' (Russell Scott).

Suggested AID birth figures are (R. Scott and J.F. Leeton):

United States of America:

until 1957 — a total of 100,000
1957-1966 — annual rate 5,000-6,000
by 1975 — annual rate 10,000
by 1979 — annual rate 20,000 (*Newsweek*, March 1979).

United Kingdom:

1977 — 22 medical centres in England performed AI. During that year, 2,400 couples were referred and 1,200 received treatment. A total of 731 pregnancies was achieved.
June 1980 — The number of AI centres has grown to 38.

Australia:

prior to 1970 — No medical reports of any AID practices, except for a few clandestine treatments.
1973-1976 — Several hospitals reported on AID work: In 1973, the Crown Street Hospital for Women (Sydney) reported 60 pregnancies from 114 patients receiving AID treatment with fresh semen. In 1976, the Adelaide Centre (Dr Colin Matthews) achieved 42 pregnancies from 111 women.

It may be noted that the 1973 pregnancies in Sydney were the results of an average of two inseminations per month over a 6.5 (menstrual) cycle period using fresh semen. The pregnancies reported from Adelaide in South Australia in 1976 occurred after an average 2.8 cycle period. But, at the same time, only two pregnancies were achieved with the use of frozen sperm after a 9.5 cycle period.

In 1977, the first Australian workshop on AID was held at the Royal Women's Hospital in Melbourne. Over 100 interstate delegates attended this meeting, during which an 'informal national body' was formed. Since 1977, annual meetings of this organization have been held. In other countries, there have been similar conferences on AID.

At present, approximately 600 women in Australia's 14 clinics are being treated by AID yearly. About 10,000 AID children under the age of 15 have already been born. But the problem of male infertility seems to be much greater than these figures might imply. The suggested (1976-78) figures relating to 'infertile couples', where the problem of infertility was with the male, were:

> **United States of America:**
> 2.25 million marriages. Between 230,000 and 340,000 married couples are infertile. Of these, 10-15% are infertilities due wholly to the husband (that is, 1-2% of all marriages were infertile due to male infertility).
>
> **United Kingdom:**
> 0.5 million marriages. The same figures and percentages as mentioned for the USA seem to be applicable.
>
> **Australia:**
> 100,000 marriages. 3% of all marriages are infertile due to a male factor.

These figures suggest that in Australia the infertility problems of married couples due to the husband outnumber those found in the USA and UK. The reasons for this disparity in estimated figures seems to be unknown.

The recruitment of donors for AID takes place through personal contact or by means of leaflet-advertising. A recent example of such a distasteful leaflet, issued by the 'Reproductive Endocrinology Unit' of one of the major hospitals in South Australia, entitled *sperm donors required*, reads as follows:

> The Queen Elizabeth Hospital Infertility Clinic requires sperm donors for its Artificial Insemination by Donor (AID) Programme.
> Within our community, 10% of all marriages are infertile; that is, a pregnancy does not occur within twelve months of attempting pregnancy. Of these couples, 24% are unable to have children because the husband is the infertile member. The option for them is to either adopt or seek help with AID. As there is a five to seven-year waiting list for adoption, AID is the more commonly preferred course for these patients.
> So that adequate donor material is available, a continuing supply of donors is necessary. Semen specimens are stored in liquid nitrogen and therefore can be kept for a number of years. Six donations are collected from each donor.
> Donors are paid $10 per specimen and it is paid in cash after the sixth donation.
> Donations are always a matter of absolute privacy.
> Prospective donors are required to have a physical examination, semen analysis and certain blood tests. An appointment can be arranged by telephoning Dr Bruce Ward, 45 0222, 8 am — 4 pm Monday to Friday.
> If accepted into the programme, the donor will then liaise with the scientist in charge of the Sperm Bank, regarding the collection of specimens, and the Sperm Bank will arrange appointments which fit in with the donor's own working schedule.

We recommend the programme to all those who may be interested in contributing to a worth-while community service.
The need is great and all prospective donors are welcome.
If you are aged between 18 and 40 telephone Dr Bruce Ward, 45 0222, 8 am — 4 pm Monday to Friday.

Such AID programs clearly pose a number of problems. The first of these is the legal status of the AID child. At present, children already born (or about to be born) as the result of AID in Australia 'cannot be regarded as legitimate', which 'means that in the eyes of the law these children are second-class citizens' (see *News Release* 3/7/80 issued by the Attorney-General of New South Wales). In addition to that sober fact, the leaflet cited above raises a number of serious socio-moral questions.

On the one hand, hospitals are trying to create a 'donor pool' from a very wide cross-section of the community to satisfy the desire of women to achieve pregnancy. On the other hand, the same hospitals provide abortion facilities to cope with an annual number of about 100,000 women in Australia seeking termination of their pregnancy at the expense of the life of their preborn children!

These ethical inconsistencies in medical policy and practice come even more into focus when we hear the irresponsible view put forward by 'busy clinicians' who say that 'the arguments of the moral philosophers opposed to AID often seem vague, irrelevant, and out of touch with reality' (William A.W. Walters). The best interests (*sic*) of AID-patients are not simply served by the technical skills of a doctor. The woman seeking treatment is a human being who is morally responsible for her actions, and who must therefore consider all aspects of the AID procedure in relation to her personal, marital, and parental responsibilities — including those which affect the status and welfare of her child.

The **selection of donors** (after family history, educational achievements, and the motivations for participating in an AID program have been considered) heavily depends on the results of a clinical analysis of the donated semen. Sperm count and motility ('at least 60% with good forward progression') are basic criteria; however, 'the general profile with particular regard to sperm morphology is also considered' (I. Johnston). The method of selection may differ from clinic to clinic, but certain laboratory screenings must be carried out to detect real and potential risk factors.

Most clinics, for practical reasons, use liquid nitrogen sperm banks so that instant suitable sperm supply can be guaranteed. There are at present three techniques for freezing sperm: the use of 'ultra deep-freeze units set at -96°, nitrogen-vapor sitting above liquid nitrogen, or controlled freezing chambers, all followed by immediate immersion in liquid nitrogen' (I. Johnston). A detailed scientific account of 'cryopreservation of human semen' is given by M. Mahadevan and A.O. Trounson in *Artificial Insemination By Donor* (ed. C. Wood, Melbourne, Australia, n.d., 19ff).

The time of insemination with frozen semen (after it has been thawed) must take place during a woman's fertile days. Those days can be determined through the use of temperature charts and cervical mucus assessment (women familiar with Natural Family Planning will know the symptoms associated with their fertile and infertile days during the timespan of their natural cycles). According to Mahadevan and Trounson, 'the patient is inseminated on the afternoon of the LH peak [high Luteinising Hormone secretion in the blood approximately 12-24 hours prior to ovulation] and again the next morning'. These writers further maintain that

> from the information available and presented the inescapable conclusion is that all AID should be carried out with frozen semen. Freezing and preservation of semen allows sufficient quarantine time to ensure no infective or other dangerous disease be transferred from a donor to a patient; gives the clinic a reasonable chance to cross-match husband and donor to the requirements of the couple; provides safety that the donor and patient are unknown to each other and allows the donor and insemination clinics to operate completely independently; simplifies the organisation and conduct of the insemination clinic; and ensures that the practice of AID is operated at the level of efficiency and safety to the patient that is expected in current medical practice.

The **selection of AID candidates** is based on a process of 'social assessment', in addition to the required medical examination. In most clinics, a social worker, specializing in the assessment of adoptive parents, is in charge of making this social assessment of prospective AID couples. This assessment has been queried; after all, no such selection or assessment criteria are applied to parents of naturally-born children. It seems that the following guidelines apply in the selection of such couples:

1. The relationship of the husband and wife to each other within the marriage.

2. Motivation of the couple to participate in an AID program.
3. The family history of the couple, including the relationship of each partner to his or her parents.
4. Indication of emotional disturbing factors in either husband or wife.

These guidelines, based on the work of the family psychiatrist, G. Rickarby, are also used in the selection process of adoptive parents.

Others have offered guidelines for the selection of AID applicants based on criteria used by marriage guidance counsellors. These guidelines deal with the presence of marital love, the ability of the partners to communicate, sexual fulfilment, parental potential and desire, the sharing of values, and involvement in mutual support in daily life.

A. McMichael suggests the following additional criteria:

> **For the wife:** good parenting experiences in her own childhood; ability to accept the husband as infertile or as the bearer of an hereditary disease; understanding and supportive attitude to her husband; a desire to assist in the creation of a satisfying relationship between her husband and the child when born.
> **For the husband:** good parenting experiences in his own childhood; ability to come to terms with his infertility and threatened masculinity; acceptance of the insemination of his wife by the semen of another man; parenting a child not his own.

All these criteria, however, are not applicable in the case of AID *candidates who are single.* In November 1981, a lesbian woman in Sydney, Australia, gave birth to a baby 'conceived' by 'do-it-yourself artificial insemination'. The consulting physician had advised the woman about the procedure and the requirements: a sterilized jar of fresh semen (from four of her male friends), a syringe without a needle 'to fertilize the womb', and a diaphragm to act 'as a stopper afterwards'. The woman was unwilling to share her child with either a natural or even a social father.

From what has been presented so far, it is obvious that AID indeed poses moral problems to a great number of people. Apart from the ethical problems, AID has also associated problems which concern the whole community. The personal choice by married couples and single women to use AID is not the only factor involved; the community also has a right to expect personal accountability from individuals who wish to fulfil desires which require the support of the community.

Socio-moral and socio-legal problems associated with AID are far-reaching. Some of the questions in this area are:

What is the moral basis for the legal provision that 'a sperm donor shall have no right or liabilities in respect of any child conceived through use of his semen and an AID child shall have no rights in respect of its donor father'? (Recommendation from the Australian Standing Committee of Attorneys General, July 1980)
What is the moral basis for deciding that, in cases of AID, biological fatherhood begins and ends with a man being spermator without any responsibility for the health, welfare, and education of the AID child which is genetically his?
What is the moral basis for allowing a fertilization-practice which deprives the child of the important right of knowing its biological, social, and cultural 'histories'?
Who should be allowed to select donors?
Should AID be permitted only in a case where the woman is married and has her husband's consent?
On what moral basis should single women who desire to have children be excluded from participating in an AID program?
Should sperm donors receive remuneration for their 'community services'?
Why should 'do-it-yourself' artificial insemination by a married or unmarried woman be recognized as a morally legitimate way of achieving motherhood?
Should controls be introduced upon the right to hold, store, and traffic in semen? (R. Scott)
Where should the details of donor, donee, the process of the insemination, and other relevant facts be kept; and to whom, under what circumstances, and by whose authority, should access to these data be given?
Should the social father of an AID child be required by law to adopt the child as his own?

In particular, far more attention needs to be paid to the responsibility of the donor for the children he sires. Until AID became widely practised, Western societies had always insisted that the natural father of a child takes moral, social, and economic responsibility for that child. Western societies need to consider seriously the socio-moral implications of such a principle being over-ridden.

It is also important to recognize the legitimate rights and aspirations of AID children. People conceived naturally are secure in the knowledge of their biological parentage, and are often fascinated as they explore that knowledge further by an examination of their family tree. Increasingly accepted today is the right of adopted children to know who their real parents are. Yet in the case of AID children such a right is specifically denied. Some AID clinics have already destroyed any records they may have had which would enable a child to find his father.

What ethically justifies doctors taking such decisions on behalf of others? Who should have the right to decide in advance for children that they must not know who their real father is? Is the happiness and fulfilment of a couple in having an AID child of more significance than the right of that child to know its biological origins? And if AID children are to be given that information on request, will it mean an end to the AID program? Would men be unwilling to give sperm if they knew that any child conceived by them could make moral, social, and economic demands upon them?

These are not just hypothetical questions. In April 1982, it was reported that Suzanne Rubin of Los Angeles, USA, was trying to trace her father. She was an AID child, now an adult. She has formed an organization called CUB — Concerned United Birthparents. CUB is seeking to get the law changed so that Suzanne, and others like her, can find out who their fathers are. Just as community attitudes changed in relation to adopted children finding their real parents, so they can change in the case of AID.

Those who engage in AID programs and are responsible for their application should answer these and other questions which are of moral and legal importance to society. If the questions raised are not unreasonable (and the above list indicates they are not), then answers ought to be sought — even if the answers mean that we abandon AID as a proper solution to infertility.

It is significant that in Australia even the most basic legal questions concerning the status of the AID child have not yet been debated in Parliament, let alone any attempt made to introduce legislation. Is it moral reluctance on the part of legislators? Is it fear that legislation in this area will have unknown social consequences? Why is it that we tolerate (even condone) medical-technological practices involving human beings before appropriate ethical guidelines and proper social legislation have been drafted, discussed, and agreed upon by the Parliament of the nation?

Present laws in Australia, both Federal and State laws, have no provisions for the status of AID children. The social father of an AID child cannot sign as, nor can the natural mother name, the father in the official birth register. 'Father' in a birth register means 'natural, biological or genetic father'. The distinction between biological and social fatherhood in relation to AID children has not yet been legally established.

In other countries, these and other socio-legal dilemmas have at least been faced — even if the legislative answers enacted and proposed are based on a legal fiction.

USA: The *Uniform Parentage Act* deals with the legitimacy and family status of AID children. The Act, approved by the Commissioners on Uniform State Laws (1973) and the American Bar Association (1974), has been recommended for adoption by all the States. The Act says that 'a consenting husband is to be regarded in law as the natural father', and excludes the sperm donor from natural fatherhood.

Europe: The Council of Europe published in 1979 a *Draft Recommendation* on artificial insemination 'primarily for the welfare of the AID child'. The Recommendation assigns the act of insemination to physicians only, and requires the consent from donor, recipient, and husband. The consent of the husband only applies where the recipient is married. The physician, under the terms of this Recommendation, is responsible for securing the consents, checking the health of the participants in the AID procedures, and maintaining the secrecy of the parties' identities. No payment except 'reimbursement of expenses' for sperm donations may be made. The trade in semen is forbidden. The AID child is the legitimate child of its natural mother — and, if she is married, of her husband. There is no legal relationship between the AID child and its genetic father (the spermator). The Council of Europe recommended to its Member States to draw up legislation as soon as possible to 'curb any abuses of this practice'.

There are reasons why this sort of Recommendation has appeared in this form. The shortage of children available for adoption has meant a rapid increase in the practice of AID; technological developments have progressed so rapidly that AID is easily carried out; and the socio-moral attitudes of people have radically changed.

Such proposed legislative provisions are certainly beneficial to AID children of Western nations. However, they fail to address themselves to the serious moral, social, and psychological implications for all those involved in AID.

Indeed, we would agree with Russell Scott who wrote:

> It is unlikely that the continued employment of AI techniques on human beings will provoke serious opposition. By comparison with the creation and birth of a number of test-tube babies since 1978, AI looks almost old-fashioned.

In Vitro Fertilization (IVF) ('Test-Tube Babies')

In 1978, an amazed world was informed of the birth on July 25 of the first 'test-tube baby'. Her name is Louise Joy Brown, daughter of John and Lesley Brown. She was 'conceived' in a small glass dish, and born in the Oldham General Hospital in England.

This 'sensational medical breakthrough' was accomplished by the Oldham gynaecologist Patrick Steptoe and the Cambridge scientist Robert Edwards. In their book *A Matter of Life* (1980), they give their personalized story of how they achieved fertilization of human eggs outside the woman's body. The fertilizing of human eggs *in vitro* (in glass) was a major step toward the ultimate goal: the birth of a human baby conceived outside the mother's womb.

The media coverage of this event (and the subsequent 15 'test-tube' births by the end of 1981) has been massive, with many daily newspapers carrying the headline: 'Life is Created in Test Tube'. Indeed, the secular media have given an almost unqualified support to what many people describe as this 'tremendous explosion in the science of biology'. Nevertheless, there has been a variety of critical responses, ranging from reservations to outright disapproval.

This new technique of *in vitro* fertilization (IVF) involves conception outside the womb by artificial means. An egg is extracted from the woman's ovary by the doctor first making three small incisions, each about half a centimetre long, in a woman's abdomen. He inserts three instruments: laparoscope, vacuum needle, and forceps. The laparoscope is a combination of eyepiece and light, which makes it possible for the surgeon to see the ovary inside the woman's body; the vacuum needle, one millimetre in diameter, is lined with slippery coating (Teflon) to prevent the egg from sticking; the forceps search for the woman's ovaries and hold them still. After the ovum has been extracted, it is placed in a small glass dish filled with a very delicate nutrient solution, a combination of hundreds of chemicals. One of the successful fertilization solutions is the modified *Ham's F10* solution which is a combination of 180 chemicals. Collected and washed spermatozoa are added to the culture fluid, and the process of IVF may begin.

Hour 1 .... sperm penetrates the egg (insemination).
Hour 12 .... formation of the nucleus within sperm and egg, containing the genetic information from man and woman.
Hour 24-26 .... the two nuclei fuse (fertilization, the beginning of a pregnancy).

After fertilization, the newly-formed cell is transferred to a growth medium, a solution to which blood serum of the mother has been added, because without this serum human life does not continue to develop.

Hour 30 .... the newly-formed cell (*zygote*) splits into two identical, smaller cells.
Hour 40-50 .... the second division occurs: four cells.
Hour 72 .... the state of thirty-two cells has arisen (*morula*, because the ball of cells now looks like a mulberry).
Hour 96 .... the embryo reaches the blastocyst stage.
Hour 120-140 .... implantation or embedding of the embryo in the uterine wall mucosa (endometrium); ending of the blastocyst stage.

The first such baby, after having been conceived outside the womb, was placed in her mother's womb at the eight-cell stage. The second 'test-tube baby' was placed in his mother's womb at the stage of his being a sixteen-cell human embryo.

Of the first 16 'test-tube babies', three were born in England (Oldham, Glasgow, and London), 12 were born in Melbourne, Australia, and one in Virginia, USA:

Louise Joy Brown (July 25, 1978);
Alastair Montgomery (January, 1979);
Clare, the world's first 'half-caste test-tube baby', who has a Jamaican father and an English mother (October 21, 1981);
Candice Reed, Australia's first 'test-tube baby' (June 23, 1980);

Victoria Smith (March 10, 1981);
Carla Polson (March 28, 1981);
an unnamed baby girl (May 20, 1981);
Stephen and Amanda Mays, the world's first 'test-tube twins' (June 6, 1981);
David (July 3, 1981);
Sharna and an unnamed boy (July 1981);
Allison (Neris) Arnastaukas (July 16, 1981);
Pippin Jaimee Brennan (July 23, 1981);
Matthew James Allan (November 3, 1981);
Elizabeth Jordan Carr, USA's first (December 1981).

According to IVF authorities, there are likely to be about 100 such babies born into the world by the end of 1982.

The IVF program culminating in the births of such children has been founded upon the desire of scientists to expand the field of knowledge, and to be able to manipulate life to suit the demands of contemporary Western societies. Indeed, it is only within the context of society's ethical and social demands that IVF as a scientific achievement can be understood and evaluated.

In Jewish ethical thinking, opinions are divided as far as the moral approval of IVF is concerned. Since Judaism does not adhere to a doctrine of natural law as such, it has to examine IVF in the light of biblical and rabbinic teachings. There are no direct and specific prohibitions of the IVF practice, and therefore 'man is free to utilize scientific knowledge in order to overcome impediments to procreation' (J. David Bleich). The questions which are put by rabbinic scholars relate to the 'moral legitimacy of research involving fetal experimentation':

> The crucial issue is that of increased risk of chromosomal abnormalities leading to physical and mental defects when the ovum is fertilized outside of the body. It is entirely possible that some aspect of the experimental technique may cause genetic damage (Bleich).

Another question which poses problems to Jewish ethicists is the means employed in procuring a man's sperm for the purpose of IVF. Jewish law forbids ejaculation outside the context of marital intercourse. Ejaculation such as by masturbation is regarded as 'destruction of the seed' (*hoza'at zera le-vatalah*). Most teaching authorities in the Judaic tradition would advise the 'removal of semen from the vaginal tract following normal coitus' as being the 'optimal method'.

Other moral questions which present themselves are those which have already been raised with regard to children born as a result of artificial insemination.

A problem which is of particular concern to Jewish ethicists is the destruction of developing embryos after the selection of a suitable blastocyst has taken place. The removal of multiple ova to ensure the success of IVF in turn leads to the fertilization of more than one ovum, for all the surgically-removed ova are exposed to the male sperm. This ultimately results in feticide: the destruction of the 'unwanted' developing embryos. Jewish authorities in general prohibit this practice; but there are some who do not regard the destruction of an embryo before the fortieth day of gestation as morally wrong.

J. David Bleich concludes his chapter on 'Test-Tube Babies' in *Jewish Bioethics* by saying:

> The moral, genetic, and societal implications of such practices are truly awesome. Nevertheless, the distinction between capricious genetic manipulation and in vitro fertilization which simulates natural procreation and is designed solely to alleviate infertility due to abnormality of the Fallopian tubes should be readily apparent.
>
> In vitro fertilization may, in time, prove to be a highly beneficial development if properly safeguarded. Certainly, indiscriminate tampering with nature is dangerous and immoral. Utmost vigilance must be maintained lest we fashion a Huxley-type world in which eugenic selection becomes the norm. Yet, if properly controlled and not permitted to become a substitute for normal human procreation, this revolutionary technique can be a welcome means of bestowing the happiness and fulfilment of parenthood upon otherwise childless couples (80 ff).

In Roman Catholic moral teaching, IVF, like the previously-discussed methods of artificial fecundation, meets with official disapproval on the grounds of (the basic principle of) the inseparability of the unitive and generative meanings of sexual love.

In Anglican, Lutheran, and Protestant circles, we find a diversity of ethical opinions which are not subject to the scrutiny of a central teaching authority. Joseph Fletcher, the American medical ethicist, said in his paper, 'Indications of Humanhood: A Tentative Profile of Man' (*The Hastings Center Report*, Vol. 2, No. 5: November, 1972):

> A 'test tube baby', although conceived and gestated ex corpo, would nonetheless be humanly reproduced and of human value. A baby made artificially, by deliberate and careful contrivance, would be more human than one resulting from sexual roulette — the reproductive mode of the subhuman species.

For the purposes of biomedical ethics, Fletcher proposed a 'profile of man' in concrete and separate terms, and listed 15 positive and 5 negative 'human criteria'.

The positive criteria include:

intelligence (an individual who falls below the IQ 40-mark is questionably a person; below the 20-mark, not a person)
self-awareness
self-control
a sense of time, of futurity, and of the past
the capability of relating to others
concern for others
communication (completely and finally isolated individuals are subpersonal)
control of existence
curiosity
change and changeability ('all human existence is on a continuum, a matter of becoming')
balance of rationality and feeling
idiosyncrasy ('to be a person is to have an identity, to be recognizable and callable by name')
neo-cortical function ('personal reality depends on cerebration, and to be dead "humanly" speaking is to be ex-cerebral, no matter how long the **body** remains alive')

The negative criteria, according to Fletcher, are:

man is not non- or anti-artificial
man is not essentially parental ('people can be fully personal without reproducing')
man is not essentially sexual ('it is not even necessary to human species survival')
man is not a bundle of rights ('all rights are imperfect and may be set aside if human **need** requires it')
man is not a worshipper ('a viable biomedical ethics is humanistic')

Joseph Fletcher concluded his presentation by saying: 'Divorced from the laboratory and the hospital, talk about what it means to be human could easily become inhumane'.

It is not difficult to see that such bioethical views are totally foreign to traditional Jewish and Christian moral thinking. Furthermore, it is not surprising that Fletcher can justify almost everything — abortion, infanticide, euthanasia, AID, IVF, genetic engineering, research on human subjects, and so on. Biological human life is, according to him, without personal status if a human being lacks one or more of the positive human criteria.

Anyone who accepts Fletcher's 'profile of man' will want, of course, to pursue an entirely different direction in biomedicine and bioethics than the authors of this book, because of a critically different understanding of life and death issues. It is, however, a direction in which most (but not necessarily all) secular humanists wish to go. The popularization of Fletcher's thoughts, and of his foundations for normative decision-making, has had such an enormous impact that his views have rapidly become the 'humanhood agenda' of modern times.

An equally well-known American medical ethicist, Paul Ramsey, holds views opposite to those of Joseph Fletcher. In his article, 'Shall We "Reproduce"?' in *The Journal of the American Medical Association* (June 5 and 12, 1972, Volume 220, Nos. 10 and 11) Ramsey says:

> I must judge that in vitro fertilization constitutes unethical medical experimentation on possible future human beings, and therefore it is subject to absolute moral prohibition. I ask that my exact language be noted: I said, unethical experimentation on **possible future human beings**. By this, I mean the child-to-be, the 'successful' experiments when they come.

Paul Ramsey passes his negative moral verdict on IVF because of a 'right-ordered concern for the child that will be produced by the "successful" cases of these experiments'. He also maintains:

> It is not a proper goal of medicine to enable women to have children and marriages to be fertile **by any** means — means which **may** bring hazard from the procedure, **any** additional hazard, upon the child not yet conceived. To suppose otherwise is to believe couples have such an absolute right to have children that this right cannot be overridden by the requirement that we should first have to exclude any incidence of **induced** risk to the child itself. This would be to adopt an extreme pronatalist assumption that an unconceived child somehow already has a title to be conceived.

Paul Ramsey, further, quotes with approval Leon Kass, who at that time was the Executive Secretary of the Committee on the Life Sciences and Social Policy, National Academy of Sciences. Since Leon Kass is an eminent and vigorous advocate of the view that 'making babies in laboratories means a degradation of parenthood', his considerations of IVF should also be noted:

> Human procreation is human partly because it is not simply an activity of our rational wills. Men and women are embodied as well as desiring and calculating creatures. It is for the gods to create in thought and by fiat (Let the earth bring forth . . .) And some future race of demi-gods (or demi-men) may obtain its survivors from the local fertilization and decanting station. But **human** procreation is begetting. It is a more complete human activity precisely because it engages us bodily and spiritually, as well as rationally. Is there possibly some wisdom in that mystery of nature which joins the pleasure of sex, the communication of love and the desire for children in the very activity by which we continue the chain of human existence? Is biological parenthood a built-in device selected to promote the adequate caring for children? Before embarking on New

> Beginnings in Life we should consider the meaning of the union between sex, love and procreation, and the meaning and consequence of its cleavage.
>
> What is new is nothing more radical than the divorce of the generation of new life from human sexuality and ultimately from the confines of the human body, a separation which began with artificial insemination and which will finish with ectogenesis, the full laboratory growth of a baby from sperm to term. What is new is that sexual intercourse will no longer be needed for generating new life. This piece of novelty leads to two others: there is a new co-progenitor (or several such), the embryologist-geneticist-physician, and there is a new home for generation, the laboratory. The mysterious and intimate processes of generation are to be moved from the darkness of the womb to the bright (fluorescent) light of the laboratory, and beyond the shadow of a single doubt.
>
> The Hebrews, impressed with the phenomenon of transmitting life from father to son, used a word we translate 'begetting' or 'siring'. The Greeks, impressed with the springing forth of new life in the cyclical processes of generation and decay, called it genesis, from a root meaning 'to come into being'. (It was the Greek translators who gave this name to the first book of the Hebrew Bible.) The pre-modern Christian English-speaking world, impressed with the world as given by a Creator, used the term Pro-creation. We, impressed with the machine and the gross national product, our own work of creation, employ a metaphor of the factory, re-production. And Aldous Huxley has provided 'decantation' for that technology-worshipping Brave New World of tomorrow.

It is indeed salutary for us to be reminded of the warning of the Holy See (Pope Pius XII, 1951), the bitter social satire of Aldous Huxley (*Brave New World*, 1932), and C.S. Lewis's *The Abolition of Man* (1947). They all saw 'genetics, pharmacology, and experimental embryology as sources of the coming great evils'. Some people, in an attempt to make light of these works, have suggested that the Pope should be considered only as a 'minor prophet' in his 1951 condemnation of artificial insemination; that Aldous Huxley was hopelessly wrong in his calendar date as to when man would apply his new discoveries to his fellowman (632 AF — After Ford, that is, 600 years in the future); and that C.S. Lewis too was wrong when he wrote that the 'achievement of mastery over the species' would supposedly occur during the 100th century AD.

These minor criticisms, so often advanced by their critics, do not invalidate the prophetic truth of the essence of their arguments. C.S. Lewis warned us that 'we should not do to minerals and vegetables what modern science threatens to do to man himself'. The reality of 'fabricated man' is with us. Genetic laboratories have appeared and continue to be established in many of our larger cities.

On September 28, 1980, the 'godfathers' of the first 'test-tube baby', Drs Steptoe and Edwards, opened Britain's 'first test-tube baby centre with facilities for offering IVF and ET (embryo transfer) to some thirty women at a time'. The centre is called Bourn Hall, and is located in Cambridgeshire. It opened 'with a waiting list of three thousand women prepared to pay £280 for an initial investigation and £1,400 for a ten-day course of treatment' (Russell Scott). 'Test-tube baby' clinics have been set up in various public hospitals both in Britain and Australia.

The British IVF program has been given approval to continue without restrictions, following scrutiny by the British Medical Association's ethics committee (see *The Australian*, February 12, 1982). This decision was reached against the advice of the BMA chairman, Dr Michael Thomas, who had called for a moratorium to allow more debate on the legal and moral issues. The BMA decision is, however, provisional upon the British Government's ultimate assessment of the program, which still continues.

The situation in the USA is different. In 1975, the US Federal Government prohibited the Department of Health, Education and Welfare (HEW) from providing funds for IVF and ET experiments. The 'unofficial nationwide moratorium' was due partly to a delay in the appointment of a national ethics advisory board by the Secretary of HEW (who did not act until 1978), and partly to the fear felt by the American physicians and scientists of being faced with lawsuits if a 'test-tube pregnancy' went wrongly.

However, in December 1981, America's first 'test-tube baby' was born in the Norfolk General Hospital in Virginia. This birth brought a sharp response from the prestigious American College of Obstetricians and Gynaecologists. The College acknowledged that 'the recent birth of children in Britain, Australia and now in the US through the process of in vitro fertilization is a significant scientific breakthrough', but also pointed out that 'there are still technical and ethical issues to be resolved on this subject'. The College, further, urged infertile couples to continue to seek help in 'normal' directions, rather than to turn to test-tube birth.

As far as the fear of lawsuits is concerned, Russell Scott in his *The Body as Property* (1981) writes:

> At the very time of Louise Brown's birth, a damages suit for $1.5 million was being heard in New York in which a husband and wife were suing a medical practitioner (among other defendants) who had destroyed a fertilized egg which one of his colleagues had produced in a

> culture in 1972 and intended to implant in the wife's uterus. The defendant, the head of the department of obstetrics and gynaecology at a university medical centre, said that he had destroyed the specimen because he felt that the skills necessary for success had not been developed at the time and that a monstrosity could have resulted. In addition, the hospital's committee on human experimentation had not approved the action. A jury gave the husband and wife a verdict for $50,000. Irrespective of the possibility that this and similar verdicts could be overruled on appeal, the chances of being dragged into litigation certainly gave American researchers reason to proceed with caution. Malpractice suits by test-tube children against their parents and against the doctors who created them can be easily imagined. The legal status of an egg fertilized *in vitro* must also be considered. Is it alive or not? Can it be discarded and thrown away? A medical practitioner would be ill-advised to embark upon treatment without offering comprehensive advice and obtaining careful documentary clearance from the patient (219,220).

There is at present almost no effective legal control of IVF. There are no specific laws dealing with 'test-tube' children. Sperm and ovum may have been provided by their 'social' parents, in which case they are also the child's 'biological' or 'genetic' parents. However, if the father's sperm and/or the mother's ovum were not 'used' in the IVF procedure, to whom is the child genetically related? Who is by law authorized to fertilize human ova in a laboratory? Who is responsible for the embryo and its welfare? Who is authorized to destroy, freeze, provide, and store human embryos obtained by scientists following an IVF laboratory process? Who owns these embryos?

There are 20,000 married women in Britain, 140,000 women in the USA, and many thousands of women in other parts of the world, all with defective Fallopian tubes. Who will provide them with IVF techniques to satisfy their desire to become pregnant?

It is becoming increasingly obvious that IVF abuse has an enormous potential, and that its inherent problems are almost beyond socio-legal solutions.

It is no secret that the chairman of the Australian Law Reform Commission, Mr Justice Kirby, has repeatedly called for a review of the ethical and legal consequences of the 'test-tube baby' program. He reportedly said in Melbourne on September 29, 1981:

> Let it not be the epitaph of our generation that we proved ourselves brilliant in a dazzling field of scientific endeavour but so morally bankrupt and legally incompetent that we just could not bother or did not have the courage to sort out the consequences for our society and for the human species.

Justice Kirby further said, speaking at the Queen Victoria Medical Centre which conducts an IVF program, that

> questions had arisen as to how frozen embryos could be identified, how they would be used and for how long they could be frozen. Is it acceptable that a child of our generation should be born decades or even centuries hence? I am not unaware of the natural tendency in a democracy for politicians to steer clear of debates such as this. The chief enemies are apathy, indifference, timidity, and the ever-present willingness to underestimate our ability to face up to and answer hard questions in law and morality.

Justice Kirby concluded his address in a rather pointed manner when he said:

> Is it realistic to envisage that the end product of Professor Wood's work will be the human hatcheries in Aldous Huxley's Brave New World? Is there really a fear that poor people will carry the children, fertilized *in vitro*, of wealthy, elegant women who worship sterility? Modern medical techniques imposed unreasonable burdens on doctors, and the law had a duty to make clearer the responsibilities of doctors. It should not be left to hospital committees to muddle along.

The Australian Family Association, at its 1981 National Family Seminar (November 21,22) held at the University of Melbourne, supported Mr Justice Kirby's sentiments by calling for a moratorium on Australia's 'test-tube baby' program. In so doing, it acted upon the advice of a few ethicists and legal authorities who believed that the medical community would show no more 'sense of collective moral responsibility' for the welfare of the unborn than they have already shown in the abortion and euthanasia debates.

There are sound reasons for calling a moratorium on IVF programs. These were outlined by one of the present authors (D.Ch. Overduin) in October 1981. These reasons are:

> the socio-moral and medico-ethical questions re the nature, implications, and consequences of IVF research and practice have not yet been publicly considered;
> the legal status of the test-tube human embryos has not been defined under Australian law;
> the life of human embryos developed under culture conditions is continually threatened because of research and other technological difficulties and failures in the process of their manipulation;
> the ongoing destruction of human embryos grown under culture conditions amounts to the killing of human life;
> the laboratory experimentation with human life, including the freezing of human embryos and the implantation of same in surrogate mothers, has inherent dangers to our human society, which have not yet been discussed but have nevertheless been articulated by a number of reputable medical ethicists;
> the inherent dangers include the associated problems of IVF research

and practice in the context of the multi-faceted field of genetic engineering which have not yet been faced and considered, so that neither adequate legal regulations nor socio-moral guidelines have been drafted and adopted by the appropriate authorities;
the costs of these IVF programs in Australia far outweigh their positive value for the common good of all.

In *Reform* (January 1982, no. 25,32 issued by the Australian Law Reform Commission) it was argued that 'a number of problems that remain to be considered' are:

the use of test-tube fertilization to promote embryonic sex selection;
the potential for genetic engineering and medical experimentation;
the use of surrogate mothers;
the period of the retention of fertilised ova and the effect on retention of death and divorce;
the property and status complications of the birth in future generations of a child conceived in our generation;
the costs of the technique, against other uses of the medical dollar.

On the face of it, the practitioners of IVF seem willing to discuss the ethics of this procedure. Professor E.C. Wood, head of Melbourne's 'test-tube baby' research team, pointed out the enormous technical improvements achieved when he said that 'Australia's test-tube embryos now have a 20% chance of survival compared with as little as 1% in 1979'. Nevertheless, on November 22, 1981, he called for 'legal guidelines on the ethical implications of test-tube research — including the freeze/thaw process of storing embryos'. He also called 'for a national body to set medical standards for the research'. He further commented on the 'improvement' of all aspects of IVF, but was convinced that IVF was 'here to stay'. According to Professor Wood, 'community feelings should dictate the question of scientists making "spare" embryos'. These embryos could be killed for the purpose of scientific study.

We cannot but feel that Professor Wood and others have got it all back to front. The techniques they are using were first devised as a part of animal husbandry. Before they started experimentation on human beings, should not the doctors first have asked for ethical guidelines? Is there something uncandid and insincere about doing something first, and then asking the community later what they think about its being done?

This unsatisfactory state of affairs was further emphasized by the response of doctors to the call by the Roman Catholic Church in Australia for a halt to the 'test-tube baby' program. Its call followed a statement by the

Anglican Church's Social Responsibilities Commission, which had expressed its concern at experiments with human life 'without any debate of the ethical issues involved and without any legal limits'. In reply, Professor Douglas Saunders, who heads the infertility clinic at Sydney's Royal North Shore Hospital and its IVF program, said that the demand by infertile couples was so great it was too late to stop the program.

It would seem that it is the demand created by the 'success' of the IVF program that is to decide the future of IVF, and not its ethical propriety. In referring to 'this conservative backlash', Professor Saunders said: 'We do not want to have a moratorium for the sake of the Church'.

The question, then, is: How serious are IVF practitioners in wanting a public discussion of the ethics of IVF? Have they already decided that it is a *fait accompli*? Is all the talk about discussions on ethics no more than an exercise in public relations?

Notwithstanding the meagre public discussion, the Attorneys General in Australia are presently preparing legislation to define the legal status of 'test-tube children' and 'babies produced by artificial insemination'. The Attorney General of one of the most populous Australian States recently wrote:

> Whilst AID has been in widespread use throughout Australia for many years, in vitro fertilization is a new aspect of medical technology whose implications are not yet clear. The problems which this new technique is capable of creating are of much greater complexity than AID and will no doubt give rise to considerable community discussion which I would encourage as there are many issues of social, as well as legal, importance of which the community should be aware.
> There has as yet been no decision by the Government on the need to legislate in relation to in vitro fertilizations. I understand that this technique is as yet only available in Melbourne and on a limited scale, but I am mindful of the need to monitor developments in this area very closely and this I shall do (F.J. Walker, New South Wales Attorney General).

One way of finding out what the public thinks is by opinion poll. Two Gallup Polls have been carried out in Australia, one in August 1978 and the other in March 1980. These showed that the majority of all people (66 and 74% respectively) approve of 'test-tube babies' for 'couples who can't have children'. The polls do not, however, discover how well informed people are about the nature, implications, and possible consequences of the IVF program. Indeed, such polls may only reflect the favourable and largely uncritical press coverage which has accompanied news of the first 'test-tube babies'. Poll results, therefore, should not be taken as positive indicators for society's moral and legal decision-making in favour of *in vitro* fertilization.

Account should rather be taken of criticisms made by those in a position to criticize. A few years ago, the US specialist in ethics and social philosophy, Dr Paul Ramsey (quoted above), gave testimony on *in vitro* fertilization before the Ethics Advisory Board, US Department of Health, Education and Welfare, established in 1978. He gave four reasons in support of his view that IVF procedures should not become standard practice in the United States:

> I offer four reasons in support of this verdict: 1) the need to avoid bringing further trauma upon this nation that is already deeply divided on the matter of the morality of abortion, and about when the killing of a human being (at tax expense) can occur; 2) the **irremovable** possibility that this manner of human genesis may produce a damaged human being; 3) the **immediate** and not unintended assault this procedure brings against marriage and the family, the **immediate** possibility of the exploitation of women as surrogate mothers with wombs-for-hire, and the **immediate** and not unintended prospect of beginning right now to 'design' our descendants; and 4) the remote — but still very near — prospect of substituting laboratory generation from first to last for human procreation. We ought not to choose — step by step — a world in which extracorporal gestation is a possibility. Since I wish to testify to things distinctively characteristic of embryo manipulation, reasons 2), 3), and 4) are more significant, in my opinion.

Those who fear that modern technological skills could be used in the service of a *Brave New World* social philosophy will no doubt find such fears confirmed in Dr Ramsey's testimony.

On the other hand, IVF is, according to its ardent supporters and practitioners, a source of hope to millions of infertile couples. One of Australia's leaders of the IVF program, Dr Alex Lopata, said in June 1980 that the 'technique could eventually become a readily available treatment for infertility'. One in fifty married women seems to be afflicted with diseased or blocked Fallopian tubes; IVF is hailed as the cure for such infertility. Further, the minute embryos developed in these glass dishes in laboratories can be used as 'donors' of cell colonies; that is, the human embryos can be grown for the purpose of using the cell tissue for the treatment of certain ailments. The human embryos are useful not only for pregnancy but also 'for the alleviation of certain human disorders' (Robert Edwards). There is even the suggestion that 'parentless' embryos can be grown for experimentation, and for growing organs for organ-transplants.

It is true that the living children, born as a result of a successful IVF process, are witnesses to one of the greatest technological advancements of the closing decades of the twentieth century. Of course, it must be remembered that, after pregnancy was established, they were allowed to go on to birth only if they passed a series of tests. These tests consisted of bio-chemical measurements, ultra-sound checks to ensure normal development, and the testing of the amniotic fluid (amniocentesis) at 16 weeks of pregnancy to detect possible mongolism (Down's Syndrome) and spinal defect (*spina bifida*).

It is equally true that IVF and embryo transfer (ET) will never be 100% successful. Professor Carl Wood stated in an interview with Ann Westmore in Melbourne (June 1980) that 'even in totally natural circumstances only about 30% of human eggs exposed to sperm survive to birth . . . So even with the best IVF and ET techniques and the most suitable couples, we could not expect a success rate greater than about 25%'.

Apart from the fact that the comparison between 'natural' success rates and 'manufactured' success rates is fraught with difficulties as far as its moral validity is concerned, there are other implications of the IVF project. Soon after the birth of Australia's second test-tube baby on March 10, 1981, it was announced that the head of the medical team, Professor Carl Wood, 'had built up a bank of frozen human embryos'. A member of the fertilization team, Dr Kovacs, was interviewed on ABC's program 'Nationwide' on April 6, 1981 by Mr Peter Couchman. During that interview, the following was said concerning the frozen embryos (*News Weekly*, 15/4/81):

Mr Couchman:	What do you intend to do with them?
Dr Kovacs:	Well, the plan is that these embryos, if they are shown to be healthy and viable after they are defrosted, will probably be planted into the same woman in a subsequent cycle with the aim of producing a pregnancy for that woman.
Mr Couchman:	Well, you have the possibility of doing more than that, don't you?
Dr Kovacs:	I guess there are all sorts of theoretical possibilities.
Mr Couchman:	Can we look at some of these possibilities? . . . If another woman comes to you, a woman who has

no contact with the woman who produced those eggs, if the woman comes to you and asked you to implant one of those embryos into her body, you would have to do it, wouldn't you?

Dr Kovacs: Well, I don't know. These are very difficult problems and it is to solve problems such as these, which are not medical problems, that the bio-ethics committee was set up — or the ethics and the bio-ethics committee was set up at Monash . . .

Mr Couchman: But shouldn't those decisions have been taken before you actually created this bank of human embryos?

Dr Kovacs: It is a problem that has arisen as a by-product of the project and it wasn't one that was necessarily contemplated . . .

Mr Couchman: Do you know the men who contributed the sperm that fertilized these eggs?

Dr Kovacs: Yes, in most cases it was the husband.

Mr Couchman: In most cases, but not all?

Dr Kovacs: Not all. If we are doing the fertilization outside the body in a couple where the husband is infertile, then we would have to use semen from a donor, the same as we do through artificial insemination.

This extract from an interview with a member of an Australian IVF team is in harmony with the expressed conviction of Dr Alan Trounson, a senior reproductive biologist 'who handles the eggs through their laboratory fertilization and implantation', and who works with the Monash University Bioethics Committee.

Dr Trounson said in Melbourne on July 5, 1981 that 'Australia's pioneering program to produce the world's first baby from a frozen embryo was an "extremely ethical approach"' (*The Australian*, 6/7/81). For a full year before it became known publicly, 'researchers had been freezing three-day-old embryos and then thawing and implanting them in women'. Twelve thawed embryos had been implanted during that period, but no pregnancy had resulted from these experiments. Nevertheless, according to Dr Trounson, the experiments were 'entirely within ethical guidelines'. He did not state who drafted these guidelines, nor did he say what these guidelines were. He talked about the 'ownership of the eggs', and said that, since the patient-owners have the right to decide what happens to the eggs, 'there are no ethical worries'. Since Dr Trounson seems to have pioneered this technique, his knowledge about it is acknowledged; but his program of freezing, thawing, and implantation of embryos raises serious ethical issues which do have to be questioned. Apart from the present statistical reality that only about one in ten embryos is likely to 'take', there are fundamental human life issues which have to be subjected to rational and critical scrutiny.

The procedures of IVF and of the freezing-thawing-implantation of human embryos are fraught with serious ethical problems. These procedures are the concern not only of those who perform them and of their patients; they are also the concern of the community at large which is being asked to fund them and to approve of them. It is not the scientists concerned who should make the final decision as to whether or not their experiments are morally justified, acceptable, and responsible. This is not to say that they should be excluded from the debate on the ethical implications of their work; we simply wish to underline the fact that a training in science does not necessarily make one's ethical judgments immune from error.

We take the stance that their 'ethics of aiding nature' is, in fact, an 'ethics of assaulting nature', and shall attempt to substantiate this argument despite the 'findings' of public opinion polls and the modern inclination to stand in awe and wonder at the technological achievements of medical and veterinary scientists.

The moral responses to the IVF 'successes' may be divided into four categories: affirmation, anathema, accommodation, and apprehension.

The **affirmation response** looks at the success of the experiment and refuses to contemplate any further questions. The 'benefit' of the technique to childless couples justifies the external fertilization process. The **anathema response** is inspired by grave misgivings related to a number of issues. These include the possibility of future embryo transfers into the wombs of 'surrogate' or 'host' mothers; the fertilization of an ovum with the sperm of a man other than the woman's husband (the problem is an extension of the current practice of AID); the destruction of unwanted embryos; a conception divorced from the marital act of sexual intercourse; difficulties of a legal nature (for example, the parents' right in relation to IVF embryos); and, last but not least, the fear that the dystopian prophecies of Aldous Huxley's *Brave New World* will become dire realities. The anathema response poses its definite No against the categorical Yes of the affirmation response.

The **accommodation response**, expressed by many contemporary ethicists and moral theologians, takes the view that, if natural conception cannot be achieved in the case of a married couple, IVF should be accepted as a morally justifiable alternative. After all, there is now hope for the millions of couples in the world who cannot have children. In this view, ethical reflection should be determined by man's scientific insights and successes rather than the reverse. Avoidance of technological horrors will be guaranteed by man's need for survival and by his rational considerations in both the social and politico-economic spheres. This is a kind of optimism which seems to be closed to the reality of moral evil. The **apprehension response** is inclined to put the burden of proof on those scientists who want to continue with 'test-tube' procreation. It holds that such scientists ought to be accountable for the moral implications of their technological experiments.

We know that IVF has had 'results' since 1978. We also know that the fertilization of eggs in a laboratory is a scientific development related to the tissue-culture field.

> As far back as the 1940s, Dr John Rock, in the course of experiments to develop a birth-control pill, succeeded in fertilizing a human egg with sperm in a test tube. Following fertilization, the egg went through several divisions. A decade later, Dr Landrum Shettles of Columbia Presbyterian Hospital repeated Rock's success. His microphotographs of the union of an egg and a sperm in vitro appeared in dozens of medical textbooks. But, like Rock's, his embryo lived only a short time. In 1961, an Italian biologist, Dr Daniele Petrucci, announced he had had considerably greater results than his predecessors. In a still-controversial experiment, Petrucci fertilized an egg and allowed it to grow outside the human body for fifty-nine days. He claimed that 'a heartbeat was discernible' but he was forced to destroy his creation because 'it became deformed and enlarged — a monstrosity'. Petrucci, a Catholic, went so far as to give his embryo conditional baptism and extreme unction, but this was deemed insufficient by Italian authorities and the Church hierarchy. Under orders from the Pope, Petrucci finally gave up his attempts to grow life in vitro (Ted Howard and Jeremy Rifkin, *Who Should Play God*?, 106,107).

'Playing God' in the laboratory is no longer a myth. In an age when the Christian faith is increasingly disregarded by the Western intelligentsia, scientists are taking on the role of creator, and are shaping society accordingly. Nevertheless, the Christian faith is the religion which is claimed by most members of most Western societies. And that faith involves a belief in 'one God, the Father, the Almighty, maker of heaven and earth, of all that is, seen and unseen' (The Nicene Creed). In the light of that fundamental belief, which is still assented to by most Westerners, how should Christians respond to the 'fabrication' of human life in test-tubes? How should they view the freezing, thawing, and implantation of human embryos in the womb of their natural or 'surrogate' mothers?

The Bible does not give a definitive blueprint for the formulation of a simple ethical response to these questions. IVF was not known to Moses, or to the prophets and the apostles. There is no command which says: 'You shall not practise *in vitro* fertilization'; there is no apostolic decree which explicitly forbids embryo transfer. Nevertheless, Christian humanism provides the firmest basis on which to assess the ethical soundness of the external fertilization process and its related issues, for such a humanism is rooted in a Christocentric faith which acknowledges the validity of the natural law and which recognizes the splendour of the laws of nature.

The fertilization process outside the woman's womb affirms the scientific fact that human life begins at conception. This immediately raises questions about the status of the human embryos fabricated in test-tubes.

If we acknowledge that human life has a unique value in the eyes of God (a fact which can easily be derived from the biblical data), and that the right to life of every human is recognized by international covenants of the United Nations (presumably in response to a rational consideration of the natural law), then serious thought must be given to the morality of willingly destroying human embryos if they cannot be 'used', or if they develop contrary to scientific goals or expectations.

If we acknowledge that the gift of a new human life is destined by God to be received in the context of a loving union of husband and wife, and that this can be verified from natural law, then consideration must be given to the morality of initiating external conception even if the sperm and ovum were taken from husband and wife.

If we acknowledge that the conception and birth of a child put the responsibility for its care and upbringing on the shoulders of both its father and mother, we should consider if it is morally right to produce 'fatherless and motherless' embryos in the incubators of university and hospital laboratories.

If we acknowledge (with Paul Ramsey) 'the remote — but still very near — prospect of substituting laboratory generation from first to last for human procreation', we ought to consider if it is morally right to support the IVF and ET programs.

If we acknowledge the contemporary pressures which are major factors in the break-up of family life in our country, we ought to evaluate the moral implications of manipulating external conception as a substitute for the natural process of fertilization.

The Australian research program costs approximately $200,000 per year, and the capital investment in this program exceeds $1 million. Is such a research program a higher priority than other research programs desperately in need of money — for example, those geared to the treatment of cancer and heart disease? And is it morally right to continue funding a 'life-creation' project when Australia allows the tragic destruction each year of more than 100,000 naturally-conceived, preborn offspring through abortion? (To those annual 100,000 abortions must, of course, be added the destruction and death of many embryos externally conceived in glass dishes.)

If we accept that the conception of human life is an act of God to which he has added the blessing of our humble and joyful 'cooperation', we should even further consider if it is morally right to separate procreation from a loving sexual communion.

Since the primary principle of medical ethics is 'Do no harm', it is essential for us all to understand the moral implications of *in vitro* fertilization and human embryo transfer, and its potentially disastrous consequences for humanity.

Paul Ramsey, in his 'Testimony on In Vitro Fertilization' presented to the US Ethics Advisory Board, leaves us with a grim warning:

> Members of the Ethics Advisory Board may wish to perform the following experiments on themselves. Turn off the tube. Don't pick up the newspaper for two days. Instead, read the third of C.S. Lewis's space-science trilogy, *That Hideous Strength.* The final assault upon humanity is gathering in Edgestow, a fictional British college town. The forces of technology, limited no more by the Christian ages, are trying to combine with pre-Christian forces, represented by Merlin the Magician whose body is buried on the Bracton College grounds. Only the philologist Ransom can save human kind from the powers of the present age concentrated in the National Institute for Coordinated Experimentation (acronym NICE).
>
> It is NICE that the Browns have a wonderful baby girl; her middle name is Joy. Lewis need not have thought of his fictional college, Bracton. Cambridge University is NICE too. So is Vanderbilt. To give couples a baby sexed to their desire will be NICE. Every other step taken will certainly be NICE. Finally, *Brave New World* is entirely NICE. For everyone is happy in Huxley's pharmacological, genetic

and womb-free paradise. Only there is no poetry there. Nor does a baby have the right to be a **surprise.**

The authors believe that the questions and arguments raised in this chapter are sufficient to justify a call for a moratorium on IVF programs and for legally-enforceable ethical guidelines in regard to experimentation on human life.

Surrogate Motherhood

A new 'test-tube (embryonic) baby' in search of a womb... Such an idea sounds far-fetched, but it is a real possibility.

There are women who would be capable of carrying a baby to term, but who are unable to produce normal ova. If they wish to become pregnant, a number of options are open to them.

Such a woman may have a fertilized ovum of another woman implanted into her uterus. The egg may have been fertilized *in vivo* (literally, in living tissue; here, in the uterus of a donor) by means of artificial insemination, using the sperm of the recipient's husband. Or, if preferring *in vitro* fertilization, the woman will ask the physician to use an ovum (or ova) of a donor and the sperm of her husband.

There are also women who have perfectly healthy Fallopian tubes and ovaries, but who do not want to go through a pregnancy. They may look for a 'surrogate mother' who is willing to have the fertilized ovum implanted into her womb (after it has been surgically removed from the donor's uterus to the test-tube), and to carry the baby to term either as a favour or for a fee. After birth, the surrogate mother gives the baby back to its biological or genetic mother.

Surrogate motherhood is not a modern idea; it even has a biblical precedent. An Old Testament passage (Genesis 30:1–6) relates the following story:

> When Rachel saw that she bore Jacob no children, she envied her sister; and she said to Jacob, 'Give me children, or I shall die!' Jacob's anger was kindled against Rachel, and he said, 'Am I in the place of God, who has withheld from you the fruit of the womb?' Then she said, 'Here is my maid Bilhah; go in to her, that she may bear upon my knees, and even I may have children through her.' So she gave him her maid Bilhah as a wife; and Jacob went in to her. And Bilhah conceived and bore Jacob a son. Then Rachel said, 'God has judged me, and has also heard my voice and given me a son'; therefore she called his name Dan. (Dan = He judged.)

It is true that Bilhah's natural motherhood was 'surrogate' only in a symbolic sense (Bilhah became Jacob's wife along with Rachel). The idea, however, of bearing a child for another woman is present in this story.

The practice of wet-nursing in England and in France, widespread in the seventeenth century, and often resulting in the death of the babies because of appalling conditions, also bears some resemblance to 'surrogate' mothering (after birth only).

At the beginning of 1981, the practice of surrogate motherhood in the USA ran into problems when a number of surrogate mothers told their stories to newspaper and television audiences. The practice in question involves an agreement between a childless couple and a woman willing to bear a child for them: the woman allows herself to be artificially inseminated with sperm from the man whose wife is infertile, and agrees to let the couple adopt the child at birth (usually for a prearranged fee).

One of the legal problems involved relates to the payment of fees, an action which is regarded as 'legally tantamount to the buying and selling of children'. Another problem is the legality of 'surrogate mother' contracts. The most difficult problems are the ones which arise out of conflict between the parties involved. A well-known example of this kind of difficulty was the following case which was widely reported in newspapers:

> Mrs Nisa Bhimani, a 29-year-old Californian woman, a widow with three children of her own (some newspapers reported that she was divorced and used a different name) contemplated 'surrogate motherhood'. In March 1980 she read about an attorney, named Noel Keane, who arranged surrogate parentings. She wrote to the attorney that she was 'interested'. In April 1980 she flew from her home in Pasadena, California, to New York City for the artificial insemination 'at a cold, impersonal sperm bank'. It did not work the first time but Mr and Mrs Jim and Bjorna Noyes asked her to try again. The second time it worked and she became pregnant with James Noyes' baby. About two months into her pregnancy she wrote to the attorney of the Noyes's

that she would keep the baby. She gave birth to the baby ('Ricky') on April 4, 1981. She was ordered into court for a custody hearing since Mr and Mrs Noyes demanded the child (she was summoned the first time before the birth of the child!). The court hearing set for June 4, 1981 had an amazing ending because Mr Noyes 'agreed to withdraw his suit provided he be listed as the father on Ricky's birth certificate. He and his wife would have no visitation rights.' The day before Mrs Bjorna Noyes had admitted in a court deposition that she was a transsexual(!). She was in her youth Robert Lawson who dreamed of three things: to be a woman, a wife, and a mother (*National Enquirer*, July 7, 1981, 28,29,31).

There are tragic aspects of this case. Apart from questioning the morality of surrogate motherhood, it is apparent that there are a number of issues which ought to be considered before this practice is condoned.

The New York reporter Diana Callander, in her newspaper article 'Wrangles over "rent-a-womb"' (April 21, 1981), raises the following questions:

If the surrogate mother is single, is it proper for her to bear a child who will be illegitimate?
Is it proper for surrogates to have children to be turned over to single people or to homosexual couples?
Does the impregnation of the surrogate by a married man amount to adultery?
What if the surrogate mother decides to have an abortion?
What if the adoptive parents die or get divorced before the birth, or decide they do not want the baby at all?
What if the child is born defective?

These and other questions are hard to answer, especially if the practice is tolerated in society. Some lawyers demand that legislation be introduced to 'legalize' the practice of surrogate motherhood. Others are opposed to the legal sanction of a 'rent-a-womb' business because they regard the practice as immoral, and fear grave socio-legal complications for those involved.

The American ethicist, Joseph Fletcher, has said:

To be men we must be in control. That is the first and last ethical word. For when there is no choice, there is no possibility of ethical action. Whatever we are compelled to do is amoral.

Such views have been welcomed by some as the ultimate in moral freedom. Others, however, see these words as indicators for moral anarchy.

Biomedical practices should be guided by profound bioethical rules. Enterprises like those of the 75-year-old Californian millionaire, Robert Graham, who runs a sperm bank for Nobel Prize winners and other 'geniuses', for the purpose of producing 'super-intelligent infants', are morally repugnant and scientifically unsustainable.

There is one issue in relation to surrogate motherhood which is certainly worth considering. This is the one raised by the authors of *Health Care Ethics*, Benedict M. Ashley, O.P. and Kevin D. O'Rourke, O.P. (1978). They write:

> Although artificial fecundation is illicit, it would seem that artificial gestation might be licit provided that there would be sufficient reason for so extraordinary a procedure. If a couple conceive a child in the natural way, and if for one reason or another the woman would not be able certainly to carry the child to viable term, it would assist the natural process, rather than subvert it, to transfer the child to an artificial womb and thus protects its life.
> Would it also be licit to transplant an embryo naturally conceived from the uterus of its mother to a foster mother for the good of the child or because of serious danger to the mother? Would the foster mother be justified in thus lending her womb to carry the fetus of another? Though one study group has rejected this form of artificial gestation, some say that it does not seem beyond the realm of ethical intervention. Certainly, it would not be mutilation of the woman's sexual organs, nor would it destroy her personal bodily integrity. It would be similar to the age-old custom of the wet nurse, which in cases of real necessity seems entirely justified (292).

There can be no doubt that a conception marks the very beginning of a new human life. It is and should remain 'the expression of the conjugal will to parenthood'.

Careful consideration of the ethical, moral, and legal problems associated with the 'fabrication' or 'artificial beginning' of human life may well lead to the view that the call for a moratorium on AID, IVF, and surrogate motherhood is morally and socially justified.

3

CHAPTER

THE PREVENTION OF PROCREATION

Contraception

Sterilization

Contraception

'Contraception is the mother of abortion.' This statement is a general indication of what has happened in the world this century. Furthermore, it has become apparent that there is a growing disillusionment with contraceptives on medical, moral, and social grounds. However, this disillusionment does not necessarily mean people will readily accept alternatives if this involves having to rethink and re-evaluate their sexual relationships.

The separation of the unitive and procreative aspects of sexual intercourse by means of contraceptives has resulted in an unprecedented upsurge in promiscuity in almost all countries of the Western world.

Within the philosophical and moral framework of promiscuity, it is not surprising that pornography, venereal disease, sexual exploitation and assault, unwanted pregnancies, abortion, marital breakdown, and other crises in inter-personal relationships, have increasingly become major symptoms of a seemingly-incurable moral sickness in contemporary Western societies. Of these symptoms, the abortion-mentality arising out of the contraceptive mentality is the most serious because it reflects society's denial of the sanctity of human life.

Contraception and Family Planning

Contraception is not the same as family planning. If couples decide on or before their wedding-day to use contraceptives, that does not necessarily mean, of itself, that they are involved in responsible conception regulation or responsible parenthood.

In this connection, it is critically important to distinguish between two attitudes of mind. On the one hand, there may be the desire to exercise responsible parenthood. On the other hand, the couple may have decided to engage in unrestricted sexual intercourse *per se.* The contemporary emphasis on sexual self-fulfilment at the expense of total self-giving in service to the other has been pursued with considerable harm to the spiritual, mental, and social well-being of individuals.

Contraception often prevents a couple from looking seriously at the nature, purpose, and methods of responsible family planning. Indeed, many young couples using contraceptives to prevent a first pregnancy have no idea if they are fertile and able to conceive.

Family planning has as its focus loving and responsible parenthood; contraception is by its very nature divorced from a couple's anticipation of becoming parents. Family planning is the legitimate concern of the married since that is the only place where a family should be started; contraception, however, is usually regarded as a means of eliminating extra-marital pregnancy as a possible consequence of sexual intercourse between a man (or boy) and a woman (or girl).

This distinction between contraception and family planning we will carefully maintain throughout this chapter. People who are accustomed to using the words 'contraception', 'contraceptives', and 'family planning' interchangeably should note the careful definition of terms employed so that the ethical issues can clearly emerge.

Before turning to contraception, we will deal with **family planning** or responsible conception regulation without the use of artificial means. This kind of planning on the part of a married couple is called Natural Family Planning. The various methods of this planning can really be understood only against the background of its basic philosophy.

This philosophy may best be summarized as 'family purity' — a term which may mean different things to different people. In Jewish thought and practice, it refers to the tradition of periodic abstinence. Some have called it

'Jewish rhythm', although this tradition is geared more to achieving conception than to contraception. Family purity for an orthodox Jewish couple means that they have no sexual intercourse during the days of the woman's menstrual flow (approx. 4-5 days) and her seven 'clean' days following that period. At the end of this 12-day time-span, the wife immerses herself in water (*mikvah*, the gathering of water, which points to the origin of baptismal immersion) while reciting a blessing in praise of her God. On the evening of that day, wife and husband 'are reunited' in the loving act of physical intimacy. This reunion is called *mitzvah*, a virtue and a fulfilment of a religious 'command' (in the sense of blessing).

The Jewish way of life, lived under the moral mandates of *taharat ha-mishpahah* ('the purity of the family') prevents the married couple from being routinely engaged in sexual intercourse. The *Talmud* 'considers the pairing of couples as difficult as the splitting of the waters of the Red Sea; and the miracle there was not so much the separation of the waters as the keeping them apart so that the Exodus might proceed successfully' (Rabbi Dr Norman Lamm). This implies that to stay married is even more difficult than getting married. Family purity in Jewish orthodox tradition has, according to the *Talmud*, priority over public prayers, and even over the reading of the *Torah* itself. Those who observe this tradition experience 'the dream of love-without-sexual-contact followed by the loving union of husband and wife'. Their being together is 'repeated every month'. The husband is not allowed to relate to his wife as if she were a 'thing', an 'object for the fulfilment of his desire', or an 'it'. She is his 'closest neighbour', a 'person with dignity', and the 'thou' to whom he ought to relate with love, care, understanding, and respect.

For Christians, the concept of 'family purity' is rooted in the New Testament 'marriage catechism' or 'family handbook': Ephesians 5:21 - 6:4. This passage of Scripture expresses the various traditions of purity by referring to being made holy, clean, and glorious through bath and Word (living word).

New Testament passages like Colossians 3:18,19, 1 Peter 3:1–7, and Titus 2:3–6 also contain encouragement, advice, counsel, warning, and praise for husbands, wives, and children so that they might know what is pleasing to God and beneficial for their marital and family relationships.

For Christians this knowledge is essential in their pursuance of family purity.

Among those who do not adhere to the beliefs of Judaism or Christianity, we may also find a sense of 'family purity' which springs from a 'natural' and noble appreciation of the goodness inherent in the gifts of marriage and the family.

Conjugal harmony, loving acceptance of children, and devotion to their welfare are signs of 'family purity'. It is in the ethical concept of 'family purity' that family planning should find its natural foundation.

Methods of Natural Family Planning

There are many publications dealing with the methods of Natural Family Planning (NFP). The last two decades have been marked by contraception, abortifacient and abortion 'explosions'. In response, some medical scientists, sometimes on the request of bishops, pastors, and concerned laypeople, have engaged in serious research of 'natural fertility control'.

Since women are the main targets of contraceptive pill and device manufacturers, they are the ones whose physiological functions are affected and interfered with. The desire for natural methods of family planning is, therefore, primarily found among married women, especially when their husbands are prepared to be consciously involved in responsible conception regulation.

There are four main natural methods of family planning. These are: the Rhythm or Calendar Method, the Basal Body Temperature Method, the Sympto-Thermal Method (simply described for instance by Ingrid Trobisch in her *The Joy of Being a Woman*, 1977, p. 44ff.), and the Ovulation Method (most adequately described for self-study purposes by Dr Evelyn Billings and Ann Westmore in *The Billings Method*, 1980).

The **Rhythm or Calendar Method** is based on the fact that the woman experiences recurring cycles of fertility and sterility during each of her menstrual months. If the average length of her menstrual month is 28 days, ovulation usually takes place round about day-14. If couples want to avoid the possibility of conception, they must abstain from sexual intercourse one week prior and one week after ovulation-day. Since this method is fraught with uncertainties as far as the exact determination of the length of the recurring fertility and sterility cycles is concerned, this method has generally been abandoned by most NFP-instructors as being 'outmoded'.

The **Basal Body Temperature Method** is based on the natural phenomenon that women at the time of ovulation may observe a rise in basal body (waking) temperature of approximately 0.5°C. This temperature rise is caused by increased progesterone production (being thermogenic). Ingrid Trobisch describes this phenomenon in a rather novel way when she writes:

> The two ovaries produce the sex hormones of the woman, of which there are two main ones, estrogen, which I would like to call here simply the hormone of femininity, and progesterone, which I would like to call the hormone of maternity. There is a change in the balance of both hormones during the cycle. The hormone of femininity (estrogen) is more active during the first part of the cycle and reaches its peak just at the time of ovulation. The maternity hormone (progesterone) is more active during the second part of the cycle. Progesterone helps prepare the lining of the uterus to receive a fertilized ovum. This explains also why a woman's temperature is at a higher level after ovulation than before ovulation. Progesterone also prepares the breasts to make milk, so that they are larger and more tender during these latter days of the cycle, just as they are during pregnancy (*The Joy of Being a Woman*, 36,37).

This method also has its shortcomings because the woman's waking temperature may be affected by illness, less than a usual amount of sleep, eating late the previous night, and so on. The use of alcohol is also a factor which influences basal body temperature. Couples who use this method must carefully record the waking temperature readings of the woman, taken under resting conditions (which is not always possible if couples have children). If they wish to avoid pregnancy, they are advised to restrict sexual intercourse to the days following the temperature rise.

The **Sympto-Thermal Method** is a combination of the Basal Body Temperature Method and the Ovulation Method. It involves a 6-12 months' study of the history of a woman's cycle lengths, the observation of cervical mucus, and the taking of the waking temperature. This combination of methods has strong advocates, especially among those who wish to observe all possible indicators of a woman's fertile days: ovulation mucus, morning temperature, ovulation pain (*Mittelschmerz*, middle pain), and cervix change. Critics of this method point out that 'if different signals of ovulation are in disagreement, confusion, anxiety and abstinence tend to result, and fertility control becomes much more complicated than it need be' (E. Billings).

The **Ovulation Method**, developed by John and Evelyn Billings, Melbourne, Australia, is based on the woman's awareness of the mucus produced by her cervix and the recognition of its symptoms. The teachers of this method claim that the mucus provides the woman with 'a recognizable and scientifically validated guide to her state of fertility. The method is applicable to all phases of reproductive life — regular cycles, irregular and anovulatory cycles, breastfeeding, approaching the menopause, and coming off the Pill.'

The choice of method by those who use NFP often seems to be determined by reported (and sometimes vigorously disputed) 'effectiveness' and 'failure' rates.

The World Health Organization initiated a study into the effectiveness of NFP. Five countries (New Zealand, India, Ireland, the Philippines, and El Salvador) participated in this study. The results seem to be rather 'complex', according to a December 1981 report. This was due to 'some significant differences in the results from the five nations' (J. Swann, 22/12/81).

The preoccupation by the promoters and teachers of NFP with 'effectiveness' and 'failure' rates of the various NFP methods has its dangers. It can easily lead to a loss of the ethical soundness of the essential nature of natural family planning in favour of the 'contraception-mentality'.

An 'unplanned' or 'surprise' pregnancy should never be classified as a 'failure'. The advocates of contraception speak of 'failure rates'. Teachers of NFP, who are certainly obliged to teach a method or methods thoroughly, should not without qualification introduce into their vocabulary terms like 'effectiveness' and 'failure' rates. It is in Huxley's womb-free paradise that a baby does not have the right to be a surprise!

If we practise natural family planning without relating it to family purity, responsible parenthood, and joyful acceptance of both 'planned' and 'surprise' children, we are simply nurturing a contraception mentality, and reinforcing a popular notion that NFP is 'another method of contraception'. The 'safe-period'-consciousness 'may well be a disguise adopted by those who cannot resist the tidal wave of the present contraceptive mentality' (see D.Ch. Overduin, 'NFP: A Mutual Venture of Faith and Love' in *International Review of Natural Family Planning*, Vol.I, Number 1, Spring 1977).

NFP centres have gained increasingly-wide acceptance in recent years. In Australia, there are now 140 natural family planning centres, with 450 teachers, 45 doctors, 120 support staff, and 8 directors. In 1981, some 15,000 people received individual instruction, and a further 41,000 participated in group instruction. This all compares very favourably with 1968, when there were only 3 services operating with a total staff of 10, and instructing a small group of interested people.

The Australian Council of Natural Family Planning Inc. is an affiliate of the International Federation for Family Life Promotion (IFFLP). This is not to be confused with the World Organization of Ovulation Method Billings (WOOMB), which operates its own 'Ovulation Method Centres' in Australia, USA, and other countries (for their listing see *The Billings Method*, 225-229).

Contraception in an Historical Perspective

Our contemporary permissive (and yet pessimistic) socio-moral climate is one which is characterized by the contraception-mentality. A brief historical overview will help us identify some of the principal factors which have brought about the permissive society and its negative attitude to procreation.

From ancient times to 500 BC: Man was involved in what is called the *participation mystique*, a human consciousness which was related to God, man, and nature. There were nature gods, house gods, village gods, indeed, gods which related to every aspect of human living. Individuals and families were deeply influenced by the religious symbolism evoked in their consciousness.

500 BC: This century marked the beginning of what the philosopher Karl Jaspers (1883-1969) has called the *Achsenzeit* — the beginning of the mythical era: Lao-tse, Buddha, Zarathrustra, the Greek philosophers, and the appearance of the *logos*, the thinking and speaking subject. A search began for the blending of faith and reason.

The sixteenth century AD: This is the age of the 'second fall' of Western society, namely, the collective fall into the 'sin' of a selfish individualism which in turn resulted in our twentieth-century materialism. Whatever the good which can be said about the Polish astronomer, Nicolaus Copernicus (1473-1543), and his revolutionary discovery published in 1543 that the earth is not the centre of the universe, it is a fact that since that time there has been a drastic change in the collective consciousness of mankind. What had been regarded as the holy temple of the universe now became a mechanism of a gigantic clock. The earth and mankind were no longer the centre of God's universe. Indeed, man was just an insignificant speck in the great impersonal cosmos. For insignificant man to find meaning for his life, he had to find it within himself, in his own ideas, needs, wants, and desires. So man began his pilgrimage to the barren places of social loneliness and isolation.

Copernicus's scientific discovery could not, in the mind of many Christians, replace the real centre of their Creator's universe, namely, the Cross on Calvary. It is the Cross which constitutes the connecting link between the three spheres of heaven, earth, and hell. Without this 'centre of faith', people may embrace one, two, or all of the three great but heretical 'systems of the world'. These systems can be described as 'nothing-but' philosophies:

Charles Darwin	(1809-1882)	:	man is nothing but a biological product of natural selection.
Karl Marx	(1818-1883)	:	man is nothing but a product of social-economic structures.
Sigmund Freud	(1856-1939)	:	man is nothing but a product of lust-desires and lust-satisfaction.

These 'nothing-but' philosophies in their multiple manifestations and modifications have created the 'new morality', in which love is separated from sexual intercourse, and sexual intercourse is separated from procreation. The three 'natural' stages of our relational development — courtship, marriage, and family — are no longer seen as part of a natural continuum. Marriage does not necessarily mean that the couple will have a family; nor does having children mean that the couple are married. And courtship has widely been abandoned in favour of an immediate sexual relationship with a 'friend' without any thought of marriage.

These 'nothing-but' philosophies were condemned in a prophetic way by the Anglican bishops at the 1948 Lambeth Conference when they said:

> The real enemy of Christianity and of all free and liberal civilisation is the professedly godless creed of secularism. This treats man, in theory and in practice, as no more than a product of natural forces, whether biological or economic, within which his experience is confined and by which his motives are determined. Wherever it goes, this view corrupts and sterilizes all the higher activities of spirit, cheapens and depersonalizes man, and turns him away from the guidance of God. **It is in fact going far to produce a new and sinister kind of human being with no inner life and no non-material interests, clever, ruthless, cruel and irresponsible** (*emphasis ours*) (Committee Report, *The Christian Doctrine of Man*).

Within the framework of this very briefly-sketched historical development, the origins and growth of the birth control movement may be understood.

1860s — George Drysdale founded a Malthusian League in England which foundered. The league was named after Thomas Robert Malthus, an English economist and theologian (1766-1834) who became famous through his studies on population and economic issues, their principles and effects on the future of society.

1878 — A new Malthusian League was formed, which proved to be viable. Its leaders promoted the ideals of birth control abroad, and this led to the forming of 'Malthusian Leagues' in Holland (1882); Germany (1889); France (1898, thereby revitalizing the old League which was started in 1865); Spain (1901); Brazil (1905); Belgium (1906); Cuba (1907); Switzerland (1908); Sweden (1911); Italy (1913). The movement spread to Japan (1912) and India (1936) and a number of other countries.
In 1913, Margaret Sanger, the 'founder of modern society', began her activities. As a result, a strong birth control movement grew up in the USA which was officially organized in 1921 (see the authors' *Wake Up, Lucky Country!*, 25).

1920s — Great Britain, Germany, Holland, and some American States established birth control clinics.

1931 — Formation of birth control societies in Czechoslovakia and Poland.

1935 — By 1935 some 200 types of mechanical contraceptive devices were being used in Western societies. In addition to these devices, a wide range of chemical solutions was being employed as spermicides or occlusive (obstructing) agents.

The birth control movement, because of its international character and support, organized a number of world congresses in Paris (1900), Liege (1905), The Hague (1910), Dresden (1911), London (1922), and New York (1925). The Dresden conference produced the slogan: 'rational regulation of population will produce peace'; New York invented the cry: 'overpopulation produces war'.

The first international clinic on contraceptive methods was held in Zurich in 1930. Population conferences and tribunes have been held in Geneva (1927) and Bucharest (August 1974). At present, the 'population planners' are still very active — and on a large scale. The target of their activities is not only the West, but also the 'developing countries'.

One of the most powerful organizations working in the area of birth and population control is the International Planned Parenthood Federation (IPPF). This organization has consultative status with the World Health Organization and assists in the work of Family Planning Associations in about 80 countries.

It is interesting to note that, for many years, Australia had only one small Family Planning Clinic in Sydney, established in 1927. It operated under the name 'Racial Hygiene Centre' until 1933, when it became known as a 'birth control clinic'. It is ironic that, apart from the mid-1970s, 1933 was the year that Australia showed its lowest number of births per 1,000 married women (131) and its lowest total fertility rate per woman (2.159).

There is no doubt that family planning should be a concern to many people. Health care is needed by men, women, and children (before and after their birth). It is a fact that in our world today an estimated 15 million children younger than five die each year (this figure, of course, does not include the 50 million whose lives are terminated before birth). The vast majority of these born children who die so young belong to families living in the Third World. In addition to these deaths, about 500,000 women in the developing Third World countries die during pregnancy or childbirth, 'leaving at least one million children without mothers' (Deborah Maine in *Family Planning: Its Impact on the Health of Women and Children*, published by the Centre for Population and Family Health, College of Physicians and Surgeons of Columbia University, New York, 1981).

From these statistical facts, we should readily recognize the need for family planning instruction in such countries as part and parcel of responsible 'aid'. However, we should beware of using the Western kind of sex education or contraceptive advice, which has produced the socio-moral disaster and grave demographic problems found in the West. People who have a profound respect for the values of marriage and the family are the best family planning 'missionaries' in places where there is a crying need for better nutrition, improved medical care, and genuine help in responsible family formation.

Deborah Maine, writing on 'Family Planning in Developing Countries', says:

> Since the mid-1960s, when the oral contraceptive and IUD began to be widely used, and organized family planning programs were begun in many countries, there has been what can truly be described as a 'contraceptive revolution' in many parts of the world.

Indeed, but at what price? There is ample evidence that women in their desire to control their fertility have become dependent on contraceptive pills, devices, sterilization, abortifacients, or abortion. This dependence can often cause physical and psychological problems. It leads to a loss of personal dignity, moral integrity, and social responsibility.

The Christian Response to the Secular Understanding of Birth Control

In 1908, the Lambeth Conference of Bishops of the Anglican Church condemned contraception (Resolution 41,43); in 1920, the Conference again condemned contraception (Resolution 68). In 1925, the House of Bishops of the Protestant Episcopal Church in America condemned contraception. However, the absolute prohibition by the Anglicans of contraception under all circumstances came to an end on August 14, 1930 during the 1930 Lambeth Conference. By a vote of 193 to 67 (46 participants did not vote), Resolution 15 was adopted. This resolution reads as follows:

> Where there is a clearly-felt moral obligation to limit or avoid parenthood, the method must be decided on Christian principles. The primary and obvious method is complete abstinence from intercourse (as far as may be necessary) in a life of discipline and self-control lived in the power of the Holy Spirit. Nevertheless, in those cases where there is such a clearly-felt moral obligation to limit or avoid parenthood, and where there is a morally sound reason for avoiding complete abstinence, the conference agrees that other methods may be used, provided that this is done in the light of the same Christian principles. The Conference records its strong condemnation of the use of any methods of conception control from motives of selfishness, luxury, or mere convenience.

The Lambeth resolution has often been misconstrued; some have thought the Anglican Church was generally in favour of the use of contraceptives in family planning. In fact, the Lambeth resolution recommends 'abstinence from intercourse' as the 'primary and obvious method'. And the Conference, in the Report on which the resolution was based, accepted the following:

> Children are the primary end of intercourse to which marriage leads. Married people do wrong when they refuse to have children whom they could train to serve God and add to the strength of the nation. But intercourse has also a secondary end within the natural sacrament of marriage. Where for any morally sound reason the first end is to be ruled out, it does not necessarily follow that the secondary end must be ruled out also, provided that self-control is exercised, and husband and wife have truly examined their consciences upon the matter.

The Lambeth doctrine, then, is patient both of a 'prohibitionist' view of contraceptives as well as of the view which might allow the use of contraceptives in certain difficult circumstances, not as a first but as a last resort, and only if the couple concerned are convinced that the method used is in accordance with 'Christian principles'.

On December 31, 1930, Pope Pius XI issued *Casti Connubii*, 'a small summa of Christian marriage', which, among other things, was a reaction to the 1930 Lambeth Conference vote. The Encyclical Letter said in the directly relevant part:

> Since, therefore, openly departing from the uninterrupted Christian tradition some recently have judged it possible solemnly to declare another doctrine regarding this question, the Catholic Church, to whom God has entrusted the defence of the integrity and purity of morals, standing erect in the midst of the moral ruin which surrounds her, in order that she may preserve the chastity of the nuptial union from being defiled by this foul stain, raises her voice in token of her divine ambassadorship and through Our mouth proclaims anew: any use whatsoever of matrimony exercised in such a way that the act is deliberately frustrated in its natural power to generate life is an offence against the law of God and of nature, and those who indulge in such are branded with the guilt of a grave sin.

These are indeed strong words in defence of the 'moral purity' of the sexual union between husband and wife. The Roman Catholic Church continues to uphold its complete rejection of contraception.

The 1958 Lambeth Conference developed this understanding of family planning further, again insisting that

> sexual love is not an end in itself nor a means to self-gratification, and that self-discipline and restraint are essential conditions of the responsible freedom of marriage and family planning (Resolution 113).

The Anglican bishops then expressed the view that

> the responsibility for deciding upon the number and frequency of children has been laid by God upon the consciences of parents everywhere: that this planning, in such ways as are mutually acceptable to husband and wife in Christian conscience, is a right and important factor in Christian family life and should be the result of positive choice before God. Such responsible parenthood, built on obedience to all the duties of marriage, requires a wise stewardship of the resources and abilities of the family as well as a thoughtful consideration of the varying population needs and problems of society and the claims of future generations (Resolution 115).

Again, while the bishops are clear that Christian conscience is the determining factor, they do not spell out in detail what methods may or may not be used by a couple in their family planning. It is evident, though, that the Anglican Church does not hold that the complete separation of the unitive and procreative aspects of intercourse is licit for a Christian couple. Nor indeed is there any talk of 'limiting' the size of the family for purely selfish reasons.

Rather, the whole emphasis in the Lambeth documents is that restraint and abstinence are the normal means by which Christian couples may plan their family, while allowing the freedom to use artificial means if it seems good to the couple and 'Christian conscience'. Further, the whole notion of family planning is very much a qualified one, since

> all problems of sex relations, the procreation of children, and the organisation of family life must be related, consciously and directly, to the creative, redemptive and sanctifying power of God (Resolution 112).

On July 25, 1968, Pope Paul VI issued his Encyclical Letter *Humanae Vitae*, 'On the Regulation of Birth'. This letter, in discussing the question of responsible parenthood, uses the following phrases: 'mind and will in full control of instincts and of passions'; 'that God is not forgotten, or his laws'; 'a couple recognize their duties towards God, towards each other, towards their family, and towards society as well'.

Pope Paul VI further stated in this Encyclical:

> Regulating birth is wrong when it involves directly some interruption of the procreative process once begun. The first thing this rules out is all direct abortion, even of a therapeutic kind. The next thing this rules out, as taught so often by the Church, is sterilizing either sex permanently, or for a while. All actions are forbidden which stop the natural effect of any marriage act, whether done before the act or during it.

The Pope also maintained that 'if spacing out a family must be done, because of how that family has to live, the use of natural rhythm is allowed'.

Humanae Vitae is one of the most controversial encyclicals of modern times. It has been met by much opposition among clergy and laity. Many attempts have been made to reinterpret its contents. Many Roman Catholics have ignored the study of this 'prophetic' document, and some have even hoped that the Church would 'change' its attitude to the generally-accepted contraceptive practices by married and unmarried people alike.

Recent history has shown that the Roman Church has not changed its mind. On November 22, 1981, Pope John Paul II issued his Apostolic Exhortation *Familiaris Consortio*: 'To the Episcopate, to the Clergy and to the Faithful of the whole Catholic Church regarding the Role of the Christian Family in the Modern World'. (The full text appeared in *L'Osservatore Romano*, N. 51,52 (715), December 21,28, 1981.) It consists of four major parts, with an introduction and a conclusion. It is very comprehensive, well documented, and of far-reaching significance.

The paragraph dealing with 'The Church as Teacher and Mother for couples in difficulty' (33) says in part:

> The gift of the Spirit, accepted and responded to by husband and wife, helps them to live their human sexuality in accordance with God's plan and as a sign of the unitive and fruitful love of Christ for his Church. But the necessary conditions also include knowledge of the bodily aspect and the body's rhythms of fertility. Accordingly, every effort must be made to render such knowledge accessible to all married people and also to young adults before marriage, through clear, timely and serious instruction and education given by married couples, doctors and experts. Knowledge must then lead to education in self-control: hence the absolute necessity for the virtue of chastity and for permanent education in it.

In various other paragraphs, the Exhortation clearly reaffirms the teachings of *Humanae Vitae* with regard to the respect for life (par. 30: 'The Church stands for life'), the rejection of contraception and the moral acceptability of a 'recourse to periods of infertility' (par. 32). It is interesting that the Pope made an urgent plea to the theologians 'to provide enlightenment and a deeper understanding' because 'doubt or error in the field of marriage or the family involves obscuring to a serious extent the integral truth about the human person, in a cultural situation that is already so often confused and contradictory' (pars. 30,31).

The Roman Catholic Church continues, then, to take a strong position against the prevailing contraception mentality and practices, and urges its members to heed the call to a true family apostolate.

The Lutheran Church of Australia, at its Convention of the General Synod held on October 12-17, 1968, adopted a statement entitled 'Attitude to Birth Control'. It says in its concluding paragraph (9):

> All avoidance of parenthood for selfish reasons, such as unwillingness to assume the responsibilities and sacrifices of bearing and rearing children, is opposed to the will of God. We warn especially against a

self-indulgent use of contraceptives. The problem is not so much the use of birth control itself but its abuse.

The responses to the secular understanding of birth control by these Christian churches or communions show different emphases, and greater or lesser degrees of theological depth. They have, however, as their common basis the conviction that Christian principles should govern marriage and family life.

Among these commonly-understood principles is, first, the opposition to the separation of the unitive and procreational aspects of the sexual union between husband and wife which results in the rejection of parenthood for selfish reasons, and, secondly, an acceptance that the primary (but not the only) purpose of sexual intercourse is procreation.

The Jewish attitude toward contraception 'by any method is a non-permissive one if no medical or psychiatric threat to the mother or child exists' (Fred Rosner). The *Talmud* discusses four methods which could be used by a woman to prevent conception: intercourse during the infertile period during her cycle; twisting movements following intercourse in order to spill the husband's semen; 'an oral contraceptive'; and 'the use of absorbent material during intercourse'. While the woman is allowed under certain circumstances to drink a 'cup of roots' (oral contraceptive), the husband is not allowed to take anything in order not to be fertile, because in doing so he would violate the commandment of procreation which rests primarily on the husband.

Finally, the concept of 'family purity' in Jewish tradition is hardly reconcilable with a contraception mentality or practice.

The Apparatus of Contraception

In the latest (5th) edition of the *Family Handbook for Doctors* (IPPF publication, 1980), the writers speak of systemic, intra-uterine, and barrier contraception. In the 1977 Report of the Royal Commission of Inquiry on Contraception, Sterilization and Abortion in New Zealand, chapter 4 deals with the 'Techniques of Contraception' (92-105). The Australian Federation of Family Planning Associations Inc. in 1980 published *The Control of Human Fertility, A Text for Health Professionals* (edited by John Porter). In addition to these publications, there are many popular booklets, tracts, and other materials dealing with the apparatus of contraception. A book highly recommended by the Family Planning Association is John Guillebaud's *The Pill* (Oxford University Press, 1980).

The incompatibility of responsible family planning with the contemporary contraception ideology is clearly evident in these publications. Since the family (*mishpahah*) should be concerned with its purity (*taharah*), it is very difficult to view contraception as a responsible means of enhancing our understanding of the nature of marital love and family relationships. References to contraception as a 'personal decision', 'being better and more in use by the young', and 'now freely available to everybody', are supposed to convey to the individual and society that 'progress' is being made.

However, 'we are being asked to swallow fantasies', to quote Claire Evans in *Freewoman* (1979) — and 'sizeable' fantasies, at that (23 ff).

The first fantasy:

> We were asked to believe that, once the principle of contraception had been accepted for extreme cases, the demand would stop of its own accord at a reasonable point. The facts of human nature already show clearly that it would do nothing of the sort.

The second fantasy:

> Contraception offers an alternative to abortion. After ten years of more and more liberal use of contraceptives a vociferous campaign has been launched to obtain the right to free abortion.

The third fantasy:

> The West's solution for the moment (to an overpopulation problem) is to dissociate sexual pleasure as completely as possible from the act of creation. Promiscuity is encouraged, procreation discouraged.

Claire Evans concludes her brief chapter, 'Fantastic', with the words:

> So to fantasy there is an alternative. Genesis tells the story of the fantasy which Eve was the first to listen to. But the Genesis story ends with the promise that the woman will one day crush the serpent's head.

This 'fantasy' world is nevertheless a very exploitative world. The Australian Federation of Family Planning Associations has decided that 'family planning is for everybody — teenagers too', so they recently produced *His'n hers sex kits*. It was announced that these kits would be 'out in time for Christmas 1981'. The kit (officially called *Double Check*) 'should make an ideal Christmas present', according to the Federation's executive officer, Wendy McCarthy. The kit, which is similar to the one produced in Britain, contains 10 lubricated condoms and 10 spermicidal pessaries. Combined use of condom and a spermicidal 'has a protection rate second only to the pill'. The $4.50 kits are chiefly produced for the purpose of giving young people increased access to contraceptives.

The apparatus of contraception may be technologically very sophisticated; it certainly is very profitable for the manufacturers. The marketing of contraceptive products seems to be easy because the contraception ideology has been readily accepted by many millions of consumers. Under the disguise of the respectable phrase 'family planning', the morally-abhorrent contraception propaganda has steadily snowballed, becoming even more blatant, aggressive, and deceitful.

A public drive for 'family purity' would be of far greater benefit to the young than the sale of sex kits. Purity does not exploit! Responsible love does not destroy the dignity of one's partner! Abstinence from sexual intercourse does no harm to boys and girls! Virginity is not something to be ashamed of! Young people should not have need of sex kits. But, because we have encouraged them to be 'sexually active' (meaning that they should engage in sexual intercourse), we have subjected our younger generation to a most harmful form of exploitation.

The purveyors of the contraception-mentality among the young and unmarried react badly to any criticism of their activities. They claim that the critics are 'out of touch with modern youth', and that 'it is better to contracept than to have an abortion'. They fail to accept responsibility for the undeniable fact that increasing availability of contraceptives among the young has led to increased promiscuity, venereal disease, and abortion. Indeed, various 'family planning' associations recommend abortion as a back-up to contraceptives.

Contemporary sex education is often completely divorced from the concept of 'family purity'. Sexual intercourse is *not* a mere physical act; it involves *moral* decision-making. The apparatus of contraception carries no advice as to how to love my neighbour (partner) with sincerity, respect, willingness to sacrifice, and self-discipline (ability 'to wait').

Christians in particular should ponder the words of St Paul in Romans 6:3–6,15,17,18 and 22. These passages speak of walking in newness of life, of being under God's grace and not under law, of being no longer slaves of sin but of righteousness and of God. It is in the light of these Scripture verses that the ever-expanding apparatus of contraception might fairly be judged.

Systemic Contraceptives (until now for females only)

Since 1960, **combined oral contraceptives**, or 'birth control pills', have become the most common form of contraception, and are currently being used by an estimated 50-60 million women in the world. These pills are oral preparations of two synthetic hormones (oestrogen and progestogen), taken in constant amounts for 20, 21, or 22 days. Being 'on the Pill' is for many women the only 'security' against a possible unwanted pregnancy.

The ordinary combination pills (OCPs) do three things: they prevent ovulation; produce cervical mucus hostile to sperm (the latter cannot penetrate and migrate); and change the inner lining of the uterus in such a way that implantation cannot occur.

The primary action of the combination pill is prevention of ovulation. A woman's hypothalamus (the major control centre of her body situated at the base of her brain) interacts with the closely-located pituitary gland to produce, among other important hormones, the two hormones essential for her ability to conceive. These two hormones are FSH and LH. FSH (the Follicle Stimulating Hormone) stimulates the woman's ovaries to produce mature egg cells and oestrogen hormones. LH (the Luteinising Hormone) stimulates the rupture of the follicle, the fluid-filled structure within the ovary that contains the developing ovum, so that the egg can be released (ovulation) for fertilization.

The first action of the OCP is to stop the normal hormone changes of the menstrual cycle because the hypothalamus and pituitary gland are 'kept inactive'. The pill 'fools' the pituitary gland into 'thinking that the woman is already pregnant' (*The Pill*, 27). This being 'fooled' is caused by the presence of enough oestrogen and progesterone (the female, pregnancy-supporting hormone produced as a result of ovulation) so that the 'signal' from ovary to pituitary gland reads: 'Switch off'. As a result, this gland does not produce FSH, and therefore the woman does not ovulate and cannot conceive.

The second action of the combination pill (namely, to produce cervical mucus hostile to sperm) is a 'back-up mechanism' if an ovum should be released. The synthetic hormone progestogen, present in the pill, changes the slippery fertile-type mucus which flows from the cervix into a 'scanty, thick material which produces a quite effective barrier to sperm'.

The third action of the combination pill (also a back-up mechanism) makes the inner lining of the uterus unsuitable for the implantation of the embryo. This third action, in case conception occurs, makes the pill function as an abortifacient.

Other pills, classified as 'Low Dose Pills' and 'Mini Pills' (POPs), contain either lower doses of one or both of the component synthetic hormones oestrogen and progestogen, or, in the case of the 'Mini Pill', only a single synthetic hormone (namely, progestogen; POP = Progestogen Only Pill). Studies seem to have indicated that these particular pills prevent ovulation only 50% and 40% of the time respectively. They may also affect the contractions of the Fallopian or uterine tubes so that they do not effectively transport the ovum. Since the chance of these pills acting as abortifacients is, therefore, much higher, they consequently present a serious problem to those who regard as a grave moral evil the destruction of a human life once begun.

The effectiveness of the Pill, if taken as prescribed, is almost total; pregnancy hardly ever occurs. This does not mean, however, that the Pill is without health-hazards.

Responsible health care demands that women know the facts about the Pill, its possible short- and long-term side-effects, and when and under what circumstances this contraceptive should not be taken. The adverse effects of Pill-use on the health of women have been studied, discussed, and published. These adverse effects have also caused changes in the formulation of the various contraceptive pills. In the USA, the Federal Food and Drug Administration (FDA) has produced detailed warnings of possible side-effects of Pill-use. These warnings are in print, and must be supplied with each Pill prescription.

Apart from the moral issues related to the use of contraception, it is of medical and social importance that these adverse effects be seriously considered by the physician during the contraception-counselling of the patient. It is known that a number of doctors refuse to prescribe the Pill, especially to young girls.

Non-restrictive distribution of contraceptive pills, including the withholding by the consulting physician or health agency of relevant information about the possible adverse effects on the woman's health, is highly irresponsible. The appropriate authorities should see to it that, as in the USA, Pill-using women receive adequate information and warning about the workings and effects of the contraceptive pill.

Uncommon and common, major and minor side-effects are described in varying details in both *The Pill* (57ff) and *The Billings Method* (160ff), as well as in other publications dealing with the subject.

Women who do not want to become pregnant, and have chosen to use oral contraceptives, often put up with the minor side-effects of the Pill. Yet, for the sake of their health, women should immediately stop using the Pill and seek sound medical advice if they suffer serious illness or experience major side-effects due to a long-term use of contraceptive pills. When women stop taking the Pill because they want to become pregnant, it is advisable for them to delay attempts to achieve pregnancy until their physiological functions have returned to normal (natural).

It is a responsible practice for women using the Pill to have regular medical check-ups. This statement does not imply that we recommend contraceptive pills. The use or non-use of the Pill should be viewed within the context of our approach to contraception, and judgment made on the basis of both the positive aspect of nature's gift of 'fruitfulness', and the negative aspects of the current contraception mentality and the hostility toward children, our natural offspring.

The development of oral contraceptives continues. In September 1981 it was reported that a new triphasic pill, developed jointly by pharmaceutical firms in America and West Germany, has fewer side effects than other fixed-dose oral contraceptives. The new pill is called 'triphasic' because its low synthetic hormone content changes three times during the woman's cycle, and thus mimics the natural changes in the menstrual cycle.

An earlier report (in *Sweden Now*, Vol. 15:4, 1981) mentioned birth control capsules which are 3cm long and 2.4mm thick. Six of these are inserted in the arm of a woman, and prevent ovulation for at least six years. The method (called *Norplant*) 'has been tested on more than 100 women in Sweden with positive results'. These birth control capsules are said to be 'safer' than normal contraceptive pills.

Research on 'effective' contraceptives both for males and females is sponsored from public and private moneys. However, what is overlooked in the wider context of such research is the medico-moral thrust of the contraception enterprise.

The possible production of 'male Pills' containing ingredients of the infertility-causing drug sulphasalazine; the invention of the 'sex chip', a tiny micro-chip built into a special thermometer, which will 'flash a green-for-go signal if it is safe to have sex without risking pregnancy'; and other possible 'discoveries' and 'inventions' will neither hide nor stop the misery caused by the ideology of sexual permissiveness.

This misery refers not only to the 'biological effects of sexual freedom' (*The Lancet*, February 7, 1981), namely, the dramatic increases in the incidence of sexually-transmitted diseases (STD), but also to the increase of pregnancy in adolescence to near-epidemic proportions'. (See the reference to a WHO study of 14-to-18-year-olds in the *Australian Family Physician*, Vol. 9, August 1980, 556.)

Among the sexually-transmitted diseases, Herpes II (although not 'notifiable') is taking an increased toll among teenagers. Millions of young people throughout the world suffer from this still-incurable disease. Many victims suffer frequent and painful attacks; and, apart from burning pains, the disease itself may cause blindness, cervical cancer, birth defects, brain damage, and even death of newborn babies who are infected by the disease during their delivery (*Newsweek*, November 10, 1980, 56: 'The Misery of Herpes II').

The answer to the ideology of sexual permissiveness is not contraception, but a powerful No!

> Leading London papers have been commenting on the ultimate answer to promiscuity, saying No! The stimulus was a pamphlet called *Saying No Isn't Always Easy*, recently published by young people for young people (*Youth Concerned*). The warning is especially for teenagers, and the pamphlet [available from an English organization called The Responsible Society] succinctly highlights the blandishments of today's society which deceive the unwary, many of whom genuinely seek the best for themselves and their peers. The world says, 'Be liberated', 'It's the way everybody lives now', and 'If you are not actively heterosexual you are probably a repressed homosexual', and note must also be taken of high pressure sales in the contraceptive business. Some of the myths about sex are exposed in the pamphlet: 'So long as you've got contraceptives you're OK', 'VD is a minor problem', 'Loving means having sex', and so on. To say No is evidence of a whole personality and a sign of personal freedom, and — to quote — 'Saying "no" isn't negative - "no" to "having sex" is saying "yes" to a real care relationship for the future' ('Commentary' in *In the Service of Medicine*, The Journal of the Christian Medical Fellowship, Vol. 27:1, No. 105, January 1981).

In the end, it is the young themselves who have to deal with the 'great temptations' of the age of permissiveness, for society itself is unwilling to do anything but foster the spirit and practice of the age.

Another recent approach to contraception is the use of **injectable steroids.** These injections of long-acting progestagens (or progestogens) given at intervals varying from one to six months are dangerous. The intramuscular injectable progestagens are the subject of heated controversy. This contraceptive, marketed under the name of *Depo-Provera*, is being vigorously promoted by the contemporary 'population planners', especially in the developing countries of the Third World.

Finally, mention must be made of **postcoital preparations** (progestagen and other substances). These are not contraceptives in the sense of 'prevention of conception'; they act as abortifacients, for they prevent blastocyst, the implantation of the fertilized egg in the uterus.

Since **intra-uterine devices** are abortifacients, they will be dealt with in the next chapter of this book.

Among the **barrier contraceptives**, there are the diaphragm (a rubber cap fitted diagonally across the vagina); the cervical cap; rubber condoms (for the male) and spermicides (creams, jellies, foams, pessaries, foaming tablets, and others).

Prevention of conception is also achieved (but not always!) by *coitus interruptus* (better, *coitus abruptus!*). This method has a very long history, and involves 'withdrawal of the penis from the vagina just before ejaculation'. This 'method', from an 'effectiveness' point of view, has grave limitations and causes sexual dissatisfaction, especially for the woman.

Christians often refer, when speaking of *coitus interruptus*, to the acts of Er and Onan mentioned in Genesis 38:7–10. Genesis 38 is regarded as the classic passage dealing with this contraceptive practice. However, according to Jewish interpreters, the acts of Er and Onan were acts of unnatural intercourse; 'Er wanted to preserve his wife's beauty by preventing her from becoming pregnant, and Onan sought to frustrate the Levirate law.' Jewish authorities simply state: 'It is forbidden to expend semen to no purpose'.

Reference may be made here to **masturbation** (by oneself or by one's partner) — an act which is, in fact, a sexual fantasy-relationship. It certainly cannot cause pregnancy;

however, its practice should never be encouraged. The orthodox Jewish ethicists, on the basis of Jewish law, regard masturbation 'as equivalent to killing a human being'. For the justification of their opinion they refer to Isaiah 1:15: 'Your hands are full of blood'.

Contraception is different from responsible conception regulation or family planning. In the context of family planning we can speak of the art and virtue of **continence**, periodic abstention from sexual intercourse. Continence should be a voluntary decision on the part of *both* husband and wife. Reasons for periodic abstinence may include spiritual preparation, mental concentration, psychological growth, or physical self-control. Continence in this sense is very beneficial to one's total health!

In a way, a Talmudic reference to Psalm 51:5(7) is an excellent summary of what we have described as family planning and family purity: 'And in cleansing [*not* 'in sin'] did my mother conceive me'. This is a beautiful reference to the Jewish woman's ritual immersion, her 'bridal bath', of which we have spoken before. It is also a reminder that in the marital, coital embrace the unitive and procreative aspects should not be artificially and completely separated.

Sterilization

Surgical sterilization is a form of mutilation or of incapacitation, and is a decision 'in favour of permanent prevention of conception' (Helmut Thielicke). It is a method of family planning (*sic*) or a form of contraception which for most Christians is morally unacceptable. Sterilization 'is a fundamental life change' (E. Billings) for the lasting prevention of procreation. Reversal attempts are in most cases not successful. When people consider sterilization, they should understand that it will mean the end of procreativeness for them.

Various procedures are in use for female and male sterilization.

The most common practice for female sterilization is **tubal ligation.** 'There are two ways of doing this, both requiring a local or general anaesthetic. In one, a fairly large abdominal incision is made, a piece of each Fallopian tube is cut out, and the two ends are tied off and folded back into the surrounding tissue. This method is often used immediately after childbirth. The second method involves entering the body through the vagina and cutting the tubes.* After these procedures, menstruation continues as the uterus is still intact' (*The Billings Method*, 181). It is estimated that approximately 40,000 women have a tubal ligation in Australia each year.

* No longer practised in Australia.

Bilateral salpingectomy is a serious operation, which involves the removal of both Fallopian tubes.

Another form of female sterilization is **diathermy**, which is carried out by the endoscopic or electro-coagulation technique, and involves the cauterizing (burning) of the Fallopian tubes with a small instrument. The danger of this technique is that other tissue may be burnt.

The use of **fallope rings** (or clips) amounts to tubal occlusion or the closing off of the uterine tubes. Since only a very small portion of the tube is destroyed, it is possible in a certain percentage of cases to reverse this type of sterilization by means of microsurgery. However, any woman who agrees to this form of sterilization should reckon with the possibility of being permanently sterilized.

When a woman has a **hysterectomy**, which involves the removal of her uterus (and usually the cervix also), she is permanently sterile. She continues to ovulate, but she no longer menstruates.

Possible complications of tubal sterilization include 'severe bleeding, pelvic infection, and ectopic pregnancies'. Complications following hysterectomy are mostly of a psychological nature, and include depression and sexual dysfunction. 'Fears concerning a hysterectomy tend to be deep-seated. They may centre around a possible loss of femininity, loss of childbearing ability and effects of sexuality' (E. Billings).

Vasectomy is the common form of male sterilization. Vasectomy literally means the excision of a vessel. The popular reference to male sterilization is 'clipping the cords' because it involves the cutting of the two *vas deferens*, the tubular ducts that carry the sperm from the testes to the penis.

Male sterilization is a safer and simpler technique than the sterilization of a woman. It requires less surgical equipment, is performed in approximately half the time necessary for female sterilization, and can be done by medical personnel other than gynaecologists.

Possible complications of vasectomy include infection, haemorrhage, and disorders caused by the production of antibodies as the broken down sperm (not ejaculated from the body) passes into the man's bloodstream. A number of men who have had a vasectomy seem to suffer from psychological problems such as anxiety and loss of self-esteem.

It is an undeniable fact that pharmaceutical and technological intervention has produced effective contraceptive means, techniques, and conditions. However, many women and men have been adversely affected, and suffer decline in their physical, psychological, and social health and well-being. Nature does not always take kindly to being attacked!

The World-wide Practice of ('Voluntary') Sterilization

Sterilization figures on a global level are rapidly increasing. It has been reported that 'almost half the world's voluntarily sterilized couples are in China'. *Population Reports* (issued by Population Information Program, The John Hopkins University in Baltimore, Maryland, USA) in its March/April 1981 issue (Series E, Number 6) featured 'legal trends and issues in voluntary sterilization'. Certain data from this research publication and other related sources are important in drawing an overall picture of what is happening.

The estimated global numbers of couples who have been sterilized for contraceptive purposes were 20 million by the end of 1970, and 100 million by the end of 1980.

The breakdown of the 1980 figures shows the following estimates:

China	40 million	Europe	11 million
India	24 million	Latin America	4.5 million
Rest of Asia	5 million	Canada	1 million
USA	13 million	Africa	1 million

The legal situation with regard to voluntary sterilization (VS) for contraceptive purposes is determined by four legislative categories within the global legal system:

1. Countries where VS is permitted by special provisions of law. These include Singapore, Panama, Japan, the Scandinavian countries, Yugoslavia, Austria, and some States of the USA. (No State in the USA has declared VS illegal.)
2. Countries where VS is legal because no law prohibits it. These include virtually all English-speaking 'common law' countries — and a number of others as well, such as India and China.
3. Countries where special statutes or decrees make VS a criminal offence. There are five such countries: Burma, Saudi Arabia, Somalia, Spain, and Turkey.
4. Countries where it is unclear whether VS is legal. These include some 'civil law' countries of continental Europe and Africa, and most Central and South American countries.

In many countries in the world, changes in the legal status of voluntary sterilization for contraceptive purposes came about during the 1970s. The influence of the International Planned Parenthood Federation (IPPF) has undoubtedly helped to achieve law reforms so that people could act 'legally' in accordance with IPPF's three guiding principles as to the availability of VS:

> Each individual (as a matter of human rights) has the freedom of choice to control his or her fertility. Indeed, freedom of choice in this area is guaranteed by many national constitutions.
> Where there is no law forbidding voluntary sterilization, it is legally permissible to perform the procedure.
> Under normal circumstances, consent voluntarily given legitimizes a medical operation.

The high numbers of sterilized couples in the world (the reported estimates may even underestimate the real numbers) show that sterilization is one of the most popular means of contraception.

Even so, it must be also stated that **compulsory sterilization** of people (including 'institutionalized persons, minors and incompetents') for reasons of eugenics (reproductive fitness), or economics (poverty, underdevelopment), or population control, is morally abhorrent.

Compulsory sterilization is justified, however, by those who believe in lifeboat ethics and the ethics of triage. The term 'lifeboat ethics' is derived from the allegory of the two lifeboats: one for the rich nations (well-maintained and well-stocked), and one for the poor nations (too crowded and ill-provisioned); the 'ethics of triage' is derived from the World War I practice of sorting (French, *triage*) the wounded soldiers into three groups because of limited medical supplies; only the wounded who could be saved if treated immediately were given the necessary medication. Using arguments drawn from these allegories, some have sought to make out a case for the compulsory sterilization of people in poor countries, of the poor in rich countries, and of those who are so disabled as to be 'unproductive' economically.

But the application of these allegories is false. There are no two lifeboats; we all are in the one and the same boat. And it is cruel. There are enough resources of food and other staple needs in the world for all of us. Lifeboat ethics and the ethics of triage are to be rejected if we want socio-moral decision-making which does not trample on human rights and values.

While we acknowledge that individuals in society may choose voluntary sterilization for contraceptive purposes, we believe that society should vigorously resist any (subtle or less subtle) pressures on medical, moral, political, economic, or social grounds which may make people feel obliged to seek sterilization.

As far as the Christian churches are concerned, sterilization has traditionally been unequivocally condemned as an act of self-mutilation, as a sin against the community by making procreation impossible, and as a sin against God who alone has full rights over man. The only exception to this blanket condemnation has been if the mutilation was necessary to rid the body of a diseased member so that the body as a whole could be healthy again (St Thomas Aquinas, *Summa Theologica*, 2a 2ae, Q. 65, a.i.).

This is still the position of the Roman Catholic Church, as reiterated in 1930 in *Casti Connubii* by Pope Pius XI. The Lambeth Conference of 1958 also warned Anglicans that sterilization

> is a major and irrevocable abdication of an important area of responsible freedom. It has psychological and physiological consequences that are as yet unknown and unmeasured, and represents as well a violation of the human body, a body which is God's gift and trust, and only in a limited sense ours to do with as we wish.

The same Lambeth Conference found 'compulsory sterilization as a means of population control' unacceptable to the Christian conscience. The attempt by later Anglican committees to justify sterilization as a government solution to a population problem runs counter to the Lambeth Conference, and to the Christian tradition.

If even voluntary sterilization involves the 'abdication of an important area of responsible freedom', then the totalitarian aspects of compulsory sterilization, and programs aimed at persuading people to be voluntarily sterilized, ought to be obvious and strenuously resisted.

CHAPTER

THE ENDING OF HUMAN LIFE

Abortifacients
Abortion
Infanticide
Suicide
Euthanasia
Natural Death

Abortifacients

At the final (twenty-first) plenary session of the World Conference of the United Nations Decade for Women at Copenhagen on July 30, 1980 (by a roll-call vote of 94 to 4, with 22 abstentions), a 'Programme of Action for the second half of the UN Decade for Women: Equality, Development and Peace' was adopted. In the section 'Priority areas for action' under 'Health' (par. 146), it says:

> Develop, implement and strengthen child welfare and family planning programmes and family planning information for inclusion also in school curricula for girls and boys on safe and acceptable fertility regulation methods so that both men and women can take the responsibility for family planning to promote the health, safety and welfare of mothers and infants and to enable women to exercise the right to decide freely and responsibly for the number and spacing of their children. Family planning should be facilitated as one means of reducing maternal and infant mortality where high risk factors prevail, such as high parity, too frequent pregnancies, pregnancies at the extremes of the reproductive age, and the frequency and danger of secretly performed abortions.

Family planning is a major concern of governments and of people in most nations in the world. And we have already noted that we should be informed about responsible conception regulation. However, 'control of human fertility' as presently understood is not beneficial to the health and well-being of people, especially women. In addition, the term 'birth control' now includes the use of contraceptives, abortifacients, and abortion. This means that both prevention of procreation and the ending of human life before birth (*in utero*) have been brought under the headings of 'family planning', 'fertility control', and 'birth control'.

It is not surprising that there were women from a number of countries represented at the Copenhagen conference who were suspicious of the terms 'family planning programmes', 'family planning information' and 'fertility regulation methods', precisely because of their moral objections, not only to the health-hazards caused by some contraceptives, but also to the destructive interference with newly-begun human life.

In the previous chapter we drew attention to the fact that certain contraceptive pills act as abortifacients if they have failed to prevent ovulation and conception. We also mentioned postcoital preparations as being abortifacients. But the most widely used means of intra-uterine contraception, namely, **intra-uterine devices** (IUDs), are undoubtedly abortifacients.

Intra-uterine devices may be divided into two categories: bioactive and inert. Current 'second-generation devices' are made of more suitable materials than those belonging to the 'first-generation devices' made of catgut, ordinary plastic, or stainless steel.

Bioactive Devices

These devices contain copper or synthetic progesterone. There are four such devices available (the names refer to the shape and contents of the device):

Copper 7 (Gravigard) is 35.9 mm long, and 26 mm wide at its widest point. It consists of a polypropylene (plastic) carrier which carries '89 mg of copper in the form of fine copper wire wound around the stem of the device'. Like all intra-uterine devices, it should be carefully and skilfully inserted into the uterus (see Edith Weisberg's 'Insertion of intra-uterine devices' in *The Medical Journal of Australia*, October 4, 1980, 359-362). Successful IUD insertion depends on 'skill and experience of personnel inserting the device; the size and type of the device and introducer; the timing of insertion; and the insertion technique employed' (Edith Weisberg).

Copper T is 38 mm long, with a width across the horizontal arm of 32 mm. The carrier supports 120 mg of 0.25 mm diameter copper wire. The *Family Planning Handbook for Doctors* (IPPF, 1980) also deals with this device (chapter 5, 'Intra-uterine Contraception', 57-78).

Multiload is a device 36 mm long. Its polypropylene carrier 'supports 27 cm of 0.3 mm diameter copper wire wound around the vertical stem'. The device is 'pre-loaded in an inserter tube and is left in the uterus by withdrawal of the tube'.
Progestasert is the device which delivers progesterone in the uterus. It is 'T' shaped and carries a reservoir of 38 mg of the synthetic female hormone progesterone in its vertical stem.

Inert Devices (not containing active metals or chemicals)
Lippes Loop is a device made of polyethylene (light-weight plastic) and is one example of this kind of device. There are four different sizes of this IUD. Size A (length 26.19 mm, width 22.23 mm, colour of thread: blue) is most often used for nulliparous women (women who have not borne a child). Sizes B, C, and D, with differing length, width, thickness, and thread colour, are used for parous women (women who have had children) according to the size of their uterus.

The IUD affects 'the complex chain of events that takes place when the blastocyst is attached to the uterine wall'. Since the IUD 'acts mainly in the uterus, it must do so just before or around the time of nidation, that is, during the three or four days that the egg is in the uterus but is not implanted in the uterine wall'. These references from the *Family Planning Handbook for Doctors* (61) are significant because the authors regard the claim that the IUD is an abortifacient as 'still speculative'. The fact that IUDs 'work by causing an inflammatory reaction of the endometrium so that a fertilized egg cannot implant' (E. Billings) justifies the listing of these devices under abortifacients rather than under contraceptives.

From the brief descriptions given above, it is not difficult to believe that these 'foreign bodies' in the woman's uterus are capable of causing all kinds of complications. While nobody knows how the IUDs work, the claim that these devices are contraceptives is false.

At present, about 55 million women in the world use IUDs, and many suffer serious side-effects. Pregnancies can occur in women during IUD use. This may lead 'to two major problems, namely spontaneous septic abortion and ectopic pregnancy' (pregnancy outside the uterus, usually in the Fallopian tubes), and may result in the woman dying.

Among the frequently observed side-effects of IUD use are perforation of the uterus or cervix, bleeding, vaginal discharge, infection, cramping and backache. In such cases, the device may be expelled or need to be removed. Women who have had such devices fitted must be examined two months after insertion, at six months, again after one year, and thereafter annually.

The IUD as a common 'mechanical' method of preventing implantation of the tiny blastocyst presents serious personal moral issues as well as socio-medical questions. The case of the *Dalkon Shield*, an intra-uterine device which was vigorously distributed from 1972 by the US Agency for International Development (AID), is a notorious example of an irresponsible and immoral foreign policy decision by a nation. The reports from developing countries of the hazardous side-effects of this IUD caused a worldwide recall of the device in 1975. The reported hazards due to the insertion of a Dalkon Shield included 'pelvic inflammatory disease, sterility, miscarriages and — in 14 cases — death to women who used them' (Patrick A. Trueman, quoting Jeanie Kasindorf's 'The Case Against IUDs', *New West*, May 5, 1980, 31).

A social policy which would forbid abortion should also outlaw abortifacients as a legitimate means of birth control. Those who claim to be 'anti-abortion' cannot possibly condone the use of abortifacients which constitute the seemingly-hidden link between contraception and abortion (*abortus provocatus*).

Abortion

Abortion is an act aimed at the destruction of the developing human fetus. It differs from the medical procedure called therapeutic termination of pregnancy. 'It is of fundamental importance to get our terms right', according to Dr Philip R. Norris, Chairman of the British section of the World Federation of Doctors who Respect Human Life. In his 'Principles of therapeutic termination of pregnancy' (*Information Bulletin* of the Dutch Physicians' League, Vol.7, No.4, November 1980) he writes:

1. Therapeutic termination of pregnancy can never be an abortion, since abortion has as its intention the destruction of the fetus.
2. The doctor must at all times be mindful that during a pregnancy he has a duty to both mother and fetus.
3. The well-being of the fetus depends upon the health of the mother. It follows, therefore, that if the health of the mother is threatened the health of the fetus is also threatened. Steps to remove it from an unhealthy, hostile uterine environment may become urgently necessary for its survival.
4. The fetus should be removed from the uterus at a time and by a method which will ensure its best chance of survival (compatible with the safety of the mother).
5. Once removed, the fetus must receive such medical assistance as is presently available and is appropriate to its stage of development.
6. Methods of termination which, by their nature, cause the death of the fetus must never be used if an alternative is possible.
7. Medical or surgical treatment of the mother is, indirectly, treatment of the fetus. No therapeutic termination is valid if the mother has not received, before termination, adequate and proper treatment — unless the fetus is likely to be harmed by such treatment.

8. If the *intention* of the doctor is to do his best for both mother and fetus, according to circumstances, it is a true termination of pregnancy and fulfils the highest standards required of medical practice.
   If, on the other hand, it is the intention of the doctor to destroy the fetus to achieve his ends, then this is an abortion, an abomination which is unacceptable to those who respect human life and who are committed to the Geneva Declaration of 1948.
9. Therapeutic termination of pregnancy requires no legal enablement. An abortion does, since the fetus must die for it to be effective.

This very responsible medical-moral statement of principles should leave no doubt in our mind that abortion cannot be regarded as a therapeutic activity on the part of physicians or other health professionals.

Personhood of the Unborn

To argue against the thesis that 'human life begins at conception' is futile because it states a biological fact which allows no room for dispute. George F. Will in his article 'The Case of the Unborn Patient' (*Newsweek*, June 22, 1981) correctly observes that 'the argument about abortion cannot be about when human life begins'. He noted that

> in 1947, before Planned Parenthood became a pro-abortion lobby, an officer referred to the being produced by fertilization of an ovum as "the new baby which is created at this exact moment". In 1964 a Planned Parenthood pamphlet said, "Abortion kills the life of a baby, once it has begun" [a phrase now used throughout the world by the Right-to-Life movement — Ed.]. What has changed is not biology but Planned Parenthood's agenda.

Indeed, the discussion should not revolve around the question as to when life begins (we all ought to know that!); it should be about the *status of the life of a human being prior to birth*. The issue of human personhood comes sharply into focus if we look at the status of life in the womb.

The questions: 'What is a person?' and 'When a person?' are essentially philosophical (Robert E. Joyce, 'When Does a Person Begin' in *New Perspectives on Human Abortion*, ed. Thomas W. Hilgers, Dennis J. Horan, and David Mall; University Publications of America Inc., 1981, 345 ff). From a biological standpoint, a biologist may view even adult human beings as 'simply a human organism'. But philosophy is the art of intelligent reasoning which flows from a love for wisdom (the literal meaning of 'philosophy'). And philosophically we maintain that a human person is a being 'that has the natural, but not necessarily the functional, ability to know and love in a transsensible or non-material way' (Joyce). This view of human personhood is derived from an understanding of nature which endows the individual with 'a *natural* capacity' for human activities.

The 'developmentalist' interpretation of the beginning of personhood (for example, Daniel Callahan) claims that a human being (in the biological sense) is a human person (in the philosophical sense) if and when 'a *developed* capacity' for human activities (reasoning, willing, desiring, and relating to others) is present. But there is a serious flaw in the developmentalist's approach. Human beings may never attain their natural capacity for human activities; alternatively, once having attained it, they may lose it. Nevertheless, such incapacitated human beings are different from rabbits even in their embryonic stages. And since embryonic rabbits do not have the natural capacity of acting as human beings, they can never achieve such a functional capacity.

Personhood is not an *achievement*; it is an *endowment*. Nature 'does not revolve around function. Function revolves around nature.' The difficulty which many people have in accepting the personhood of the fetus is rooted in the ancient error, carried into our thinking by modern philosophers, that the 'real me' is identified only with the human 'soul', or with 'rational consciousness'. No being becomes a human person *'unless it already is a person'*. We do not develop from a 'subpersonal human animal' into a human person; we are human persons from the moment of our conception, for from that moment we have been *endowed* with human personhood!

The philosophical questions: 'What is a person?' and 'When a person?' are important because 'prebirth individuals (or persons) are now being dehumanized-by-definition through quasi-scientific and erroneous philosophical endeavours' (Joyce). In an age in which we condemn racism and sexism, we are happily accepting *natalism*, the superiority of the born over the unborn! In doing so, we stand guilty of 'polluting the atmosphere of thought'!

If we accept (as we should) that we have been endowed with human personhood from the moment of our conception (without disputing the developmental phases in our natural capacity for human activities), it is obvious that abortion involves more than the destruction of human cells, tissue, microscopic matter, and tiny human organs. It destroys a human being who has been endowed from conception with personhood, and who possesses individuality, a quality that distinguishes a person from all other persons. The fact that human beings in their early stages of development are very small does not make them less human or non-human, less a person or a non-person, less an individual or a non-individual.

Abortion is the end of a human life. Because it is a deliberate human act, it should be open to serious moral scrutiny (see D. Ch. Overduin's 'The Ethics of Abortion' in *New Perspectives on Human Abortion*, 357-386).

Jewish Attitudes to Abortion

Immanuel Jakobovits, Chief Rabbi of the British Commonwealth and the author of *Jewish Medical Ethics*, once wrote:

> The decision on whether, and under what circumstances, it is right to destroy a germinating human life depends on the assessment and weighing of values, on determining the title to life in any given case. Such value judgments are entirely outside the province of medical science. No amount of training or experience in medicine can help in ascertaining the criteria necessary for reaching such capital verdicts, for making such life-and-death decisions.
>
> Such judgments pose essentially a moral, not a medical, problem ('Jewish Views on Abortion' in *Jewish Bioethics*, 1979, 118,119).

Rabbi Jakobovits is right when he says that abortion is essentially a moral issue. This does not mean that abortion is a personal moral issue only; life-and-death decisions by individuals should not be made without reference to the potential 'victim', to society, and to the law.

In dealing with the subject of abortion, we therefore need to consider the personal-moral, socio-moral, socio-medical, and legal-ethical criteria by which abortion is either justified or condemned.

For Jewish believers, as indicated earlier, the validity of personal and communal moral values is derived from the divine revelation at Mount Sinai. The definition of these values is to be found in the 'vast and complex corpus of Jewish law, the authentic expression of all Jewish religious and moral thought'. A distinct attitude to 'all aspects of the abortion problem' is to be found in the Bible, the *Talmud*, the great medieval codes, and the authoritative rabbinical writings containing judgments founded on biblical and Talmudic principles.

The only reference to abortion in the Bible is the controversial passage in Exodus 21:22,23:

> And if men strive together, and hurt a woman with child, so that her fruit depart, and yet no harm follow, he shall be surely fined, according as the woman's husband shall lay upon him; and he shall pay as the judges determine. But if any harm follow, then thou shalt give life for life (transl. *The Soncino Books of the Bible*).

In most Jewish interpretations, the words 'no harm follow' refers to the survival of the woman after a miscarriage, and the terms 'any harm follow' and 'hurt' refer to the fatal injury of the woman.

The Christian interpretation differs because it takes into account the Greek translation of this text in the Septuagint. The Septuagint reading of Exodus 21:22,23 is:

> And if two men strive and smite a woman with child, and her child be born imperfectly formed, he shall be forced to pay a penalty: as the woman's husband may lay upon him, he shall pay with a valuation. But if it be perfectly formed, he shall give life for life.

The differences between the translated texts are obvious. Up to 1588, Catholic interpreters followed the interpretation of the African Church Father Tertullian (c. 160-220). On the basis of this text, Tertullian distinguished between an unformed and a formed fetus, and branded the killing of the latter as murder. Since 1588, the Roman Catholic Church has regarded the destruction of human life at any stage of gestation as murder.

According to some interpreters, the Exodus passage is not a reference to abortion at all, but to the premature birth of a child (*partus praematurus* or maybe *partus immaturus*). The reference in the Old Testament (Job 3:16) to an 'untimely birth', to 'infants that never see the light', is also not a reference to abortion. There have even been suggestions that there is a reference to a missed abortion in Numbers 12:12: 'Let her not be as one dead, of whom the flesh is half consumed when he comes out of his mother's womb'.

The *Talmud* condones abortion only if it is necessary to prevent the death of the mother.

> If a woman is in hard travail [and her life cannot otherwise be saved], one cuts up the child within her womb and extracts it member by member, because her life comes before that of [the child]. But if the greater part [or the head] was delivered, one may not touch it, for one may not set aside one person's life for sake of another (*Tohorot* II *Oholot* 7:6).

The rabbinical writings discuss abortion more fully, leaving no doubt that, according to the letter and spirit of Jewish law, abortion is a moral evil (see the excellent and detailed chapter 'Abortion in Halakhic Literature' by J. David Bleich in *Jewish Bioethics*, 134-177).

Judaism reflects 'an attitude of awe and reverence before the profound mystery of existence and a deeply rooted reluctance to condone interference with the sanctity of individual human life'. It 'regards all forms of human life as sacred, from the formation of germ plasm in the cell of the sperm until the decomposition of the body after death' (J. David Bleich).

An ancient Jewish prayer-like saying points to the evil of abortion in the following words:

> There are three [persons] who drive away the Shekhina [dwelling or nearness of God] from the world, making it impossible for the Holy One, blessed be He, to fix His abode in the universe and causing prayer to be unanswered ... [The third is] he who causes the fetus to be destroyed in the womb, for he destroys the artifice of the Holy One, blessed be He, and His workmanship ... For these abominations the Spirit of Holiness weeps (*Zohar, Shermot* 3b).

Christian Attitudes to Abortion

The Churches, both of the East and the West, which stand in the catholic and apostolic tradition, regard human life as sacred, and reject abortion as an unlawful and immoral ending of human life.

Pope Pius XI in his Encyclical Letter 'On Christian Marriage' (*Casti Connubii*, December 31, 1930) says:

> Those who hold the reins of government should not forget that it is the duty of public authority by appropriate laws and sanctions to defend the lives of the innocent, and this all the more so since those whose lives are endangered and assailed cannot defend themselves. Among whom we must mention in the first place infants hidden in the mother's womb. And if the public magistrates not only do not defend them, but by their laws and ordinances betray them to death at the hands of doctors or of others, let them remember that God is the Judge and Avenger of innocent blood which cries from earth to Heaven.

Pope Pius XII in his Address to the Association of the Large Families (November 26, 1951) explicitly states:

> Innocent human life, in whatever condition it may be, from the first moment of its existence, is to be preserved from any direct voluntary attack. This is a fundamental right of the human person, of general value in the Christian concept of life; valid both for the still hidden life in the womb and for the new-born babe, and opposed to direct abortion as it is to the direct killing of the child, before, during, and after birth.

> No matter what the distinction between those different moments in the development of the life, already born or still to be born, for profane and ecclesiastical law and for certain civil and penal consequences — according to the moral law, in all these cases it is a matter of a grave and illicit attempt on inviolable human life.

The 1959 *Statement on Birth Control* by the US National Conference of Catholic Bishops (November 19, 1959) says that Catholics will not

> support any public assistance, either at home or abroad, to promote artificial birth prevention, abortion or sterilization whether through direct aid or by means of international organizations.

The Pastoral Constitution on the Church in the Modern World (*Gaudium et Spes*, December 7, 1965) contains the exhortation:

> For God, the Lord of life, has conferred on men the surpassing ministry of safeguarding life — a ministry which must be fulfilled in a manner which is worthy of man. Therefore from the moment of its conception life must be guarded with the greatest care, while abortion and infanticide are unspeakable crimes.

The *Theological Report* of the Papal Commission on Birth Control (June 26, 1966) states clearly:

> Governments, which have the care of the common good, should look with great concern on sub-human conditions of families and 'beware of solutions contradicting the moral law, solutions which have been promoted publicly or privately, and sometimes actually imposed'. These solutions have contradicted the moral law in particular by propagating abortion or sterilization.

The same report says in its 'Pastoral Approaches' that it cannot be

> legitimate for anyone to attack already existing human life, even in the first moments of its existence. The Church has always condemned abortion as a particular vile form of murder in that it destroys a helpless and innocent human being.

Similar statements could be drawn from other Roman Catholic sources. However, it should be quite clear that official Catholic teachings up to the present time have clearly expressed the attitude of the Church to abortion, namely, total and unequivocal rejection!

Lutheran churches within their larger global communion of 75 million adherents differ in their publicly-expressed attitude to abortion. However, the doctrinally 'conservative' or 'confessional' churches generally stand in the catholic tradition with regard to their view on abortion. Such

Lutheran churches reject abortion, but do not oppose the socio-legal provision that a doctor may terminate a woman's pregnancy to prevent her from dying, or, to use the more familiar phrase, 'to save the mother's life'.

The views on abortion of the churches within the 70 million world-wide Anglican communion are guided by the teachings of the Fathers of the Lambeth Conferences of 1930, 1948, 1958, 1968, and 1978.

In 1930, a resolution was adopted which stated that 'the Conference further records its abhorrence of the sinful practice of abortion'. In a report on 'The Life and Witness of the Christian Community', and under the sub-heading of 'Birth Control', the bishops said: 'We strongly denounce the practice of abortion which has as its aim the destruction of life which has already come into being'.

In 1948, the Lambeth bishops defended the notion of the sanctity of life for all human beings:

> Christianity accordingly endorses every claim that can rightly be made for man ... It believes in man as no other religion could, since it knows what God can do for man and in him. Moreover, because at the centre of its faith is the conviction that the living God has Himself entered into human life, giving men 'the right to become children of God', and summoning them to an eternal destiny, it regards man's personality as sacred. In Christ all humanity is ennobled, for He shows us what God intends man to be.

At the 1958 Conference, a report commended by the following Conference in 1968, said:

> In the strongest terms, Christians reject the practice of induced abortion, or infanticide, which involves the killing of a life already conceived (as well as a violation of the personality of the mother), save at the dictate of strict and undeniable medical necessity ... The sacredness of life is, in Christian eyes, an absolute which should not be violated.

Finally, at the 1978 Lambeth Conference, the Anglican bishops, in calling 'Christians everywhere to seek the grace of Christ to live lives of holiness, discipline, and service in the world', pointed out the need for local education programs

> to emphasize the sacredness of all human life, the moral issues inherent in clinical abortion, and the possible implications of genetic engineering (Resolution 10, 2.c).

The views of Protestant churches in the Reformed tradition differ widely. In the USA, a number of these churches supported the US Supreme Court abortion decision of January 22, 1973 (*Roe v. Wade*, 410 US 113) which invalidated all restrictive State abortion laws in the USA and gave women a constitutional right to abortion.

The *Abortion Act of 1967* in Britain was also supported by some of those churches. The same can be said for Australia — particularly South Australia, where abortion was 'legalized' on January 8, 1970.

The support for less-restrictive abortion legislation is still very strong among those churches which see abortion as a sad, but morally permissible, solution to a pregnant woman's problems. These churches seem to have adapted themselves to the socio-moral changes in the community.

Community Attitudes to Abortion

Those who do not adhere to orthodox Jewish or Christian beliefs also differ in their views on abortion. The personal moral views of some have been determined by their vision of a humane society, and others by the currently prevalent spirit of permissiveness. In general, however, there is not much opposition in the secular community to legalized abortion.

Western communities are deeply divided on the abortion issue, and it seems that attitudes on both sides of the argument are hardening.

The often very active and articulate **Right to Life** movement which has been established in almost all countries of the Western world, the recently formed and well-organized **Moral Majority** in the USA, the **Festival of Light** in Britain and Australia, the growing number of conservative women's organizations in various countries, are all outspoken in their opposition to abortion. Their persistent activities have kept abortion as a socio-moral and socio-political issue very much alive, often to the chagrin of those who want to believe that abortion has been socially and politically 'settled'.

The pressures, both in favour of and against legalized abortion, will not disappear, and the deep division in society on this issue will continue to surface (for a detailed discussion on the abortion controversies in Australia during the 1970s, see the authors' *Wake Up, Lucky Country!*).

A frequently-heard argument used in the abortion debate is the one related to the question: 'Who owns our body?' Russell Scott in his book, *The Body as Property*, says:

> Another example of the assertion of direct dominion over the human body is the creed of the antiabortionist. The abortion debate stirs deep moral and religious passions and continues to rage. At the very heart of

> it is the issue of personal autonomy. Whichever way the argument is resolved for a particular community, the power to control the pregnant woman's body is at stake. If abortion is forbidden by law, women lose personal autonomy and are unable to deal with important functions of their own bodies without the risk of committing a criminal offence. If abortion is permitted by law, a woman will have the power to determine what will happen to her body and the embryo in it.
> The physical dominion we are talking about here is principally that which controls the removal of body materials for subsequent use. This kind of dominion extends to semen, ova, fetuses, ovaries, fallopian tubes, and testicles, as well as to any other tissues (252).

The basic fallacy in Scott's argument is that the ownership-question with regard to the fetus is essentially different from the one pertaining to semen, ova, ovaries, and other bodily organs. The fetus is not part, is not an organ, of the woman's body; the fetus is a separate human person, with a genetic make-up different from the father and the mother. Since its blood is probably of a different type from the mother, the fetus could not be an appendage of the mother without killing her through the feeding in of a foreign blood supply. Since the fetus is biologically and philosophically another human being, the woman's 'dominion' over the fetus living and developing in her womb can never be autonomous. Whatever the mother decides to do with her own body may well affect the unborn child within her (and, indirectly, the man who is the child's father). The often-forgotten person in the abortion debate is the father of the unborn child; his relationship to the child should militate against any autonomous dominion of the mother over the child. Furthermore, neither women nor men can ever claim unrestricted autonomy over even their own bodies. Claiming such autonomy constitutes both a grave philosophical and ethical error. Common sense also tells us that this cannot be the case. We are never 'on our own' — as secular humanists want us to believe (H.J. Blackham, *Humanism*, 1968, 13).

The questions: 'When does life begin?', 'What is a person?', 'When a person?', 'What is the value of unborn life?', and 'Who owns the body?' are a few of the very important questions which have been raised in the continuing debate on abortion, and to which we have briefly addressed ourselves.

At the root of the arguments in favour of abortion lies the question of the autonomy of the human individual. The abortion debate is fundamentally related to the collision of different philosophies of life. The abortion issue is one which must be resolved in the 'heart' of people. That is the reason why the abortion debate is so difficult in an age in which the virtues of love, faith, and hope are so often ridiculed.

It is important, therefore, that the case against abortion be argued convincingly, earnestly, and compassionately. And it is an entirely proper and laudable work for citizens who oppose abortion to strive for the legal protection of the unborn. These same people strive nobly to provide adequate counsel, help, and assistance to pregnant women and their families. In short, it is both a right and a duty of concerned citizens to be involved in responsible social action to advance a course they believe in.

However, having said all that, we reiterate the truth that the personal moral, socio-moral, socio-medical and legal-ethical criteria by which we either justify or condemn abortion are basically philosophical. That our philosophy of life is influenced by our beliefs, our cultural and social heritage, and our socio-economic environment, is beyond dispute. Any philosophy of life should affirm our human freedom, our responsibility, and our interdependence.

The autonomy of a pregnant woman, which supposedly justifies her 'right' to have an abortion, cannot be sustained if we consider her moral responsibility toward a new life entrusted to her care. A society which sanctions (and then provides facilities, resources, skills, and funds for) the destruction of human life, abdicates its socio-moral responsibilities for the welfare of its born and unborn members.

'The promotion and use of abortion clearly represents an implementation of the doctrine of using death to solve social problems' (C. Everett Koop).

Medical Attitudes and Methods of Abortion

Since the late 1960s, the death of the unborn has been morally justified if it is achieved 'in accordance with good medical practice and under circumstances that do not violate the law' (*Current Opinions of the Judicial Council of the American Medical Association, 1981*, Article 2.01). This stance is in flagrant opposition to the long-standing medical-ethical tradition embodied in a number of 'General Codes' (see the Introduction).

This 'good medical practice', which often has serious effects on the physical and mental health of women, is said to be evident in the five methods of abortion at present in use (see Berger and C. Everett Koop, *Abortion in America*, 1980;

also 'Explanatory Notes' in *Wake Up, Lucky Country!*, 60,61).

1. **Dilatation and Curettage abortion** (D & C). This method is most often used in the first thirteen weeks of pregnancy. A tiny hoe-like instrument, the curette, is inserted into the womb through the dilated cervix, its natural gateway. The physician, performing the abortion, then scrapes the wall of the uterus, cutting the fetus to pieces. This method is now used less frequently than suction.

2. **Suction abortion.** This is the most commonly used method for early pregnancies. The principle is the same as in the D & C. In this technique, which was pioneered in China, a powerful suction tube is inserted through the cervix into the uterus. The fetus and placenta are torn to pieces and sucked into a jar.

3. **Salt Poisoning or Hyper-Natremic abortion.** This method (not used in a number of countries, including Australia) is generally performed after thirteen weeks of pregnancy. A long needle is inserted through the mother's abdomen and a strong salt solution is injected directly into the amnionic fluid which surrounds the developing unborn child. The salt is swallowed and 'breathed', and slowly poisons the baby, burning his skin as well. The mother goes into labour about a day later, and expels a dead, grotesque, shrivelled baby. Some babies have survived the 'salting out', and have been born alive.

4. **Hysterotomy or Caesarean Section abortion.** This method is used in the last trimester of pregnancy. The womb is entered by surgery through the wall of the abdomen. The tiny baby is removed and allowed to die by neglect, or is sometimes killed by a direct act.

5. **Prostaglandin Chemical abortion.** This is the newest form of abortion, using chemicals developed and sold by the Upjohn Pharmaceutical Company, Kalamazoo, Michigan, USA. These hormone-like compounds are injected or otherwise applied to the muscle of the uterus, causing it to contract intensely, thereby pushing out the developing baby. Babies have been decapitated during these abnormal contractions; many have been born alive. The side-effects to the mother are many. The package insert for Upjohn's *Prostin E2* abortion suppository cautions: 'Unlike the use of 20% hypertonic saline which usually has a lethal effect on the fetus, the administration of Prostin E2 vaginal suppositories does not appear to directly affect the integrity of the feto-placental unit and, therefore, there exists a

possibility that a live-born fetus may occur, particularly as gestational age approaches the end of the second trimester' (see Richard A. Watson, *The Case Against Upjohn*, 1979). Furthermore, it is known that a number of mothers have died from cardiac arrest when the prostaglandin compounds were injected. The manufacturing company of these chemical abortion compounds has declared that 'the company will promote these abortion chemicals in India and China during the coming decade'. Is this the kind of 'humanitarian aid' we should promote?

The sanctity of human fetal life is ethically violated each time that an abortion is performed. Technologically-advanced methods of abortion, which supposedly make the operation 'safe' for the woman, do not change our first and most important duty toward our unborn fellow human beings: to safeguard their primary human right, the *right to life!*

Another issue which deserves our attention in the context of the abortion-practice is **amniocentesis**, an examination of amniotic fluid surrounding the developing child in the uterus.

Amniocentesis was devised and developed by Sir A. William Liley, research professor in perinatal physiology in Auckland, New Zealand, a person strongly opposed to abortion. Used to establish the diagnosis of birth defects, it aimed to facilitate life-saving treatment of the mother and her baby. For instance, a woman with a serious Rh problem (Rhesus factor in blood cells) must have an amniocentesis to save her and her baby's life. Such amniocentesis is done very late in pregnancy ('third trimester amniocentesis'), and enables the medical specialist to administer a blood transfusion even to a child in the womb. But every technique devised for positive health reasons has the potential to be used negatively.

In countries where legal abortion can be obtained, the grounds for abortion have been laid down in legislation or by court-decisions. The five most common grounds are: the preservation of the life of the mother; the preservation of the physical and mental health of the woman; fetal abnormality; present or envisaged social or economic hardship of the pregnant woman; and present or envisaged social or economic ill effects on those living with or caring for the mother.

Since fetal abnormalities constitute the ground for eugenic abortion, every effort is now made to discover possible defects in the developing fetus. Second trimester amniocentesis (during the 4th-6th month of gestation) is done for three reasons: to detect fetal abnormalities; to determine the sex of the child before birth; to facilitate hypernatremic abortion (salt-poisoning).

Fetal abnormalities which can be detected by amniocentesis include: the Rhesus-incompatibility disease; Down's Syndrome (often called 'mongolism' — the Mongols call it 'European feeble-mindedness' — but more accurately known as 'Trisomy 21' because of the presence of 3 chromosomes-21 instead of 2, thereby giving a human being 47 chromosomes instead of 46); neural-tube defects such as anencephaly (absence of the brain) and *spina bifida* (exposure of the contents of the spinal canal).

Pregnant women who are 30 years or over are often advised to have an amniocentesis so that Trisomy 21, if present in the fetus, can be detected. Statistical data (produced in South Australia) indicate that this risk-factor is very low:

Women 30 years	0.857/1,000 total births risk-factor: 0.08%
Women 35 years	2.611/1,000 total births risk-factor: 0.26%
Women 36-39 yrs	3.65/1,000 total births risk-factor: 0.36%
Women 40 years	6.34/1,000 total births risk-factor: 0.63%

Amniocentesis is a medical procedure which carries substantial risks. A needle is inserted through the mother's abdominal and uterine walls into the amniotic sac. A sample of the amniotic fluid which surrounds the developing unborn child is taken because the fluid contains cast-off fetal cells. The culture is examined and (after 4-6 weeks waiting) diagnosis made. If a disease or abnormality is suspected, action is taken (usually abortion).

Second-trimester amniocentesis causes a high increase in the average rate of miscarriages: from 1 in 98 to 1 in every 38 pregnancies. It can also cause damage to the fetus if the needle puncture in the amniotic sac does not close, or if the fetus itself has had direct contact with the needle. These and other risks make second-trimester amniocentesis a procedure to which women should not subject themselves.

It is depressing to read in Chapter 18 of the Second Report of the Social Services Committee presented to the British House of Commons (published June 19, 1980) that 'all mothers whose babies are at high risk of Down's Syndrome be offered prenatal diagnosis and termination of affected pregnancies ... a maternal age of 40 or more is an indication for amniocentesis' (par. 356).

It should be carefully noted 'that an amniocentesis late in pregnancy to detect Rhesus incompatibility is meant to facilitate early and effective treatment of the Rhesus-incompatibility disease and is not done with abortion in mind' (Hymie Gordon).

Abortion is not healing. It adulterates the practice of medicine.

> The sole role of medicine is to protect the individual from accidents as much as possible during the long and dangerous road of life (Jerome Lejeune).

In 1980, abortion became the 8th of the 10 most common surgical operations in Australia. Medical benefits were paid for 42,462 abortions, out of the estimated total of between 80,000 and 100,000 abortions performed during that year in hospitals and private abortion clinics in the country. Approximately 80% of abortions in Australia are performed in States which have restrictive abortion laws. These laws have been interpreted by judges, and their interpretations in turn have facilitated the growing practice of providing abortion-on-demand in the name of socio-moral freedom of choice.

We long for the day when all members of the medical profession will again adhere to the Declaration of Geneva (1948), which states:

> I will maintain the utmost respect for human life from the time of conception; even under threat, I will not use my medical knowledge contrary to the laws of humanity.

Infanticide

Professor R.B. Zachary, a British pediatrician, wrote a few years ago:

> Disregard for the life of the child in the womb, as exemplified by abortions for fetal defects, has 'spilled over' into disregard for life after birth.

These words apply not only to our modern times, but seem to have applied throughout history.

E.A. Westermarck in his 'The Killing of Parents, Sick Persons, Children — Feticide' (*The Origin and Development of the Moral Ideas*, London: 1906-1908; vol. 1, chapter 17, 393-413) gives a description of the various attitudes toward infanticide found in a number of cultures.

In primitive and less advanced societies, infanticide was common practice. Deformed, diseased, illegitimate, and unwanted children were often killed. Westermarck mentions that this was the practice in most of the South Sea Islands, Melanesia, Polynesia, in Australia among the Aborigines, and among a number of tribes in North and South America. In Africa it seems to have been less widespread (the Swahili culture was one of the few in which infanticide was common practice).

In more highly developed cultures, such as the ancient Arabs, infanticide was also prevalent. The Arabs even regarded it, in certain circumstances, as a duty. Female infanticide was common in the poorer districts of China in spite of 'the prohibition by both Buddhism and Taoism' (Michael Tooley).

On the basis of Westermarck's book, Michael Tooley gives the following summary of the practice of infanticide in Greece and Rome, the two most advanced cultures of ancient Europe (*Encyclopedia of Bioethics*, 1978, vol. 2, 742,743).

> In Greece, exposure of weak and deformed infants was an ancient custom and, in at least one state, Sparta, was required by law. Exposure of healthy infants was not generally approved, but it was practised very widely and not regarded as a grave offence.
> This attitude toward infanticide was shared by the greatest of the Greek philosophers, Plato and Aristotle. Aristotle, in the ideal legislation proposed in his *Politics*, holds that deformed infants should not be allowed to live. Plato, in the *Republic*, goes farther and advocates the destruction not only of defective children but of those who are the product of inferior parents or of individuals past the ideal childbearing ages.
> The status of infanticide in Rome was similar. The exposure of healthy infants was probably less common; however, this apparently reflects not a difference in moral outlook, but the need for a population sufficient to maintain a large army. So, while the killing of healthy infants was disapproved, it was not viewed as an especially serious crime. And the destruction of weak or deformed infants was not merely accepted but required by custom, and possibly even by law.

There is an obvious difference between the ancient, pagan societies, including some primitive cultures, and a society which has been influenced by Christianity. However, the enormous changes in moral outlook came about slowly, and long-established, socially-accepted practices such as slavery and torture of enemies were hard to eradicate.

In a Discussion Paper (No. 4) entitled *The Changing Face of Childhood* by Gay Ochiltree and Don Edgar (Institute of Family Studies, Melbourne, Australia, 1981) a number of references are made to infanticide in England and France during the period between the Middle Ages and the twentieth century. Three references in particular are useful in the context of this chapter.

The first reference concerns midwives:

> Births were handled by midwives who were both respected and subject to superstitious fears. During the seventeenth century they were licenced by the church for two reasons. Firstly, to ensure the child was baptised if it was dead or dying, and secondly, to prevent the midwife practising witchcraft. The oath taken by the midwife gives some indication of the reasons for fear — 'I will not destroy the child of any woman, nor cut, nor pull the head there off, or otherwise dismember or hurt the same, or suffer it to be so hurt or dismembered' (8).

The second reference is to the killing and abandonment of infants:

> Evidence of infanticide abounds during the period we are looking at. Essex Court records for the fifteenth and sixteenth century give many examples of infanticide where charges were actually made. According to the records babies had their throats cut, were strangled, left to die of cold, smothered, drowned and so on. But some deaths would have occurred which went unrecorded. Many of these children were illegitimate and all were certainly unwanted. Illegitimate children were frequently abandoned in both England and France. Many were simply left in the streets to die or be looked after by some charitable person or institution. From 1722 onwards, most abandoned English babies were sent to parish work-houses where the death rate was almost as high as if they had been left on the streets (9).

The third reference points to child-minders:

> Unscrupulous child minders in the nineteenth century were known as baby farmers. In many instances the babies were neglected and in some cases drugged with laudanum [an opium solution]. Many babies died as a result of this. In 1870 in London, the bodies of 276 babies were found in various places. The case of Margaret Waters who was convicted of the murder of a number of babies was given a great deal of publicity, which helped gain support for the Infant Life Protection Society in 1870. In 1872 the *Infant Life Protection Act* was passed requiring people who minded more than two children for remuneration to register their homes with local authorities, and that they should be certain of the good character of the person. The Act also required that the death of an infant in such circumstances must be registered and a death certificate from a doctor provided. The Act was easily evaded at first but was later amended (14).

These references, based on various sources, clearly show that it took a long time, even for countries deeply influenced by Christianity, to end the existing social evil of infanticide either by social action or legislation.

The Christian church has always taught parents and those responsible for children to care for them. It has strongly opposed infanticide, the deliberate killing of an infant. Care for the child does not begin with the subjective notion of 'the child being wanted', but with the recognition that, 'with the help of the Lord', the loving union of a husband and wife brings the possibilities of the conception and birth of a child.

In the Bible, the child is seen as God's blessing and enrichment of a marriage; the fulfilment of God's covenant promise; God's gift to people as a reward for their faithfulness (many children's names in ancient Israel were related to the verb *natan*, to give); an example of innocence and simplicity.

The care for the child is expressed not only in the variety of Hebrew words which indicate the age of children, but also in the instructions which guide parental and communal care for the child. According to the Scriptures of both the Old and New Testament, the child should be given:

protection (even before birth), Exodus 21:22-24
comfort, Psalm 131:2
instruction (including discipline), Proverbs 22:6; Deuteronomy 4:10; Ephesians 6:4
food, Mark 7:27
security, 2 Corinthians 12:14
pity and forgiveness, Psalm 103:13
freedom from abuse and danger of death, Jeremiah 32:35
admonition, Exodus 20:12.

Laws and activities which take away **protection** from children are against God's caring law. The anti-child mentality of modern man is utterly dangerous to the wholesome concept of total child-care. The instability of the modern family does not provide the necessary **comfort** for our children. The secularization of education and the absence of moral imperatives do not provide our children with a proper **instruction** for living. The insufficient provision of **food** and aid to millions of families causes the deaths of an untold number of children (indirect infanticide), as indicated by the grim statistics published by various organizations. The enormous increase in the divorce figures in many countries of the world has endangered the **security** of thousands of children. The increasing incidences of child-abuse shows man's inability to have **pity**.

We are living in a society which harbours a host of displaced homemakers; a high number of 'quasi-married' people, living together; an increasing number of divorced families becoming two households, a paternal and a maternal one (previously called broken homes); and a rising number of step-families, which experience far more psychological stress than contemporary nuclear families.

It has been suggested that 75% of broken marriages could be saved if partners could work through their hurts and pains. The post-divorce picture is not good because the feelings of loneliness are very real. Children involved in the process of their parents 'getting unmarried again' (previously called getting divorced) face a situation of painful stress. Social scientists talk about 'changing the form of the family' when, in fact, the family is breaking up.

This does not alter the hardship for children who are 'victims' of their parents' decision.

Many infants, children, and young people are at risk today. Infants are at risk before birth and after birth if they are unwanted, abused, neglected, or disabled. Many 'unwanted' children are killed by feticide or infanticide, before or immediately after birth; the latter is a 'logical' extension of the first.

It has now become practice in certain hospitals to withhold treatment from children who are physically or mentally disabled, whose 'quality-of-life' prospect is regarded by doctors and parents as hopeless, burdensome, or socially unacceptable.

Victor Rosenblum, a Professor of law in the USA told an International Conference on Infanticide and the Handicapped Newborn (Chicago, December 6, 1980):

> Modern society still harbors a 'fear of defectiveness'. When disabled children are killed or left to die we become idolators of the plastic, the cosmetic, the illusory, and the elitist. When on the other hand we help that child to live, we affirm our capacity to love, our respect for human difference, our dedication to the democratic values of heterogeneity [being of dissimilar kind] as instruments of creative achievement.

A statement of a different kind was issued by a Humanist Society in Australia (New South Wales) in 1973:

> *The Newborn Baby* — If a baby is born with severe mental or physical disabilities, such as are sure to make it a misery to itself or to those who have to look after it, its life should be terminable by legal process before any person becomes emotionally attached to it. Doctors may sometimes take no steps to sustain such a baby, or may even hasten its end.

This infanticide statement ignores and sets aside the fundamental principles on which all responsible socio-medical care should be based.

The moral acceptability of passive and active infanticide cannot be sustained because it involves the destruction of an innocent human person. (By 'passive' infanticide the authors mean the withholding of ordinary medical care from infants who suffer physical or mental defects, thus hastening the end of their life; by 'active' infanticide they mean the actual killing of the child.) Infanticide is nothing less than an 'abominable crime' (Second Vatican Council).

Emerging bioethical principles are trying to take into account the actual situations which physicians face in their surgeries and hospitals. Medical technologies have, on the one hand, increased and refined the possibilities and means of advanced health care; on the other hand, they have created a number of serious ethical and moral questions and problems.

These issues must be faced, and clear bioethical guidelines for society formulated. Furthermore, such guidelines ought not to contradict the nature and demands of the 'laws of humanity' — laws rooted in both the laws of nature and the natural (moral) law. These laws should not be violated.

Suicide

Suicide according to Dietrich Bonhoeffer, is 'a specifically human action'. It is the 'ultimate and extreme self-justification of man as man'. This deed 'will usually take place in a state of despair'. Suicide is 'a man's attempt to give a final human meaning to a life which has become humanly meaningless'.

> The involuntary sense of horror which seizes us when we are faced with the fact of suicide is not to be attributed to the iniquity of such a deed but to the terrible loneliness and freedom in which this deed is performed, a deed in which the positive attitude to life is reflected only in the destruction of life (Dietrich Bonhoeffer, *Ethics*, 1975 ed., 167,168).

As Bonhoeffer reminds us, Christians believe that God is Creator and Lord of life. He alone

> exercises the right over life. Man does not need to lay hands upon himself in order to justify his life. And because he does not need to do this it follows that it is not rightful for him to do it . . . Man must not lay hands upon himself, even though he must sacrifice his life for others.

Bonhoeffer concludes his brief but penetrating section on suicide in his *Ethics* with these beautiful words:

> It is not the right to life that can overcome this temptation to suicide, but only the grace which allows a man to continue to live in the knowledge of God's forgiveness. But who would venture to say that God's grace and mercy cannot embrace and sustain even a man's failure to resist this hardest of all temptations?

With Bonhoeffer we want to emphasize, from an ethical point of view, the tragedy and seriousness of self-killing, rather than the socio-moral objections to such an act (most Christians certainly regard suicide 'as a sin of lack of faith').

Statistical Information

In the USA it is estimated that more than 80 Americans a day commit suicide, and that 'between six and seven million living Americans have attempted suicide' (Daniel Maguire, 'The Freedom To Die' in *Revised Bioethics*, ed. Thomas A. Shannon, 1981, 209-218). Some research has shown that as many as 25 per cent of people who failed in an attempt to commit suicide will try it again.

Most studies on suicide show that attempted suicide is a 'cry for help'. People thinking of killing themselves are lonely, and often desperate.

> The incidence of suicide in certain groups is revealing. Suicide rates among blacks and Indians in this nation [USA] are rated as of epidemic proportions. Two to three times more women than men attempt suicide (Daniel Maguire).

In 1978, a national organization called Suiciders Anonymous was launched in California, USA, upon the request of mental health professionals and clergy of all denominations throughout the country. According to a recent report (December 1981) by one of the Regional Directors, Meta Uchtman,

> Suiciders Anonymous is for those suffering in depth, deep depressions, anxiety, stress and fears which they cannot overcome. It is for those who have attempted suicide and failed, and those who are considering taking that final desperate step.

Meta Uchtman further wrote:

> Suicide is assuming frightening proportions. In the USA in 1978 there was one suicide attempt every 16 minutes. Today there is one attempt every minute. Adult suicide has increased 400%, teenage suicide 500% ... Cincinnati Suiciders Anonymous has seen 5,620 members in the last 35 months. 4,000 of these were women. (Men use a more drastic means for suicide, are successful, and therefore we see less men.)
> Of the 4,000 women ... **1,800 or more had abortions**. 1,400 of these were between the ages of 15-24. The highest suicide rate in this country is between the ages of 15-24 *(emphasis ours).*

In the 1960s the situation in the USA was already so serious that the United States Public Health Service created the National Centre for Studies of Suicide Prevention in October 1966. There are regional suicide prevention centres throughout the country, and a periodical devoted exclusively to suicide (*Bulletin of Suicidology*, 1967 —) provides regular information on this tragic phenomenon.

Statistical data show that the situation in Australia is less severe than in the USA. In 1968 there were 1,527 suicides in Australia: 1,022 males (1.7% of total deaths), and 505 females (1% of total deaths). The methods of self-killing were listed as follows:

Poisoning by solid or liquid substances	626
Firearms and explosives	353
Hanging, strangulation, suffocating	153
Other gases	117
Gases in domestic use	112
Drowning	80
Other and unspecified means	39
Jumping from high places	24
Cutting and piercing instruments	23

Some 1970 statistics show that suicide ran high among the categories of causes of death in the following age-groups:

15-24) 25-34)	Third (behind motor vehicle accidents and all other accidents)
35-44) 45-54)	Fifth (with heart disease and cancer leading)
55+	Not in the first six places

The *Yearbook Australia 1981* lists the 1978 suicide deaths under age-groups (227), but does not state the rates for males and females separately:

Ages		Ages	
1-14	6	55-64	223
15-24	284	65-74	134
25-34	329	75 & over	66
45-54	283	Unknown	2
		Total	1,595

The most recent figures which we were able to obtain from the Australian Bureau of Statistics were those for the year 1979. Total suicides in Australia for that year amounted to 1,677: males 1,198 and females 479. Related to the total number of deaths (males 59,257 and females 47,311), the suicide rates were slightly higher than in 1968. In regard to the methods of committing suicide, males mostly used firearms (485), and females poisoning (253).

The publication entitled *Suicide and Attempted Suicide* (Public Health Papers No. 58), issued by the World Health

Organization in 1974, says in its Introduction:

> Suicide is one of the commoner causes of death and as such presents a serious public health problem. The World Health Organization estimates that at least 1,000 persons kill themselves every day, and in the developed countries of Europe and North America suicide ranks among the first 5-10 causes of death. In the last decade, suicide ranked third, fourth or fifth among causes of death of people aged 15-44 in selected countries of North America, Europe and Oceania. It was responsible for about 6.5% of all deaths in this age group ...
>
> Attempts to explain the enigma of suicide have been made in terms of race, climate, religion, social custom and economic factors, with small success ... An adequate suicide prevention programme must be based not only on the provision of appropriate treatment centres for those who have attempted to take their lives, but also on the identification of those population groups and those individuals within a community who might be most at risk.

There is, however, no accurate reporting of suicide, and 'international suicide rates are so inaccurate that no useful conclusions can be drawn from them'.

Studies of available suicide rates in the years 1968-1970 give the following picture:

> Ireland had the lowest rate per 100,000 population: 1.8, and Czechoslovakia the highest: 24.5.
>
> Other available rates: Israel 5.2; Scotland 7.6; England and Wales 8.0; Netherlands 8.1; Norway 8.2; Canada 10.9; USA 11.0; Australia 12.4; Denmark 20.8; Sweden 22.0; Japan 15.2; Sri Lanka 17.2.

There is no doubt that the attitude to death, the experience of life, and the concept of death, all play a very significant role in the formation of the idea of self-killing.

A more recent report on the situation in Denmark has this to say (December 30, 1980):

> Suicide takes more Danes than road toll — Denmark has the highest suicide rate in the Western world. Almost twice as many Danes commit suicide as die in car accidents. Government statistics for 1979 show that in a country of 5 million people, 1,318 people took their lives, compared with 730 who died on the roads.
>
> The figures show the dark side of a society that enjoys one of the most advanced social welfare systems and highest standards of living. About 10,000 Danes attempt suicide each year. While more women attempt suicide, men have a better 'success rate', the figures show.

Religious Attitudes to Suicide

The Sacred Scriptures of both Jews and Christians give a few examples of people who killed themselves.

Samson's story is well known. The end of his life is described in Judges 16:23-31. King Saul and his armour-bearer committed suicide during the final battle against the Philistines on Mount Gilboa in the 11th century BC (1 Samuel 31:4,5). Ahithophel, the corrupt adviser to King

David, hanged himself in his native town of Giloh (2 Samuel 17:23). The high-ranking officer Zimri, after his initially-successful *coup d'etat*, killed himself after the army elected General Omri as king (1 Kings 16:18).

The Second Book of Maccabees records two acts of suicide. These are the suicides of the 'most respected man in Jerusalem, Ragesh or Razis (2 Maccabees 14) and of the advocate Ptolemy or Macron, who poisoned himself (2 Maccabees 10:13)'.

From the New Testament we know that Judas, the disciple who betrayed Jesus, committed suicide by hanging himself (Matthew 27:5).

Suicides and near-suicides are mentioned in the Talmud and other ancient Jewish writings (Fred Rosner, 'Suicide in Jewish Law' in *Jewish Bioethics*, 1979, 317ff). Codes of Jewish Law make a distinction between suicides committed by adults and children, and self-killing done by wilful intention and in unusual circumstances.

Maimonides in 'Laws of Mourning' in his *Mishneh Torah* states:

> For one who has committed suicide intentionally we do not occupy ourselves at all [with the funeral rites], and we do not mourn him nor eulogize him. However, we do stand in a row for him and we recite the mourner's benediction, and we do all that is intended as a matter of honour for the living.

The rabbinic writings consider a person who commits suicide a murderer, and he who 'neglects the preservation of his health is guilty of partially murdering himself'. Some moral authorities in Judaism take the view that 'it may even be a graver sin to commit suicide than to murder someone else'. The reasons for this view are the following:

> Firstly, by killing himself, a person removes all possibility of repentance. Secondly, death in most circumstances is the greatest atonement for one's sins; however, in a suicide's death there has been committed a cardinal transgression rather than expiation. A third reason why Judaism abhors suicide is that the person who takes his own life asserts by this act that he denies the Divine mastery and ownership of his life, his body and his soul. The wilful suicide further denies his Divine creation. Our Sages compare the departure of a soul from a human body to a Torah scroll which has been consumed by fire. Thus, a person who commits suicide can be likened to one who burns a *Sefer Torah* (Fred Rosner).

Since the question of suicide is sometimes related to the issue of martyrdom, it should be noted that, in Jewish tradition, martyrdom is prohibited except for reasons of idolatry, adultery, and murder.

A classic example of martyrdom involving suicide is the Jewish stand at Masada against the Roman Empire. In this case, 960 Jewish men, women, and children withstood the might of the 5,000-strong Tenth Roman Legion for four years after the fall of Jerusalem in 70 AD.

Faced with imminent defeat by the Romans, involving almost certainly the rape of the women, the forced slavery of the children, and the torture and murder of the men, those Jewish people chose death by their own hand, in response to the speech of their leader, Eleazar:

> But outrage, slavery and the sight of our wives led away to shame with our children — these are not evils to which man is subject by the laws of nature: men undergo them through their own cowardice if they have a chance to forestall them by death and will not take it. We are very proud of our courage, so we revolted from Rome; now in the final stages they have offered to spare our lives and we have turned the offer down. Is anyone too blind to see how furious they will be if they take us alive? Pity the young whose bodies are strong enough to survive prolonged torture; pity the not-so-young whose old frames would break under such ill-usage. A man will see his wife violently carried off; he will hear the voice of his child crying 'Daddy!' when his own hands are fettered. Come! while our hands are free and can hold a sword, let them do a noble service! Let us die unenslaved by our enemies, and leave this world as free men in company with our wives and children (Flavius Josephus, *The Jewish Wars*, Book VII).

The question as to whether or not suicide can be caused by a psychiatric illness is still unresolved. And the assertion that it should be regarded as a 'human right' (or civil right) is even more controversial.

Both Christians and Jews generally reject suicide as a morally justifiable act. The refusal of Judaism and (most of) the Christian churches to accord full burial rites or honours to those who have died by their own hands (except in the case of children who commit suicide) expresses the belief that self-killing is displeasing to God.

The Pros and Cons of Suicide

Ancient Greeks and Romans both condemned and defended suicide, depending on the circumstances in which it occurred. (In Eastern cultures we encounter similar situations.) The Epicureans preferred suicide above the endurance of life 'if it had become more painful than pleasurable or peaceful' (Benedict M. Ashley and Kevin D. O'Rourke in *Health Care Ethics*, 1977, 380). The Stoics would rather die 'with dignity' than 'perish in a shameful way'. Manichaeans justified suicide as 'a laying down of the burden' of the body.

In recent times we have heard the argument that justice may be responsibly advanced by committing suicide 'for the sake of honour' or to achieve a political objective. Roman Catholic Irishmen and Buddhist Vietnamese monks have committed suicide by means of self-starvation or self-immolation (sacrifice of self).

The 'advantages and disadvantages' of suicide have been summarized as follows:

The advantages are:

1. Suicide gives the human person full autonomy since he or she can choose to live or die, to be part of society or reject it.
2. It enables someone to leave life with dignity, instead of to endure useless suffering, be a useless burden to others, and so forth, or suffer mental disease or unjustified disgrace and dishonour.
3. It may enable one to avoid temptation to treacherous or ignoble acts which destroy one's personal integrity, or which may be harmful to others, such as the revelation of secrets under torture.
4. It relieves society of burdens and also one's family, so that their resources can be used for something better.
5. It can be an act of heroic sacrifice for others, such as the Kamikaze pilots during World War II.
6. It can be a protest against social injustice, such as the Buddhist monks who burned themselves in protest against tyranny in Vietnam.

The disadvantages are:

1. It is an intrinsic evil for a person to reject living out life to its full, since as long as conscious suffering or conscious endurance is possible, there is opportunity for personal growth.
2. It is contradictory to the very basis of morality since by this act the person gives up all other moral responsibilities.
3. Suicide is not a road to immortal life, since that life is mysterious, and we do not know whether this is the proper way to enter it.
4. By suicide the individual withdraws himself from the community which has given him life and deprives it of a unique member.
5. Suicide is a rejection of God because it is a rejection of God's gift of life.
6. Suicide deeply hurts those who love us and discourages them in their own task of living (*Health Care Ethics*, 382,383).

Suicide is an act which shows that a person for various reasons regards life as no longer 'worth living'. Self-killing as a sacrifice for one's honour, or as a means of saving others, or as a protest against injustice, can probably be justified only if it amounts to martyrdom 'in the service of God and our neighbours'.

Euthanasia

The word *euthanasia* is derived from two Greek words: *eu*, meaning 'happy', and *thanatos* meaning 'death'. The more popular term for euthanasia is mercy killing. Expressions such as 'merciful release' and 'liberating euthanasia' are also used.

On the basis of a number of studies, articles, pamphlets, and other materials on the subject of euthanasia, the following distinctions should be made:

Positive, active, or direct euthanasia. This means to bring about the death of a human being by positive intervention. This intervention may take place with or without the consent of the person or patient. It is *involuntary euthanasia* if no consent has been sought or given; it is *voluntary euthanasia* if the patient has asked for or consented to the administration of death.

Negative, passive, or indirect euthanasia. At present, this means 'the omission of useless treatment, that is, not prolonging the dying process by life-sustaining machines, such as a respirator' (Andrew C. Varga, *The Main Issues in Bioethics*, 1980, 180). Passive euthanasia may also be voluntary or involuntary. Patients may refuse treatment; in most Western countries this is recognized as a right of the individual. However, there is, of course, a moral difference between refusal of health-restoring medical treatment and of 'useless' treatment. Some also speak of involuntary negative euthanasia if doctors decide to discontinue treatment without consulting the dying patient.

(In addition to these terms, we can speak of **compulsory euthanasia**, the deliberate ending of a human life not only without the consent of, but clearly against the wishes of, the patient. The term **convertible euthanasia** has also been used for cases where the patient is at the time unable to give consent, after having consented at a prior stage.)

The described meaning of the terms negative or passive euthanasia, as currently used, is dangerous because it is confusing. No person objects to the omission of 'useless' treatment or to the discontinuation of interference in the dying process. The term euthanasia implies *killing*, or 'to force death to meet man on his own terms'.

Even the terms: 'right to die', 'death with dignity', and 'extraordinary means or extraordinary treatment', in the context of the current social, legal, and medical ethos, are highly suspect. They are open to all kinds of subtle, eroding manipulation in the contemporary debates on the subject of death and dying.

We do not object to a phrase like 'death with dignity' if properly understood. We do, however, object to euthanasia in all its forms if it implies voluntary or involuntary, active or passive, positive or negative, direct or indirect (mercy) killing and death selection. In a strictly legal sense, 'mercy killing is murder' (Fred Rosner). Even the British Euthanasia Society once admitted that!

Euthanasia in Historical and Legal Perspectives

In 1980, one of the present authors wrote a comprehensive essay on the subject in which he considered the historical, social, medical, legal, and moral aspects of euthanasia, including the Christian attitude to it (D.Ch. Overduin, *Euthanasia*, Adelaide: Lutheran Publishing House, 1980). On the basis of that study and other resources, including further research and reflection on mercy killing, we will briefly look at its modern historical development and the legal attitudes to euthanasia.

It is interesting to note that Joseph Fletcher, the 'father of Situation Ethics', who is a strong and outspoken proponent of euthanasia in the USA, has introduced the term *anti-dysthanasia*, which literally means 'against difficult death'. He uses this term to draw attention to 'the problem of prolonging death'. Every human being is against a difficult death, and is grateful if such a death does not threaten him. In practice, however, this nice term means both positive and negative euthanasia.

Some examples of various forms of euthanasia in modern history are:

> October 1939:
> Hitler orders eugenic euthanasia.
> 'More than eighty thousand German and Austrian mental patients, epileptics, feebleminded and deformed persons were killed in gaschambers in 1940 and 1941. The law originally dealt only with small children but the age was raised later' (Andrew C. Varga).
>
> December 4, 1949: Death out of pity.
> Dr H.N. Sander in Manchester, New Hampshire, USA, 'ended a cancer patient's suffering by injecting into the patient a substantial quantity of air intravenously'. Dr Sander was acquitted (Fred Rosner).
>
> March 9, 1950: Death out of pity.
> Miss C.A. Paight of Stamford, Connecticut, USA, shot and killed her father who was dying of incurable cancer. She was acquitted (Fred Rosner).
>
> 1962: Infanticide out of pity.
> In the internationally-famous Liege trial of the Belgian mother, Susanna Coipel van de Put, the charge of murder of a 'damaged' child involving parents, relatives, and a physician was heard in the midst of much national and international publicity.
> 'Mrs Van de Put who had taken thalidomide during her pregnancy, gave birth to a daughter. The baby had no arms, only fingers coming out of her shoulders, her face was badly disfigured, and she had other abnormalities as well. Her mother and sister decided that the baby should not be allowed to live, and Susanna agreed with their decision. Soon after going home from the hospital, she mixed barbiturates with a honey-sweetened formula that killed the one-week-old baby. The police, tipped off by Mrs Van de Put's suspicious pediatrician, arrested her and her accomplices. The defendants did not deny the fact of the killing. They argued only that it was a merciful act because it was better than letting the baby live.
> 'The prosecution argued for a conviction on the charge of a premeditated homicide but recommended leniency. The jury of twelve men reached a verdict in less than two hours of deliberation: not guilty. The fact that a public-opinion survey ran ten to one in favour of the not-guilty verdict indicates that a large number of people might agree with involuntary positive euthanasia, at least in circumstances similar to those of Mrs Van de Put' (Andrew C. Varga).

This latter case of euthanasia (infanticide by pity) shows how strongly human emotions can influence one's actions. There is no doubt that the woman was guilty of homicide. The fact that leniency was recommended shows that the prosecution was aware of the emotional trauma in which the mother had found herself. But the not-guilty verdict of the jury did not absolve from moral guilt those involved in the killing of this child.

It is not surprising that, soon after the trial, on November 26, 1962, a Bill to legalize euthanasia for some 'damaged' children came before the Parliament of Belgium. However, euthanasia in Belgium, as in France, is still 'considered premeditated homicide' (Fred Rosner).

The USA, Britain, and Australia do not have euthanasia legislation. There are a few European countries that have rather lenient legislation; and, in at least one country, passive euthanasia has been legalized (Sweden, in 1964). The only two countries in the world which legally exempt people from penalty if they commit a homicide out of compassion, acting on repeated requests of an incurably-ill patient, are Uruguay and Peru in South America.

Humanist and euthanasia societies throughout the Western world have been very active in supporting the introduction of euthanasia legislation. In Britain, USA, and Australia, various attempts to legalize (voluntary) euthanasia in various forms have failed, but proponents continue to press their demands. Those who favour euthanasia are convinced that one day they will succeed in achieving the legal sanction of 'death-on-demand' — not only for the unborn (abortion), but also for those who are born (infanticide, suicide, and euthanasia).

The attempts to legalize infanticide in the USA have been documented by the Jewish writer David Bleich in 'Abortion and Jewish Law' which appears in the book *New Perspectives On Human Abortion* (edited by Hilgers, Horan and Mall, 1981). Bleich points out that, even before the US Supreme Court decision on abortion in 1973, 'the prominent situation ethicist Professor Joseph Fletcher argued that if the life of a mongoloid baby can be "ended prenatally, why should it not be ended neonatally (i.e., just after birth)?"'.

Since then, several prominent scientists have attempted to get around the problem that, while society regards feticide (the killing of the unborn) as morally acceptable, it also regards infanticide as morally offensive. Nobel prize-winners, James Watson and Francis Crick, wish to see birth redefined in such a way that the child would not be declared to be 'born' and 'alive' until two or three days after birth. Michael Tooley, professor of philosophy at Stanford University, would prefer the time to be extended to two weeks. All three men want this change to allow parents a second chance for an abortion of their child.

If that were to be the case, it would allow the possibility of infanticide for all children — not just those who are mongoloid.

Jean's Way

At the other end of the age scale, the evangelizing for legal voluntary euthanasia for adults was never more apparent than in the book *Jean's Way* (Derek Humphry and Ann Wickett, 1978). Derek Humphry is a British journalist and author; Ann Wickett is an American now living in Britain as Humphry's second wife. In this book, Derek Humphry gives an account of the events which led up to the assisted suicide of his first wife, Jean.

The writers use all their skills to present an emotionally-compelling justification for a husband helping his wife, desperately ill with a terminal cancer, to kill herself. But, while the book, for some, may be emotionally compelling, it flouts the rules of objective logic, and inadvertently justifies many of the criticisms of voluntary euthanasia.

Jean's request for her husband's help to kill herself was made at a time when Humphry admits 'that she was making a big effort to fight off the residual effects of the massive doses of drugs which caused drowsiness and forgetfulness' (80). He further admits that, after he had promised to help, 'she and I never discussed the matter again' (82).

That Derek Humphry did not always understand what his wife was really saying, even on important matters, is also admitted. Because she felt unable, at that stage, to have a sexual relationship with him, Jean told him to have an affair to satisfy his sexual desires. When he took her at her word and later told her of it, 'she was stunned' (104). He later admits that he 'realized that a part of her had been trying desperately to make things easier for me by encouraging me to find some form of relief, but that, underneath it all, she had never wanted it to happen at all' (104).

On the day when the lethal poison was taken (a poison provided for the purpose by a 'Harley Street doctor'), Jean raised obstacles to the whole thing. 'Aren't you breaking the law in helping me to take my own life? Won't you get into trouble?' (136). He persuaded her that it would be all right.

It should not have been difficult for the prosecution to make out a case against Humphry, given his admission that he assisted in a suicide, and given that, even from his own evidence, he may well have been mistaken as to his wife's real wishes. But there was no prosecution, because no charges were laid. Was this because the British Crown believed that they would be unlikely to find a jury to convict the man, no matter how strong the evidence?

The ready reception of this book by the media and by the public may be taken as an indicator of the increasing acceptance of the so-called 'right-to-die'.

Karen Quinlan

The tragic case of the American girl, Karen Quinlan, should be mentioned in the context of this section because of its historical, legal and socio-moral significance.

On the night of April 15, 1975, Karen Ann Quinlan ceased breathing for at least two 15-minute periods; the reasons why this occurred are still unclear. After some attempts by friends to resuscitate her, she was rushed to Newton Memorial Hospital, New Jersey, USA. When the ambulance arrived and the admitting physician examined her, Karen had a temperature of 100 degrees, her pupils were unreactive, and she was unresponsive even to deep pain. After three days, another doctor examined Karen, and found her comatose with evidence of decortication (a serious condition relating to derangement of the cortex or outer layer of the brain). She required a respirator to keep her breathing.

When Karen was later transferred to Saint Clare's Hospital, she was still unconscious, and still on a respirator, when a tracheotomy (cut in the wall of the windpipe) had been performed. In Saint Clare's Hospital, Karen received extensive and detailed examinations including various neurological tests. The result of an electroencephalogram (EEG, which measures the electrical rhythm of the brain) was characterized as 'abnormal but it showed some activity and was consistent with her clinical state'. Other significant neurological tests were 'normal in result'.

From the time that the first doctor treated Karen, she had been in a state of coma, lack of consciousness. There are basically two types of coma: sleep-like unresponsiveness, and awake unresponsiveness. Karen was initially in a sleep-like unresponsive condition; but she soon developed 'sleep-wake' cycles, which apparently occur within three to four weeks, and signal normal improvement for comatose patients. In the awake cycle, Karen blinks, cries out, and does things of that sort, but is still totally unaware of anyone or anything around her.

Attending physicians declared Karen as being in a 'chronic persistent vegetative state'; she no longer has any cognitive function. However, according to medical experts, Karen is not 'brain dead'. Her brain stem function was at that time regarded as ineffective for respiration, and therefore required the assistance of the very sophisticated MA-1 respirator to assist her breathing.

The *Quinlan Case Opinion* (Supreme Court of New Jersey), argued on January 26, 1976, and decided on March 31, 1976 (see *Death, Dying and Euthanasia*, ed. Dennis J. Horan and David Mall, 1977, 492-524), says:

> Karen remains in the intensive care unit at Saint Clare's Hospital, receiving 24-hour care by a team of four nurses characterized, as was the medical attention, as 'excellent'. She is nourished by feeding by way of a nasal-gastro tube and is routinely examined for infection, which under these circumstances is a serious life threat. The result is that her condition is considered remarkable under the unhappy circumstances involved.
>
> Karen is described as emaciated, having suffered a weight loss of at least 40 pounds, and undergoing a continuing deteriorative process. Her posture is described as fetal-like and grotesque; there is extreme flexion-rigidity of the arms, legs and related muscles and her joints are severely rigid and deformed.
>
> From all of this evidence, and including the whole testimonial record, several basic findings in the physical area are mandated. Severe brain and associated damage, albeit of uncertain etiology, has left Karen in a chronic and persistent vegetative state. No form of treatment which can cure or improve that condition is known or available. As nearly as may be determined, considering the guarded area of remote uncertainties characteristic of most medical science predictions, she can **never** be restored to cognitive or sapient life. Even with regard to the vegetative level and improvement therein (if such it may be called) the prognosis is extremely poor and the extent unknown if it should in fact occur.
>
> She is debilitated and moribund and although fairly stable at the time of argument before us (no new information having been filed in the meanwhile in expansion of the record), no physician risked the opinion that she should live more than a year and indeed she may die much earlier.

This Supreme Court case followed the denial of a request by Karen's father and his family to have the life-support mechanisms withdrawn. The doctor would not accede to the request, and the County Supreme Court would not give its permission either (November 10, 1975). The Roman Catholic Bishop, Lawrence B. Casey, who testified on behalf of his own and the Quinlan family's church, said that the request of Karen's father to discontinue the extraordinary means of treatment did not involve euthanasia, and was therefore a morally correct decision. It should be understood that the reluctance of doctors to discontinue 'useless' treatment is due to the ever-present threat of being sued for malpractice. Such lawsuits are commonplace in the USA, but not in Australia or the UK.

After a number of constitutional and legal issues were reviewed, and medical factors considered, the court ruled in its *Declaratory Relief* that 'upon the concurrence of the guardian and family of Karen the life-support apparatus being administered to her could be discontinued' on two conditions:

(1) The concurrence of the responsible attending physicians who must conclude that there is no reasonable possibility of Karen's ever emerging from her present comatose condition to a cognitive, sapient state; and

(2) The concurrence and agreement by a hospital ethics committee that there is no reasonable possibility of Karen's ever emerging from her present comatose condition to a cognitive, sapient state (Dennis J. Horan).

The legal arguments in this most famous case were complicated, and have since been criticized by various legal authorities. However, with J. David Bleich, we are of the opinion that Karen Ann Quinlan's 'tragic life and protracted death **have not been in vain**' (*emphasis ours*). Since passive euthanasia, and sometimes active euthanasia, continue to be practised ('albeit clandestinely'), the Quinlan case is useful in considering the question: 'Who is the arbiter of life and death: man or God?'

The 1976 case of Karen Quinlan, who was then 22 years old, presented three critical issues:

> Should Karen be pronounced dead?
> On the basis of medical evidence this cannot be done.
>
> May parents authorize withdrawal of treatment?
> Proxy consent is still a clouded issue, and in some legal systems this cannot be done (for example, in Jewish law).
>
> Does anyone have the right to choose death over life?
> New Jersey's Supreme Court unanimously ruled that no one has a 'right' to die.

At the time of writing, Karen is still alive. The respirator was disconnected on May 22, 1976, but she has breathed spontaneously ever since that date. She has been moved to a nursing home where she is nursed, artifically fed, and cared for. No one thought that Karen would survive the removal of the respirator, but there has been no suggestion of withdrawing her artificial feeding support, the 'ordinary means' of contemporary medical care. Her condition is considered 'medically permanent'.

Christopher Derkacz

Christopher Derkacz was a Down's Syndrome (Trisomy 21) child who was admitted to the Princess Margaret Hospital in Perth, Western Australia, on Sunday, January 21, 1979. On arrival at the hospital, Christopher was taken to the intensive care unit after a quick examination by the casualty doctor. The physician diagnosed Christopher's trouble as croup, inflammation of the organ of voice, causing difficult breathing and a hoarse metallic cough. This diagnosis was confirmed by others.

Christopher's foster-parents were very worried because of the child's persistent breathing troubles while in the intensive care unit. However, later that night, the parents left after being told that their child would be much better in the morning. When the next morning came, Christopher's foster-mother was informed by the doctor that the little 23-months-old child had died.

The parents were deeply shocked by this information, and made inquiries into the circumstances surrounding the death of their foster-child. Their personal inquiries, together with the subsequent Coroner's hearings, revealed that Christopher had died of laryngo-tracheo bronchitis, and that the post-mortem had been conducted 50 hours after his death. Furthermore, the instructions written on Christopher's card by the doctor in charge of the Intensive Care Unit read: 'not for resuscitation, not for intubation, not for external heart massage', and there were to be 'no further orders'.

Thousands of people in Western Australia demanded an open inquiry into the possible discrimination against this sick handicapped child. By mid-February, 5,000 people had signed a petition, and thousands of other people were adding their names to petitions urging the Government to support the cause of justice, not only toward the Strestik family who cared for Christopher, but also for a child who was left to die because a physician did not think it necessary and appropriate to use all available means to save the life of a mentally-handicapped child. The reading of the evidence and other related documents gives a definite impression that the life-not-worth-living concept does influence medical decision-making. To this date, no official open inquiry into Christopher's death has been held.

The ultimate medical and moral imperative for society demands that we 'maintain the utmost respect for human life'.

The Concept of the 'Right to Die' and the Living Will

In the Quinlan case, the Supreme Court of New Jersey ruled that 'no one has a "right" to die'. But many people would disagree with that legal opinion.

What are 'rights'? Rights are derived from natural needs and duties according to Andrew C. Varga (*The Main Issues in Bioethics*, 187ff):

> People having a natural need for food, clothing and shelter are obliged to provide these necessities for themselves in cooperation with others. They have a moral claim, that is a natural right, to the means by which they can procure them. It follows from this that nobody is allowed to prevent them from pursuing this goal. Is death a duty? Can a right to die be derived from that duty?

If death is placed among a series of 'natural duties' because nature has imposed death upon us, we then can speak of the 'obligation to die'. The growing idea that, if people are sick, infirm, or aged, they should fulfil their obligation to die, is not only tragic, but also misplaced.

Death is, indeed, inevitable for all of us. We should not be subjected to 'futile therapies' which frustrate the dying process, once it has reached an irreversible stage. We have the right to be informed about the nature and purpose of medical treatment if we ask the physician for such information. If we are unconscious, our next of kin should know. However, to demand that the doctor assist us in the exercise of our 'right' to die, may amount to making the physician an accomplice to self-killing.

The concept of the right to die is hardly compatible with a natural need or duty. The idea of the right to die as a natural duty is fraught with danger, absurdity, and practical difficulties. This is often shown in so-called 'natural death legislation'.

California was the first State in the USA which gave legal force to what is known as the **Living Will**. On January 1, 1977, the *Natural Death Act* came into force. Following 'California's example, seven other States have passed "natural death" legislation, assuring the right to die of terminally ill patients under carefully circumscribed legal conditions. Twenty-five more States are considering such legislation' (Andrew C. Varga).

At present in Australia, one State (South Australia, which pioneered liberalized abortion legislation) has before its Parliament a *Natural Death Bill*, while another State (Victoria) has seen the introduction of a *Refusal of Medical Treatment Bill.*

The Living Will is, according to others,

> based theoretically on the legal right that all competent persons have to refuse any treatment, and the teaching of several religious traditions that they have the moral right to refuse extraordinary treatment (Thomas A. Shannon and James J. DiGiacomo).

There are three types of Living Wills, based on the concepts of 'right to die', 'right to refuse treatment', and 'right to decide for others'.

The 'right to die' concept leads to a Living Will which authorizes active euthanasia. Relevant legislation must relate to 'voluntary request; person over 21; victim of painful, terminal illness; euthanasia administered under supervision of court or hospital panel; agent not subject to prosecution for homicide'.

The 'right to refuse treatment' concept requires a Living Will which clarifies the rights of competent patients. Relevant legislation must relate to 'right to refuse treatments; status of prior requests by now incompetent patient; locus of authority to interpret instructions; question of penalty for not following instructions; deciding on evidence with regard to refusal of treatment'.

The 'right to decide for others' concept demands a Living Will which stipulates the areas of authority for such decision-making on behalf of an incompetent patient. Relevant legislation must state on whose authority active euthanasia or discontinuation of treatment can be implemented: on the sole or combined authority of the physician, the next of kin, the guardian, or the court.

California has the longest experience with Living Wills. Such wills have to be renewed every five years to remain valid in that State. In 1978, there were more than 100,000 'right-to-die forms' distributed. Only a small number of people (approximately 0.6 per cent of recipients) are using those forms. In the case of American hospitals, the absence of a legally-executed Living Will makes a doctor sometimes very hesitant to stop even 'useless' treatment of a patient. The fear felt by hospitals and doctors of being involved in malpractice suits is very real.

If States had proper natural death legislation, the Living Will would become superfluous. The State cannot grant any 'natural rights'. If the 'right to die' is classified as being a natural right, it cannot be given to us by parliaments or courts. The State should see to it only that the right of patients to refuse 'useless' treatment is guaranteed, upheld, and respected.

Right-to-die movements have found that the words 'suicide' and 'euthanasia' have become difficult words to 'sell' to the community. Consequently, they have changed the names of euthanasia societies, and are now changing their vocabulary as well. Assisted suicide has become 'requested self-deliverance', and voluntary euthanasia is now described as 'end stage terminal illness'. However, the real motives of groups like Exit, formerly Britain's (Voluntary) Euthanasia Society, became quite obvious after they published their 'do-it-yourself suicide guide', called *A Guide to Self-Deliverance* (1980). This booklet caused such furor, scandal, and controversy that it cannot be publicly sold.

Nevertheless, the 'right-to-die' issue is still very much with us. There is no doubt that society's moral and medical attitudes toward 'self-deliverance' and continued treatment of the severely-handicapped and terminally-ill patients are changing.

Jewish and Christian Attitudes to Euthanasia

The Jewish and Christian attitudes to euthanasia have been shaped by their Sacred Scriptures. In each book of the Pentateuch (the five books of Moses) there is at least one reference to killing or murder.

> Whoever sheds the blood of man, by man shall his blood be shed; for God made man in his own image (Genesis 9:6).
>
> You shall not kill [murder] (Exodus 20:13).
>
> But if a man wilfully attacks another to kill him treacherously, you shall take him from my altar, that he may die (Exodus 21:14).
>
> He who kills a man shall be put to death (Leviticus 24:17).
>
> If any one kills a person, the murderer shall be put to death on the evidence of witnesses; but no person shall be put to death on the testimony of one witness (Numbers 35:30).
>
> You shall not kill (Deuteronomy 5:17). [Here the 5th (6th) commandment of the Decalogue is repeated.]

> Cursed be he who slays his neighbour in secret ... Cursed be he who takes a bribe to slay an innocent person (Deuteronomy 27:24,25).

The only reference to euthanasia in the Bible is the version of King Saul's death as given to David by a messenger who escaped from the battlefield:

> Then David said to the young man who told him, 'How do you know that Saul and his son Jonathan are dead?' And the young man who told him said, 'By chance I happened to be on Mount Gilboa; and there was Saul leaning upon his spear; and lo, the chariots and the horsemen were close upon him. And when he looked behind him, he saw me, and called to me. And I answered, "Here I am." And he said to me, "Who are you?" I answered him, "I am an Amalekite." And he said to me, "Stand beside me and slay me; for anguish has seized me, and yet my life still lingers." So I stood beside him, and slew him, because I was sure that he could not live after he had fallen; and I took the crown which was on his head and the armlet which was on his arm, and I have brought them here to my lord' (2 Samuel 1:5-10).

After this 'euthanasia' report, which suggests that King Saul did not immediately die after his attempted suicide (1 Samuel 31), David ordered the execution of the messenger because he had killed 'the Lord's anointed'.

The *Mishnah* clearly states that 'one who is in a dying condition (*goses*) is regarded as a living person in all respects' (Fred Rosner). And the *Babylonian Talmud* says:

> He who closes the eyes of a dying person while the soul is departing is a murderer [literally, he sheds blood]. This may be compared to a lamp that is going out. If a man places his finger upon it, it is immediately extinguished (*Shabbat* 151b).

This implies that even the 'small effort of closing the eyes may slightly hasten death' (Fred Rosner). In Jewish law it is forbidden to do anything that might hasten death.

The monumental *Talmudic Encyclopedia* (ed. S.J. Zevin; Jerusalem, 1963) deals in Volume 5 with death and dying. It is quite clear that the Jewish attitude to both active and passive euthanasia is one of total prohibition. Artificial prolongation of the dying process where a person's death is imminent (three days or less) is not sanctioned because the patient's 'soul's departure' should not be hindered.

The Roman Catholic Church condemns euthanasia (see article 27 in the Pastoral Constitution on the Church in the Modern World , Vatican II, *Gaudium et Spes*, December 7, 1965). A precise statement in the tradition of Pope Pius XII is contained in A Pastoral Reflection on the Moral Life, issued by the National Conference of Catholic Bishops in the USA on November 11, 1976 ('To Live in Christ Jesus'):

> Euthanasia or mercy killing is much discussed and increasingly advocated today, though the discussion is often confused by ambiguous use of the slogan 'death and dignity'. Whatever the word or term, it is a grave moral evil deliberately to kill persons who are terminally ill or deeply impaired. Such killing is incompatible with respect for human dignity and reverence for the sacredness of life.
> Something different is involved, however, when the question is whether hopelessly ill and painfully afflicted people must be kept alive at all costs and with the use of every available medical technique.
> Some seem to make no distinction between respecting the dying process and engaging in direct killing of the innocent. Morally there is all the difference in the world. While euthanasia or direct killing is gravely wrong, it does not follow that there is an obligation to prolong the life of a dying person by extraordinary means. At times the effort to do so is of no help to the dying and may even be contrary to the compassion due them. People have a right to refuse treatment which offers no reasonable hope of recovery and imposes excessive burdens on them and perhaps also their families. At times it may even be morally imperative to discontinue particular medical treatments in order to give the dying the personal care and attention they really need as life ebbs. Since life is a gift of God we treat it with awesome respect. Since death is part and parcel of human life, indeed the gateway to eternal life and return to the Father, it, too, we treat with awesome respect.

The Roman Catholic position has been most recently set out in a *Declaration on Euthanasia* drawn up by the Sacred Congregation for the Doctrine of the Faith, approved by the Pope, and promulgated on May 5, 1980.

Other Christian churches, too, have given a clear witness against euthanasia. In 1981 the Lutheran Church of Australia adopted a detailed statement entitled *Euthanasia or Mercy Killing*. This statement addresses itself to the 'Legislation of Mercy Killing' and 'Care for the Dying', and includes calls to the Church and to governments. The conclusion states:

> The Church also calls upon Commonwealth, State, and local governments to support the care for the dying by all appropriate means available to them, e.g., the allocation of sufficient funding for the purchase of adequate means of life-support for the terminally ill and dying patients; the provision of a 'hospice-type' environment for such patients; the support of adequate training programs for medical and para-medical personnel so that specialized care for such patients is readily available; and a firm commitment to refuse the enactment of any form of euthanasia legislation even in the face of increased pressure by influential euthanasia supporters.

The Church, if it is to be loyal to the Christian tradition, dare not remain silent if the principle of the sanctity of human life is threatened and the lives of people are endangered. The Church has a deep moral commitment to the welfare of human beings. It is because of this commitment that the Church protests against violations of justice, morality, and man's total well-being.

Natural Death

In a Jewish 'Confession of the dying' it is written:

> I acknowledge before You, my God and the God of my fathers ... that my cure is in Your hand and my death is in Your hand ... and if my appointed time to die has arrived You are righteous in all that befalls me.

Indeed, both Jews and Christians believe that life and death are in God's hands.

The Old Testament of the Christians' Bible, which is also the Sacred Scriptures of the Jews, makes it very clear that life is a gift of God (Genesis 2:7), and that God has its origin and manifestations in his hand (1 Samuel 2:6; Psalm 49:7-9). When God withholds his spirit (*ruach*, breath, spirit), all flesh (*basar*, individual being) dies (Psalm 34:14,15; 104:29). He is the living God, because his very nature is life (Deuteronomy 5:26; Joshua 3:10; 1 Samuel 17:26; 2 Kings 19:4; Psalm 36:9). God gives to every individual his or her identity (*nephesh*, power of identity). Because the individual's life is both the gift and yet the property of God, we have no right to destroy it (Genesis 4:10; Exodus 2:13; Deuteronomy 5:17).

The New Testament view of life agrees with that of the Old Testament. God is the living God (Matthew 16:16; 26:63; John 6:68,69; Acts 14:15; Romans 9:26) who 'alone has immortality' (1 Timothy 6:16), and who has life in himself

(John 5:26). God is the Lord of life and death (Matthew 10:28; Luke 12:20; James 4:15). He gives to all human beings their life (*psychē*, which appears 40 times in the New Testament and is the equivalent of the Hebrew *nephesh*). He also gives us our human existence (*zōē*, which appears 133 times in the New Testament and may also connote 'health', Mark 5:23; John 4:50).

The life of a Christian, including his or her conduct (*bios*, Luke 8:14; 1 Timothy 2:2; 2 Timothy 2:4, 1 Peter 4:3; 1 John 2:16), is liberated by the (new) life-creating and life-sustaining Spirit (*pneuma*) of God.

Natural death for Christians cannot be divorced from their faith in the resurrection (Romans 6:5; 1 Thessalonians 4:14-17 — and many more passages in the New Testament). They know that death is always at the horizon of their existence. Believers recognize that death is the penalty for sin (Genesis 3:14-19), and that this penalty affects all people in their bodies and souls (Matthew 10:28; 1 Corinthians 15:42-50). Yet, they are comforted by the beautiful language of hope which the New Testament writers use when speaking of death (John 11:11; Acts 7:60; Acts 13:36; 1 Corinthians 15:6; 2 Peter 3:4).

The Sacred Scriptures of Jews and Christians tell their readers that in ancient times people also knew about death in its tragic setting (Genesis 3:19; Psalm 22:15; 30:9; 90:5,6 Proverbs 27:20; Habakkuk 2:5). In an extreme situation people may even come to curse the day of their birth (Job 3:3,4; Ecclesiastes 4:2; Jeremiah 15:10; 20:14,15).

Natural death in the context of the Christian faith is both a tragedy and a joy; pain and relief; end and beginning. Our life in this world begins at conception and ends when we die. But it is not the fear of death which motivates believers in their concern for people with severe illnesses and those with physical or mental handicaps. It is a sense of responsibility to both the Giver and the recipients of life that makes Christians take such a deep and sincere interest in bioethics.

Legal and Medical Definition of Death

One of the great and pressing problems in contemporary bioethics is the problem of the definition of death. There was a time when defining death was a simple medical judgment. The common law defined death as the moment when life had ceased, 'defined by physicians as a total stoppage of the circulation of the blood and a cessation of the animal and vital functions consequent therein, such as respiration, pulsation, etc.'

However, such great advances have been made in medical science that the problem of the determination of death has become a real one as far as its legal definition is concerned. Having said this, it is good to remember that 'we cannot really define death since it is the absence of life which we can only describe' (Dennis J. Horan).

The American Bar Association in its Resolution, voted and approved by the House of Delegates on February 24, 1975, accepted as a definition of brain death the 'irreversible cessation of total brain function'. The Resolution, including its important preamble, reads as follows:

> WHEREAS, it is to the well-being of the public to cease all artificial life supports, respiratory and circulatory, after a human body is dead; and
> WHEREAS, it is currently medically established that irreversible cessation of brain function is determinative of death; and
> WHEREAS, in the current technology of organ transplants it is vital that the donor's gift be in the best cellular condition,
> THEREFORE, be it resolved: that the American Bar Association offers a Current Definition of Death as follows:
>
> For all legal purposes, a human body with irreversible cessation of total brain function, according to usual and customary standards of medical practice, shall be considered dead.

This means that the best definition of death available at the present time is the one which says:

> Death of the person occurs exclusively if and when brain death occurs, that is, when total and irreversible cessation of all neuronal function in all parts of the brain occurs.

This particular definition of death does not imply that a person can be declared dead who has spontaneous respiration and circulation, but who has a severe brain injury which makes him comatose (unconscious). Hydrencephalic and even anencephalic children cannot be declared 'brain-dead' under this carefully-worded definition, in spite of the reality that anencephaly (having almost no brain) is a condition incompatible with life. Such children will not live more than a few hours.

This definition also does not exclude a physician's pronouncement of death under ordinary circumstances in which he has diagnosed 'an irreversible cessation of spontaneous respiratory and circulatory functions'. However, general physiological standards do not apply if patients are assisted by modern life-support systems. It has therefore become necessary to arrive at a new standard for determining that a person has died.

The definition determines the ultimate and evidentiary fact of death; it covers the three known tests, which are brain, heartbeat, and breath deaths; it also covers death as a process (medical preference) and as a point in time (legal preference); it avoids both active and passive euthanasia and is not in conflict with theological, ethical and non-physical scientific criteria.

There is no objection to 'natural death legislation' if it simply and clearly states the definition of death. References to Living Wills, to passive and active euthanasia in all forms, ought to be avoided if society wants to uphold its respect both for life and death, for the living and the dying, the healthy and the sick, the young and the aged.

Preparation for Death

Human beings have the knowledge that one day they are going to die. Yet, we don't like to be continually reminded that this is an event which we cannot escape. In contemporary society, many people die alone in nursing homes, hospitals, or other institutions. We separate the sick from the healthy, the feeble aged from the sturdy young. The living and the dying seem not to mix.

In earlier times, the situation was quite different. People died in their homes surrounded by their loved ones and friends. Children, too, were present at the deathbed of their grandparents or parents. The physician acting as a 'messenger of death' (*nuntius mortis*) told the patient if the end of life was imminent. The priest or pastor was called to give spiritual aid, comfort, and hope to the dying person. The ministry to the dying (at some stage in history called 'euthanasia', meaning preparation for a Christian death) was an important ingredient of the total concept and practice of the Church's pastoral care of its people. A funeral service was a community event, and the rite of mourning involved the family, relatives, friends, and neighbours.

The great advances in medical technology and the secularization of our industrialized and suburbanized society have brought about a change from a personalized care to an institutionalized care for the dying. This, in turn, has meant a tremendous change in the pastoral ministry to the seriously ill and dying, for the 'environment' of the sick is no longer the home, but often a hospital room or ward with sophisticated life-support equipment. The extended use of drugs to alleviate pain often makes the patient unable to concentrate on what is happening or said.

Our hospitals were not built for the purpose of assisting the dying; they were established for the cure of diseases, after which the patient was returned to his or her own surroundings. Today many people stay in hospital until they die. However, the life-support machines do not assist the dying spiritually, and most doctors have difficulties if they are called upon to comfort, assist, or guide their patients in the hour of their death.

Because of this, many people have begun to think, speak, and write about the care of the dying. Workshops were held, first in Europe, then in the USA and Australia, at which initiatives were taken 'to transform the impersonal and businesslike atmosphere surrounding the dying' (Andrew C. Varga).

In the early 1960s, a British physician and former nurse, Dr Cicely Saunders, pioneered the idea of a modern hospice as a response to the obvious need of giving more human and loving care to the terminally ill. The hospice idea comes from the Middle Ages when travellers could rest in a *hospitium* (from the Latin *hospes*, host or guest), usually maintained by a religious order. Such places also cared for the sick.

In 1966, Dr Saunders opened her modern hospice in London and called it after St Christopher, the patron saint of travellers. This hospice is not there to provide a cure for rich people, but to offer care for the terminally ill if and when they can no longer be cared for at home. It has a home-like atmosphere; patients have plenty of freedom, and family, relatives, and friends can even come and stay. It serves as a model for 'the modern way of caring for the dying'.

There are hospice movements in various countries which try to implement Dr Saunders' ideas and ideals in their own communities. In 1971 the first hospice in the USA was established in New Haven, Connecticut. It began by providing care for the dying at home, with the support of family, relatives, and friends; seven years later, it erected a 44-bed building 'as a backup for its home care'. At present, there are more than 100 hospice organizations in the USA. Those who plan the organization of this type of service may be guided by the US National Hospice Organization.

In Australia, the hospice movement is growing steadily. In some cities hospice-type care is provided in conjunction with established hospitals. One criticism of the hospice movement is that it has still tended to institutionalize the dying. Such a tendency constitutes a total misunderstanding of the hospice idea as originally conceived. There is a strong body of opinion both within and outside the hospice movement which suggests that the best place for care to be provided is in the dying person's home, with an institution being used only when absolutely necessary.

To help members of the caring professions come to a better understanding of the problems of death and dying, a new discipline is now available, called *thanatology* (from the Greek *thanatos*, death). The practical aspects of care for the dying, including the problems of death, have been thoroughly explored by the Swiss-born psychiatrist Dr Elisabeth Kübler-Ross, whose publications are widely read. Her book *On Death and Dying* (1969) describes the 'five typical stages in the attitudes of the dying': denial and isolation; anger; bargaining; depression; and, finally, acceptance. An understanding of these 'stages' or 'phases' (some or all of which may be experienced by the dying) have been of great help to those involved in the care of people faced with the imminent ending of their life.

Our life in this world began at the moment of our conception, and it ends at the moment of our death. Between beginning and end lies our earthly pilgrimage. There are some who never face the reality of death, who seek membership in a Cryonics Society which arranges for the freezing of their bodies after death in the hope that medical science will one day find a remedy for mortality. It is better to heed the prayer of Moses:

> Teach us to number our days
> that we may get a heart of wisdom (Psalm 90:12).

5

CHAPTER

THE MANIPULATING OF HUMAN LIFE

Genetic Engineering

Cloning

Research on Human Subjects

Genetic Engineering

Contemporary biomedical technology may be divided, according to stated aims and endeavours, into three different categories:

1) Control of life and death, involving medicine which is now able to control reproduction and to prolong life
2) Control of human potentialities, involving genetic engineering
3) Control of human achievement, involving neurological and psychological manipulation.

The previous chapters have dealt with issues related to life and death control. This chapter takes up matters related to the second category, and refers to the third.

Genetic engineering involves the whole process of altering genes, the 'building blocks of life'. (The word *gene* comes from the Greek word *genesis*, descent.) It is done to achieve either a radically altered, or a completely new, human being.

As explained in Chapter II, every human being usually has 23 pairs of 46 single chromosomes (literally, coloured bodies, because they become visible by staining them with dyes). Of these 46 chromosomes, 44 are 'carriers of character', and 2 are a person's sex chromosomes. Parents and children have the same genes; but, for various reasons, they do not have the same physical characteristics.

A single chromosome looks 'like a ribbon of varying length, formed of a number of bands which are stuck together in a certain order. These bands or discs contain the real carriers of the hereditary substance, the genes' (K.H. Wrage).

We now know that the genes are made of DNA (deoxyribonucleic acid). The structure of DNA was discovered in 1953 by J.D. Watson and F.H.C. Crick. This very important scientific discovery was followed in the early 1970s by scientists discovering how to produce recombined DNA molecules. With this achievement, we entered the age of genetic engineering.

Since 1974 there have been serious debates and heated controversies surrounding the various techniques of recombining pieces of DNA.

> A set of techniques had been developed that made it possible to cut the long, threadlike molecules of DNA into pieces with the aid of certain enzymes [proteins], to recombine the resulting segments of DNA with the DNA of a suitable vector, or carrier, and to reinsert the recombinant into an appropriate host cell to propagate and possibly to function (Clifford Grobstein, 'The Recombinant-DNA Debate' in *Scientific American*, July, 1977, Vol.237, No.1, 22-33).

The gene-splicing technique known as recombinant DNA research, in spite of its great potential value in producing medicines, opens up a myriad of possibilities in the manipulation of human life. To understand this fully, it should be remembered that 'the replication of DNA is the most fundamental chemical reaction in the living world'.

> It fully accounts for the classical first principle of heredity: like begets like.
> If DNA replication always worked without error, life would be far more homogeneous than it is. Here, however, a second classical principle of heredity intervenes: the principle of mutational variation, or the appearance in the offspring of new hereditary characteristics not present in the progenitors (Clifford Grobstein).

The crux of recombinant DNA technology lies in the ability of the technologist to manipulate the basic structural compounds of DNA and their direct genetic change. In an age of 'human intervention' and of 'biocultural progression', we urgently need a public policy to control this highly-ingenious technology — especially if it is to be used to manipulate human life.

> Anyone affirming immediate disaster is a charlatan, but anyone denying the possibility of its occurring is an even greater one (Erwin Chargaff).

In October 1974, the National Institutes of Health in the United States established the Recombinant DNA Molecule Program Advisory Committee. Some 150 international scientists participated in an international conference held in February 1975 in the Asilomar Conference Grounds, Pacific Grove, California. The Conference decided that 'the voluntary moratorium should be lifted and that future research should be conducted under a set of guidelines' (Daniel Callahan, *The Hastings Center Report*, Vol.7, No.2, April 1977, 20). The Conference was well aware that this work is accompanied by real and potential biohazards. This research therefore demands stringent safety rules. The *Summary Statement* of the Report of the Asilomar Conference on Recombinant DNA Molecules (*Science*, Vol.188, No.4192, June 6, 1975, 991-994) speaks of four types of containment for the various research experiments: minimal risk, low risk, moderate risk, and high risk.

On the basis of the study of Fred Rosner, 'Genetic Engineering and Judaism' (*Jewish Bioethics*, 409-420), some of the potential advantages and hazards of recombinant DNA research are listed here.

Potential advantages:
Some genes can now be copied and their precise structure more easily studied.
Bacteria can be directed by an implanted gene to assemble valuable protein for human beings.
Insulin, antibiotics, antiviral agents, and numerous other drugs, chemicals, and vaccines may be synthesized in large quantities by the technology of genetic engineering.
Patients with absent or defective genes suffering from certain genetic disorders may be given a replacement gene.
Clones of nitrogen-producing bacteria may be useful for agriculture.
Specially-engineered bacteria are envisaged at factories for the production of numerous important substances for medicine and industry.

Potential hazards:
Genes of products which cause diseases may be transplanted into bacteria deliberately or inadvertently.
Unexpected genetic alterations may occur.
Accidental release into the environment of organisms which carry extraneous genetic material may cause disastrous infection of plant or animal life.
Recombinant DNA may be taken up by human cells in such a way as to produce cancer or other diseases.
Nitrogen-fixing bacteria could devastate soil ecology; once created they can't be destroyed.

The possibility of gene manipulation in a human sperm or human ovum by microsurgical techniques raises ethical questions of great importance. Even more urgent are the moral questions raised in the further possibility of gene manipulation in fertilized ova for both therapeutic and eugenic reasons. On the other hand, there can be no ethical objection to the technological feasibility of curing genetic diseases by gene surgery.

However, the concept of gene transplantation, involving the transplantation of genes from one person into the sperm or ovum of another person, raises a number of serious moral questions. For instance, is the child conceived from a manipulated sperm or ovum related to the gene donor? And should gene transplantation be viewed in the same way as kidney, heart, and other organ transplants?

Genetic engineering has certainly opened another chapter in the history of healing or health care. We agree with Rabbi I. Jakobovits who wrote in his *Jewish Medical Ethics*:

> It is indefensible to initiate controlled experiments with incalculable effects on the balance of nature and the preservation of man's incomparable spirituality without the most careful evaluation of the likely consequences beforehand ... Without prior agreement on restraints and the strictest limitations, such mechanisations of human life may also herald irretrievable disaster resulting from man's encroachment upon nature's preserves.

It is interesting that Theodore Friedmann and Richard Roblin in their paper, 'Gene Therapy for Human Genetic Disease?' (*Science*, 3 March, 1972, Volume 175, 949-955), said in their conclusion:

> We therefore propose that a sustained effort be made to formulate a complete set of ethico-scientific criteria to guide the development and clinical application of gene therapy techniques. Such an endeavour could go a long way toward ensuring that gene therapy is used in humans only in those instances where it will prove beneficial, and toward preventing its misuse through premature application.

Moral Attitudes to Genetic Engineering

Four basic theses regularly appear in the literature on the subject of genetic engineering:

> A scientist has the moral right to do anything he has the technical capacity to do in research.

> A scientist has no right to intervene in the natural processes of human life, because it is sacred.

> A scientist has no right to intervene in the natural processes in such a way that he might alter what men believe to be, and value as, the most distinctively human characteristics.

> A scientist has the right to intervene in the course of human development in such a way that the uses of his knowledge foster growth of those distinctive qualities of life that humans value most highly, and remove those qualities that are deleterious to what is valued (James M. Gustafson, Thomas A. Shannon, James J. DiGiacomo, and others).

These basic premises, which describe four different moral views on scientific research and its application, can all be supported by more or less sustainable arguments.

As far as the first of these positions is concerned, we willingly agree that knowledge is valuable; the 'right to know' is an ingredient of human freedom. However, there must be moral boundaries to human activities, even research activities. The fact that we have the capacity to do something does not necessarily mean that we *ought* to do it.

The second position starts from the proposition (with which we would agree) that human life is sacred. It is not clear, however, how the conclusion is reached. Indeed, intervention in natural processes occurs on almost all levels of our human existence. This position amounts to a blanket prohibition of all scientific work, and is ethically and logically untenable.

The third and fourth positions are the soundest, and therefore the most attractive. There are moral boundaries and ethical demands which simply cannot be ignored. If genetic engineering amounts to 'self-creativity' (Karl Rahner) without limitations, it will become a highly dangerous enterprise. In 1961, Pierre Teilhard de Chardin wrote in his *The Phenomenon of Man* (229):

> We have become aware that, in the great game that is being played, we are the players as well as being the cards and the stakes.

In addition to the ethical issues raised so far, genetic engineering also affects our understanding of nature. There are basically three different views of nature.

The first view regards nature as 'a sacred reality to be revered and respected'. Nature is part of God's creation and therefore should be nourished, rather than moulded or changed according to a human blueprint dreamt up by scientists. The second view denies the existence of a Creator, but accepts that nature has both logic and purpose. This view also does not permit a limitless or 'unbridled intervention into nature'. The difference between the first and second view is that it is not the Creator, but the 'inherent meaning of nature itself' which demands moral prudence from all of us. The third view regards nature as alien and independent of the human person. It has 'no inherent value and is dominated by impersonal forces and causes'. This view permits people to do with nature as they see fit; the only limitation is our lack of knowledge of the workings of nature.

It is clear that the ethical boundaries of genetic engineering will be determined by our view of man and nature. If people are allowed to do whatever they can to manipulate nature and the natural processes, they may achieve a degree of mastery about which we at this stage can only speculate.

Not so long ago, a writer (Cynthia Scott) asked: 'Genetic Engineering: Menace or Mandate from God?' The answer to this question may well be: It is both mandate and menace. Genetic engineering can serve therapeutic purposes; it can also be misused as a tool for eugenic manipulation, behaviour modification, and socio-political power.

Ray Bolin in his article, 'Sociobiology Cloned from the Gene Cult' (*Christianity Today*, January 23, 1981, 16-19), reminds us that the workings of sociobiology are based on three concepts: human social patterns are shaped by evolutionary processes acting on genes ('our genetic make-up influences our behaviour'); the 'reproduction imperative' is inherent in the human organism ('love your children is an effective means for making more DNA'); and the individual is meaningless ('the individual reproduces and dies, but its genes persist into the next generation').

Genetic engineering may easily serve the ideals of modern sociobiology and its moral implications. The era of human engineering has begun. Biological, psychochemical, and electro-computer engineering will further develop. But, in the meantime, who will make responsible public policy regulations? This is a vital question for Australia as well, now that a national genetic engineering research centre has been set up in the national capital, Canberra (August 1981).

A new set of socio-medical and bioethical issues has emerged now that the era of genetic engineering has begun. The underlying questions for all societies are: How far are we prepared to let man's scientific achievements rule man, and how far is man prepared and able to exercise control and dominion over the experiments and achievements of genetic engineers?

Cloning

Cloning belongs to the field of reproductive technologies. It is asexual or non-sexual reproduction, 'a common mode in simpler life forms'. The progeny (offspring) of a single cell or organism reproducing asexually is a clone. All the individuals of a clone are genetically identical.

The word *clone* comes from the Greek word *klōn*, meaning a twig or slip; it is a botanical term used for a cutting. The word 'colony' is one of its cognates.

> Clonal reproduction means vegetative or asexual reproduction. Not all reproduction of vegetative forms is, of course, asexual or the result of cuttings or dispersal from a single source; but there are natural clones in plant life that seem to have advantages under certain luxuriant environmental conditions. Examples of clonal or asexual biological reproduction are the growth of an intact worm from each of the segments when an earthworm is cut in two, and the growth of identical twins from the segmentation of a single genotype in man (Ramsey, *Fabricated Man, The Ethics of Genetic Control*, 1970, 64).

Clones can be artificially created (for example, commercially-produced chrysanthemums and orchids, the leopard frog, and, recently, mice). More than 20 years ago, it was shown by Drs R. Briggs and T.J. King that

> by some deft microsurgery on the leopard frog it was possible to replace the nucleus of a fertilized egg with a nucleus taken from a tissue cell of another frog. The cell containing the genotype of the developing embryo — the cell which resulted from the normal chance combination of parental genes — was 'renucleated'; that means, its nucleus was replaced by one having the genotype of a single already existing

individual of the species. The new frog made by 'nuclear transplantation' would have been the identical twin, a generation late, of but a single 'parent' (Ramsey, 66).

According to the Religious News Service Correspondent, Richard DuJardin, in his 'Human Cloning: Question's not whether one can, but whether one should', the dream of the cloning of human beings may no longer be unthinkable because the first successful cloning of genetically identical mice from mouse embryos has recently been achieved (*Lutheran World Information* 6/81, 10).

As early as 1970, Paul Ramsey wrote:

> Mankind has not evidenced much wisdom in the control and redirection of his environment. It would seem unreasonable to believe that by adding to his environmental follies one or another of these grand designs for reconstructing himself, man would then show sudden increase in wisdom. If genetic policy-making were not miraculously improved over public policy-making in environmental and political matters, then access to the Tree of Life (meaning genetic management of future generations) could cause grave damage.
> It could cause the genetic death God once promised and by his mercy withheld so that his creature, despite having sought to lay hold of godhood, might still live and perform a limited, creaturely service of life. Then would **boundless freedom** and self-determination become **boundless destruction** in its end results, even as its methods all along included the unlimited subjugation of man to his own rational designs and designers. No man or collection of men is likely to have the wisdom to rule the future in any such way (96).

The cloning process is extremely difficult if we think of it in terms of cloning human beings. In a simplified schematic presentation, we may be able to imagine what would happen:

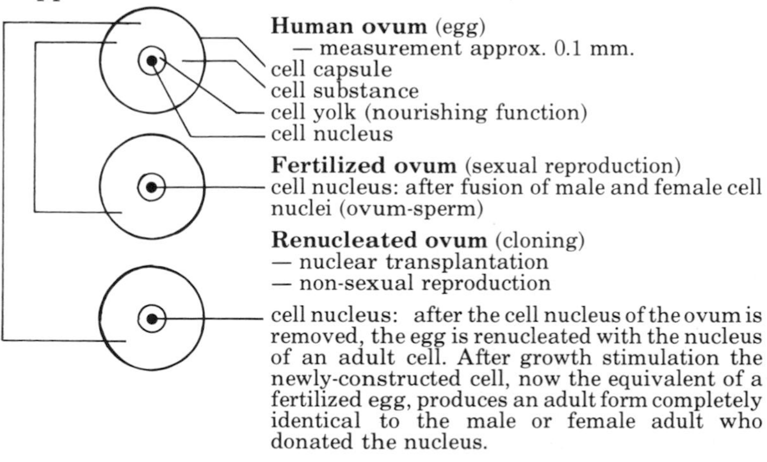

Since 'many nuclei could be obtained from the cells of one adult and each transplanted into an appropriate egg cell, a large number of genetically identical organisms could thereby be produced by this cloning process' (Robert L. Sinsheimer, 'Asexual Human Reproduction' in *Encyclopedia of Bioethics*, Vol.4, 1452).

The technological road involving the manipulation of human life could well lead from *in vitro* fertilization — via embryo transfer and cloning — to fabricated man according to a genetic model of our liking.

Among the leading proponents of cloning (the 'xeroxing of people' is the phrase of Robert T. Francoeur) are Drs Joshua Lederberg, microbiologist and Nobel Prize winner, and Joseph Fletcher, both living in the USA. They believe that 'man himself must be in control of human evolution'. This thinking comes very close to that of evolutionary humanists who believe that humanity 'is not here by design and special creation but only by evolutionary chance'.

The secular humanistic arguments in favour of cloning, according to Lane P. Lester and James C. Hefley (*Cloning, Miracle or Menace?* 1980, 46-56) are:

Cloning is a great way to perpetuate genius.
Cloning can provide soldier and servant classes of people.
Cloning can improve the human race.
Cloning can prevent genetic disease in a selected posterity.
Cloning can exchange body parts and experience enhanced social communion.
Cloning can provide a genotype of one's spouse, living or dead, of a deceased parent, or of some other departed loved one.
Cloning can provide a form of immortality for donors.
Cloning can determine the sex of future children.
Cloning can increase scientific knowledge about human reproduction.

These are the nine most often used scientific arguments in favour of human cloning.

The possibility of human cloning becoming a reality, once the many existing technological difficulties can be overcome, is nevertheless frightening. The arguments put forward in favour of human nuclear transplantation clearly show that some contemporary scientists and ethicists have a mentality which can only be described as the desire to 'play God'. Some advocates of parthenogenesis (literally, virgin birth; non-sexual reproduction) in human beings also claim that cloning would be a liberating event for women because they 'could assert their independence by their freeing themselves from male participation in the process of procreation' (Andrew C. Varga).

Arguments in favour of human cloning have multiplied since David Rorvik wrote his famous book, *In His Image: The Cloning of a Man* (1978). In this book the author tells the story of a bachelor millionaire who asked a number of scientists to produce his clone. Initially they failed, but later they allegedly succeeded, with a young Asian woman carrying the cloned embryo to viability, and giving birth to a baby-boy who is a 'Xerox copy' of the millionaire. According to Rorvik, the boy is doing fine.

This story cannot be verified because David Rorvik is allegedly bound by a promise of secrecy not to reveal the names and identities of the people involved: the millionaire (the gene donor), the scientists (the gene manipulators), and the woman (the gene recipient). Many regard this story as a hoax, and they may well be right in their judgment. Nevertheless, apart from the question of the genuineness of the alleged technological event, it raises the important question of the moral legitimacy of human cloning. If we strip the arguments in favour of human nuclear transplantation of their fantasy-ridden presuppositions and dream-like expectations, this kind of scientific experimentation still leaves us with vital bioethical questions.

Clonal reproduction of humans is morally different from clonal reproduction of plant or animal species. While cell fusion and clonal reproduction have many advantages in horticulture, agriculture, and animal husbandry, the authors believe that the attempts to achieve human cloning are morally wrong, not only because of many unforeseen and unknown dangers, but also because such attempts violate both the laws of nature and the natural law (the moral law of all humanity).

Human cloning does not aid nature. Nor does it enhance our moral consciousness about the origin, nature, and purpose of our existence as human beings.

Many scientific achievements have first been conceived in the minds of science-fiction writers; *in vitro* fertilization is perhaps the best example of this. And when the science-fiction dream became a reality, few of us were prepared for it; the scientists secretly did their work first, leaving society to worry about the ethics of it all after the event. Are we being confronted with a similar situation here?

It is possible that the cloning of human subjects has already taken place, or that plans for it to be achieved are already advanced. Given what has been happening —

secretly, and at uninhibited speed, the community in all countries would be wise to press for immediate legislative action to prohibit human cloning. It would be very foolish to imagine that nothing need be done in the belief that it could never happen.

Our view on this matter is shared by the Chairman of the Australian Law Reform Commission, Mr Justice Kirby. Addressing the National Science Forum in Canberra, Australia, Mr Justice Kirby drew attention to a report in an American journal which suggested that nuclear transplantation in men would be technologically possible within the next 10 or 20 years. Under an intensive development program, the report said that cloning would be achieved 'virtually overnight' (see *The Australian*, March 5, 1982). Mr Justice Kirby said that it was naive to think that cloning would never happen:

> Such sceptics should read our recent human history, not least the way in which the distinguished German medical profession was diverted into Hitler's experimentation.
> It is but 40 years since there was talk of a master race and experiments were conducted on live humans ...
> Without legal regulation it is sure that scientists somewhere will continue this experimentation.
> Meanwhile, the law and the lawmakers sleep on this subject.

The Western world has been frequently warned of the dangers of human cloning happening secretly. For the moment it seems that there is a general lack of will in the community and in the political process to place restraints on the activities of the medical technologists.

Research on Human Subjects

Medicine is by its nature an experimental science, and 'the history of human experimentation is as old as the history of medicine' (Andrew C. Varga). The very complex field of medical research and experimentation on human beings calls for, and to some extent is getting, a critical ethical evaluation.

Ancient physicians realized that the dissection of the dead did not provide them with sufficient or adequate knowledge about human anatomy and bodily malfunctions. Encouraged by the views of the great philosopher Aristotle (384-322 BC), who in his lectures laid the principal stress on biology, the physicians experimented with vivisection (research on the living) to advance medical science. The human subjects of vivisection in those days were exclusively condemned prisoners. This practice originating in Egypt was followed in later centuries by doctors in Europe.

When the International Military Tribunal conducted the 1945-46 Nuremberg trials, the physician Karl Brandt and 22 other German doctors were on trial. During those post-World War II trials, it became clear that experiments had been conducted on human beings who were prisoners. For these experiments on inmates of concentration camps, the German doctors stood accused of 'war crimes and crimes against humanity'. Their defence was based, in part, on the fact that human experimentation has been going on for many years in other countries.

The judges who had to formulate their judgment were helped by a 'special court opinion concerning the conditions under which experimentation on human subjects may be approved and ethically carried out'. This opinion, known as the **Nuremberg Code** (1946), is a ten-point statement which delimits permissible medical experimentation on human subjects. Its emphases include informed 'voluntary consent of the human subject' (1), 'fruitful results for the good of society' (2), the avoidance of 'all unnecessary physical and mental suffering and injury' (4), protection 'against even remote possibilities of injury, disability, or death' (7), the conduct of the experiment being done 'only by scientifically qualified persons' (8), the 'liberty of the human subject to bring the experiment to an end' (9), and the preparedness on the part of the scientist 'to terminate the experiment at any stage' if the experiment 'is likely to result in injury, disability, or death to the experimental subject' (10).

The Nuremberg Code later became the basis for the **Declaration of Helsinki**. This document contains recommendations for conducting experiments on human subjects. It was revised and adopted by the 18th Assembly of the World Medical Association at Helsinki, Finland, in 1964. The Declaration was again revised by the 29th World Medical Assembly held in Tokyo, Japan, in 1975.

The 1964 and 1975 documents consist of four parts: Introduction; Basic Principles; Clinical (Medical) Research Combined with Professional Care; and Non-Therapeutic Clinical (Biomedical) Research (Human Subjects).

There are some remarkable differences between the original and the revised versions of the Helsinki Declaration, which medical ethicists ought to consider very carefully. The present authors are of the opinion that the 1975 document shows less ethical sensitivity than the 1964 Declaration.*

---

* In the *Encyclopedia of Bioethics* (Warren T. Reich, Editor in Chief, 4 vols; New York: The Free Press, A Division of Macmillan Publishing Co., Inc., 1978) Vol.4, 'Appendix' (1721-1815), Section II (1764-1781) appear the full texts of the various 'Directives for Human Experimentation'. These are: Nuremberg Code (1946); Responsibility In Investigations on Human Subjects, Medical Research Council, Great Britain (1963); Experimental Research on Human Beings, British Medical Association (1963); Declaration of Helsinki, World Medical Association (1964 and 1975); Ethical Guidelines for Clinical Investigation, American Medical Association (1966); US Guidelines on Human Experimentation (Institutional Guide to DHEW Policy on Protection of Human Subjects, 1971).

The public is now more aware of what is happening in the field of medical research, especially in the USA where a series of immoral experiments carried out in secret have now been made public. It is important, therefore, that the formulation and application of medical-moral and socio-legal guidelines be treated as high priorities on the legislative agenda of governments.

Henry K. Beecher of Boston, USA, wrote a 'special article' entitled 'Ethics and Clinical Research' (*The New England Journal of Medicine*, 274; 1354-60, 1966) in which he listed 22 'examples of unethical or questionably ethical studies'. Dr Beecher concluded his article by saying:

> An experiment is ethical or not at its inception; it does not become ethical *post hoc* — ends do not justify means. There is no ethical distinction between ends and means. In the publication of experimental results it must be made unmistakably clear that the proprieties have been observed. It is debatable whether data obtained unethically should be published even with stern editorial comment.

A widely-publicized case of immoral research on human subjects is the **Tuskegee Syphilis Study** carried out in the USA. It is reputed to be the 'longest non-therapeutic experiment on human beings in medical history'. This study, begun in 1932, came to light 40 years later when a reporter, Jean Heller, exposed the experiment to public view. This appalling practice of 'racial medicine' was carried out in Macon County, Alabama.

US Public Health Service physicians experimented on two groups of black males to study the natural course of untreated syphilis. One group consisted of 400 (399) syphilitic men who remained untreated, and who were not informed of the nature of this most severe and contagious venereal disease. Another group of 200 (201) who did not have syphilis also took part in the experiment. All 600 men received periodic injections with a harmless substance (placebo); they all were supposedly tested and treated for 'bad blood'. When penicillin (an effective remedy for the disease) became available in the 1940s, the men were not treated with it or given any other helpful medicine.

In return for subjecting themselves to extremely painful spinal taps, the men received a free meal, a free hospital bed, and a last chance for free treatment. When 'the subjects' wives contracted the disease and their children were born with congenital syphilis, the project did nothing'.

The idea 'to observe the effects of untreated syphilis in blacks — did it differ from the effects on whites?' originated with Dr Taliaferro Clark, who saw this experiment as an 'unparalleled opportunity' for research on human subjects. The real answer — which was No — came from autopsies!

In 1973 a special *ad hoc* government committee declared that the experimentation has been 'ethically unjustified'. Only 74 men were known to have survived the ordeal. Litigation on behalf of the survivors and the heirs of the deceased resulted in an out-of-court settlement in 1974 of $10 million. Syphilitic survivors received $37,500 each, and living non-syphilitic participants in the experiment received $15,000 each from the US Government.

James H. Jones publicized this case of immoral research in his book *Bad Blood* (reviewed by Jean Strouse in *Newsweek*, July 20, 1981, 43).

> Jones's instructive case study of closed medical ranks, institutionalized racism, and hermetically sealed bureaucracy is both appalling and heartbreaking. One survivor, told he'd been used as a 'guinea pig', said, 'I don't know what that means . . . I don't know what they used us for. I ain't never understood the study' (Jean Strouse).

Research and experimentation on human beings has greatly increased. Of course, some of those research projects have been, and will be, advantageous for the common good. One example of this was the massive experiment with polio vaccine in the USA in 1954 and its consequent successful development. Certain drugs which promise to stop diseases must be tested on human beings. The problem is: Who is to be selected for experimental purposes, and who should do the selecting? These and other questions need to be answered.

Types of Research

First, we need to carefully distinguish between therapeutic and non-therapeutic experimental research.

> Therapeutic experiments are designed and conducted for the benefit of the subject, either to diagnose or to treat his illness.
> Non-therapeutic research refers to an experiment not designed to benefit the research subject directly but only to gain knowledge that can be used in the treatment of other persons (Andrew C. Varga).

This distinction has recently been abandoned by the US National Commission for the Protection of Human Subjects of Biomedical and Behavioral Research because of the fact 'that some types of research cannot be clearly defined as either therapeutic or non-therapeutic'. This is one of the principal reasons for the abandonment of the distinction which we find in the various 'Directives for Human

Experimentation'. Research designed to explore the cause of a disease can be put on the borderline between therapeutic and non-therapeutic experiments because we are not sure if a patient may or may not benefit by the research.

The Commission in the USA decided to use the terms 'standard, accepted, routine practice and nonvalidated practice of medicine'. This new distinction is, in our view, not very helpful for ethical evaluation of particular research projects; unusual or non-validated treatment may well be therapeutic in certain circumstances.

This change in terms is reminiscent of the change in the versions of the Declaration of Helsinki. The 1964 Declaration says in I. 'Basic Principles' par.1:

> Clinical research must conform to the moral and scientific principles that justify medical research and should be based on laboratory and animal experiments or other scientifically established facts.

The 1975 Declaration says in I. 'Basic Principles', pars.1 and 2:

> Biomedical research involving human subjects must conform to generally accepted scientific principles and should be based on adequately performed laboratory and animal experimentation and on a thorough knowledge of the scientific literature.
> The design and performance of each experimental procedure involving human subjects should be clearly formulated in an experimental protocol which should be transmitted to a specially appointed independent committee for consideration, comment and guidance.

The differences between the original paragraph and the enlarged 1975 section are very obvious: There is no longer reference to 'moral principles'; and the 'experimental protocol' (medical etiquette and precedence) can mean anything and everything — although it 'should always contain a statement of the ethical considerations involved' (I.12).

Secondly, it should be remembered that, in all medical research, total respect for human life should prevail. On January 26 and 27, 1981, the US Department of Health and Human Services and the Food and Drug Administration published in the *Federal Register* the final regulations amending the previous agency policy governing research involving human subjects. These regulations came into effect on July 27, 1981 (for summary texts and comments, see *The Hastings Center Report*, April and June, 1981).

The regulations apparently commit the researchers 'to respect for person and equity and to the independent necessity for adequate consent, confidentiality, and the like'.

However, Robert M. Veatch in his 'Protecting Human Subjects: The Federal Government Steps Back' (*The Hastings Center Report*, Vol.11, No.3, June 1981, 9-12) remarks:

> The specific details of the new regulations suggest that serious moral problems may be lurking in the fine print. Whenever the more abstract moral requirements stand in the way of pursuing the greater good of the research enterprise, **these concerns seem to give way to the principle of benefit of the knowledge to be gained** *(emphasis ours)*.

These remarks summarize the concerns of the present authors with regard to contemporary research on human subjects.

The duty to obtain voluntary informed consent is stressed in the relevant declarations and regulations. However, when is voluntary consent *voluntary*, and when is informed consent *informed*?

When is research on human beings truly beneficial for the common good of all? At what cost in terms of moral integrity, physical and mental health, and social benefit, is the current research on human subjects being advanced, funded, and carried out? Are the ethical considerations of biomedical scientists beyond reproach?

If we read the **Declaration of Oslo**, the Statement on Therapeutic Abortion, adopted in 1970 by the 24th World Medical Assembly in Oslo, Norway, we may draw the conclusion that modern medical practice is no longer determined by medical ethics according to the letter and spirit of the Hippocratic Oath. Medical practice seems to be determined by the changing and prevailing socio-moral 'attitudes and rules of any particular state or community'.

Another important issue involves the research on unborn human subjects or the 'use of fetuses and fetal material for research'. It is evident that the question of 'voluntary informed consent' of the subject cannot apply here. In Britain, such research is guided by a code of practice recommended by the Advisory Group (the 'Peel Committee') of the Department of Health and Social Security. The **Recommended Code of Practice** (London: H.M.S.O., SBN 11-320478 — 7, 1972) reads as follows:

> This code has no binding legal force but is the result of a careful consideration of all relevant factors in the light of the available evidence. It is hoped that it will prove acceptable to the bodies statutorily responsible for the disciplinary matters in the medical and nursing professions.

1. Where a fetus is viable after separation from the mother it is unethical to carry out any experiments on it which are inconsistent with treatment necessary to promote its life.
2. The minimal limit of viability for human fetuses should be regarded as 20 weeks' gestational age. This corresponds to a weight of approximately 400-500 grammes.
3. The use of the whole dead fetus or tissues from dead fetuses for medical research is permissible subject to the following conditions:
   i) The provisions of the Human Tissue Act are observed where applicable;
   ii) Where the provisions of the Human Tissue Act do not apply there is no known objection on the part of the parent who has had an opportunity to declare any wishes about the disposal of the fetus;
   iii) Dissection of the dead fetus or experiments on the fetus or fetal material do not occur in the operating theatre or place of delivery;
   iv) There is no monetary exchange for fetuses or fetal material;
   v) Full records are kept by the relevant institution.
4. The use of the whole pre-viable fetus is permissible provided that:
   i) The conditions in paragraph 3 above are observed;
   ii) Only fetuses weighing less than 300 grammes are used;
   iii) The responsibility for deciding that the fetus is in a category which may be used for this type of research rests with the medical attendants at its birth and never with the intending research worker;
   iv) Such research is only carried out in departments directly related to a hospital and with the direct sanction of its ethical committee;
   v) Before permitting such research the ethical committee satisfies itself (a) on the validity of the research; (b) that the required information cannot be obtained in any other way; and (c) that the investigators have the necessary facilities and skill.
5. It is unethical to administer drugs or carry out any procedures during pregnancy with the deliberate intent of ascertaining the harm that they might do to the fetus.

In Australia, research on human fetuses and fetal tissue is also carried out. There are no legal guidelines regulating research involving fertilized ova, human fetuses or embryos, and human fetal tissue. The *Transplantation and Anatomy Ordinance 1978* (Australian Capital Territory, No.44 of 1978) does not contain 'a reference to fetal tissue, spermatozoa or ova' (II,6).

An editorial in one of the major Australian newspapers (*Sunday Telegraph*, September 13, 1981) said:

> Many people will be concerned at the news that scientists in Canberra are to use aborted fetuses in a research program to fight diabetes. And rightly so ... Without doubt the benefit of the program, if successful, will be enormous. But a great danger lies in the fact that at present there are no guidelines for such research ... And when the guidelines are established, those involved must still proceed with caution — and take steps to explain what they are doing to the people they are ultimately responsible to — the public.

There are a number of socio-moral issues involved here:

> Why was the fetus aborted?
> Who owns the aborted fetus?
> Who must give (proxy) 'consent' for the use of the fetus?
> Are only dead aborted fetuses to be used, or also 'surplus' living embryos, fetuses, and fetal tissue from the 'test-tube baby' laboratories?
> Must the research related to a possible cure of diabetes necessarily be carried out on aborted human fetuses or their tissue?
> Why are the Australian authorities not responding to the advice of the Law Reform Commission given three years ago that guidelines were necessary?
> Which are the bioethical principles used to justify this kind of research?

These and related questions ought to be publicized, faced, discussed, and answered before scientists are allowed to engage in this kind of research.

Henry K. Beecher, a pioneer among US physicians concerned about the ethics of research, once said: 'Man is the final test site'. Indeed, scientific medicine is a 'new' science.

> The revolutionary advances based on knowledge of physiology and biochemistry have come in the past 40 years, and they came from research (Bernard Barber, 'The Ethics of Experimentation with Human Subjects' in *Scientific American*, February 1976, Vol.234, No.2).

There is ample evidence that scientists can be either morally strict or ethically permissive as far as such research work is concerned.

The therapeutic benefit for human subjects is, in many cases, non-existent or very small. The risk factors associated with such research can be either minor or very great. These facts also deserve ethical consideration.

> The ethical problems that attend medical research with human subjects are representative of an entire class of problems created by the impact of professionals and professional power on the general public and on public policy. In the area of research with human subjects the medical investigators are not alone; there is a tendency in other fields too for humane concerns to be left at the laboratory door (Bernard Barber).

Jewish and Christian Views on Research on Human Subjects

Ethical evaluations of modern medical procedures by Jewish and Christian ethicists seem to be still in a preliminary stage of development. The rapid expansion of biomedical technology and its implications has made it very difficult to give definite and detailed moral views on some of its more-technically-complicated methods and subsequent results. A 'good' result often obscures the moral nature of the experimental and research methods used.

It is often taken for granted that the organ-transplant technology is morally sound, and that obtaining tissue from the dead without prior consent does not need ethical consideration and socio-legal guidelines. As far as the 'claim upon dead bodies' is concerned, we are, according to Russell Scott, faced with four main choices:

> A legal prohibition may be placed on the removal of any human tissue from a corpse without specific consent from both the deceased and his close relatives.
> The state may be given power to remove any tissue from any dead body irrespective of the wishes of the deceased and the family.
> State power may be softened by allowing the deceased to make an effective veto during his or her lifetime. This is the new European concept, which allows a veto by the deceased but not by the family.
> If there is no indication of attitude by the deceased one way or the other, the family may be given power to consent, to refuse, or to permit removal of organs by indicating non-objection (*The Body as Property*, 229).

The donation of bodily organs is also an issue of moral magnitude to a great number of people. There are a number of choices available which deserve ethical consideration.

> Should there be any legal restriction upon the power of an intelligent, mature person to give his or her body tissues to save another, or should the law stay completely out of it? If the law should play a role, should distinctions be made between different kinds of tissue? Should the law forbid the gift of a vital organ like the heart, or one that will grossly disfigure the donor such as an eye? Should the community foot the bill by providing social service benefits to a citizen who deliberately depletes himself or herself in this way?
> Should a difference be drawn between adults and minors, or should the only standard be the maturity and intelligence of the donor?
> Should limits be placed upon the uses to which tissue donations from living persons may be put?
> Should a legal difference be made between donations of regenerative and nonregenerative tissues, between vital and nonvital parts, and between paired and unpaired organs? (*The Body as Property*, 236,237).

These and other biomedical and biotechnological issues ought to be viewed in a socio-moral context. It is in this context that both Jewish and Christian ethicists ought to make their contributions, for the benefit of both the members of their communions and the community-at-large. Research methods and results cannot be divorced either from their technological interrelation or from their bioethical and socio-legal context.

The Jewish author and ethicist, Immanuel Jakobovits, in his 'Medical Experimentation on Humans in Jewish Law' (*Jewish Bioethics*, 377ff) lists the 'ten basic Jewish principles' affecting the issue of research on human subjects:

> Human life is sacrosanct, and of supreme and infinite worth.
>
> Any chance to save life, however remote, must be pursued at all costs.
>
> The obligation to save a person from any hazard to his life or health devolves on anyone able to do so.
>
> Every life is equally valuable and inviolable, including that of criminals, prisoners, and defectives.
>
> One must not sacrifice one life to save another, or even any number of others.
>
> No one has the right to volunteer his life.
>
> No one has the right to injure his own or anyone else's body except for therapeutic purposes.
>
> No one has the right to refuse medical treatment deemed necessary by competent opinion.
>
> Measures involving some immediate risks of life may be taken in attempts to prevent certain death later.
>
> There is no restriction on animal experiments for medical purposes.

From these ten principles, Jakobovits 'tentatively reached' the following criteria in regard to research and experimentation on human subjects:

> Possibly hazardous experiments may be performed on humans only if they may be potentially helpful to the subject himself, however remote the chances of success are.
> It is obligatory to apply to terminal patients even untried or uncertain cures in an attempt to ward off certain death later, if no safe treatment is available.
> In all cases it is as wrong to volunteer for such experiments as it is unethical to submit persons to them, whether with or without their consent, and whether they are normal people, criminals, prisoners, cripples, idiots, or patients on their deathbed.
> If the experiment involves no hazard to life or health, the obligation to volunteer for it devolves on anyone who may thereby help to promote the health interests of others.
> Under such circumstances it may not be unethical to carry out these harmless experiments even without the subject's consent, provided the anticipated benefit is real and substantial enough to invoke the precept of 'Thou shalt not stand upon the blood of thy neighbour'.
> In the treatment of patients generally, whether the cures are tested or only experimental, the opinion of competent medical experts alone counts, not the wishes of the patient; and physicians are ethically required to take whatever therapeutic measures they consider essential for the patient's life and health, irrespective of the chance that they may subsequently be liable to legal claims for unauthorized 'assault and battery'.

> Wherever possible, exhaustive tests of new medications or surgical procedures must be performed on animals. These should, however, be guarded against experiencing any avoidable pain at all times.

Christians may not necessarily agree with all the ten principles and the tentative conclusions as put by Jakobovits. It should be remembered that Jewish law emphatically maintains that serious moral questions such as those pertaining to research on human subjects and related issues

> cannot be resolved simply by reference to the fickle whims of the individual conscience or of public opinion, but only by having recourse to the absolute standards of the moral law which, in the case of Judaism, has its authentic source in the Divine revelation of the Holy Writ and its duly qualified interpreters.

Christians also believe that God alone has supreme authority over life and death. They maintain that moral questions should be answered in the light of revelation: the teachings of Christ and his apostles, to which the Church ought to remain faithful. Although Christians may differ in their views on specific biomedical and biotechnological issues, they recognize that in matters of life and death no moral compromise ought to be tolerated.

The manipulation of human life has inherent moral dangers. At this point in history, Christians must search for greater wisdom, deeper moral insight, and stronger courage so that they may give a more powerful witness to the prophetic and apostolic words:

> All flesh is like grass
> and all its glory like the flower of grass.
> The grass withers, and the flower falls,
> but the word of the Lord abides for ever
> (Isaiah 40:6-8; 1 Peter 1:24,25).

CHAPTER

AN ETHICAL APPRAISAL

The Foundations of Medical Ethics
The Essence of Medical-Moral Decision-making
For the Common Good

The Foundations of Medical Ethics

Foundations are bases upon which something stands, rests, or is supported. The word *ethics* (Greek, *ethos*) in its original meaning refers in the most elemental sense to human activities in accordance with customs, traditions, or prevailing habits. Such activities, generally seen as being 'normal', may in time become 'normative', that is, required or binding on people. Medical ethics can be described as the behaviour or activities of physicians in accordance with their professional traditions, customs, or etiquette.

Three questions should be raised at this point:

> Is there an ultimate norm or principle at the centre of medical ethics?
> Are there definite rules or concrete standards of behaviour in particular types of medical situations?
> Is the forming of the character of the doctor, to enable him or her to make the right medical decisions, a paramount concern of medical ethics?

The first question explores the possibility of medical ethics being lifted above medical-moral individualism. The second question investigates the desire to avoid merely intuitive decisions in medical situations in favour of using rules as objective standards for medical-moral decision-making. The third question probes the moral disposition of the physician, the decision-maker.

Any reflection on medical ethics will depend on our perception of certain relations: the relation of physician to self; the relation between physician and patient; the relation of physician to society; and the relation of the physician to the 'power that made him'. In other words, the doctor may be viewed as person, healer, citizen, and creature. Should medical-moral standards be determined by the moral disposition of the individual physician, by ethical codes adopted by medical conventions, or by socio-legal guidelines promulgated by society's legislative authorities?

We will answer this question by using a medical-moral issue as an example.

ABORTION

as viewed by:	*as determined by:*	*accepted as morally justified:*
the physicians	their consciences	both no and yes
the medical codes	their contents	both no and yes
the society	its attitude	both no and yes
the law	its provisions	both no and yes

If the moral rejection of abortion depends on the **consciences** or personal moral attitudes of physicians, then we will never be able to determine the moral rightness or wrongness of medical-moral standards as they affect abortion. It is a fact that there is no longer a moral agreement among physicians on this controversial issue.

If the moral rejection of abortion depends on the contents of such **medical codes** as the Oath of Hippocrates and the Declaration of Geneva (1948), we can confidently say that abortion cannot be justified. However, if our moral view is based on the Declaration of Oslo (1970), we can no longer say that abortion is *always* wrong; in that medical code there is no longer clarity on the issue of abortion and on the medical-moral standards of behaviour which physicians should maintain.

If the moral rejection of abortion depends on the prevailing **attitudes** of the members of our society, again we would be in doubt because of the wide diversity of moral opinions among people on this socially-divisive issue.

If the moral rejection of abortion depends on the **laws** of the country, we can no longer regard abortion as a moral evil because in most countries the legal protection of the unborn is almost non-existent. Many nations in the Western world have either passed very liberal abortion laws, or have by court-decisions rendered unenforceable what legal protection there is.

It is clear that abortion has created moral conflict for physicians, medical assemblies, society, and legislators. The issue has caused sharp divisions among people, including doctors, nurses, ethicists, lawyers, clergy, and politicians.

It is true that the Declaration of Oslo (1970) says that 'if the doctor considers that his convictions do not allow him to advise or perform an abortion, he may withdraw while ensuring the continuity of (medical) care by a qualified colleague'. However, this allowance for conscientious objection does not solve the existing moral conflict in its wider context.

The moral dilemma with regard to abortion is very real. The moral rejection or justification of abortion cannot be upheld by making abortion a matter of a woman's choice, or an issue of the physician's conscience, or a directive from a medical assembly, or a decision by legislators supported by a relatively-uninformed public opinion.

If any objective moral judgment is to be formed about this fundamental medical-moral issue, then abortion as a concern of medical ethics must be viewed from a different perspective.

The Declaration of Geneva (1948), the 'medical vow' and reformulation of the ancient Hippocratic Oath, points to the sound foundations of its medical ethics when it says:

> I [the physician] will maintain
> the utmost respect for human life,
> from the time of conception;
> even under threat,
> I will not use my medical knowledge
> contrary to the laws of humanity.

The laws of humanity are not laws made by man, but laws by which humanity remains human. These laws can be identified as the laws of nature and the natural law. These laws do not lose their validity at any time, in any place, or under any circumstances.

Physicians throughout the ages have understood and recognized this. The above 'medical vow' reflects this understanding and recognition.

'Utmost respect for human life': This moral virtue is not based simply on a social contract between doctors and patients. It is founded on and grounded in the natural law (the moral law). People, including doctors, 'doing by nature what the law requires' and showing 'that what the law requires is written on their hearts, while their conscience also bears witness' (Romans 2:14,15) are living as morally responsible people.

If people live according to the natural law, they *know* that there is a Lawgiver (Romans 1:18ff), and they *know* that they ought to have respect for their fellow human beings: Honour your parents — don't kill — don't violate a human relationship — don't take what is not yours — don't lie — and don't lust after someone or something belonging to another person (Exodus 20:12-17, an excellent summary of the natural law).

'From the time of conception': These words reflect a knowledge of the laws of nature. A human being is human from the moment he or she is conceived. We all have human parents. If we have children, they are human offspring. Only human beings can say, in the words of an ancient poet:

> You have made man inferior only to yourself [O Lord];
> You crowned him with glory and honour (Psalm 8:5 TEV).

or

> You created every part of me [O God];
> you put me together in my mother's womb ...
> you knew that I was there —
> you saw me before I was born (Psalm 139:13-16 TEV).

The laws of nature have not changed. But, while we still have knowledge of these laws, our willingness to accept the moral implications of them seems to have diminished.

'Even under threat': This statement reinforces the noble commitment to uphold the laws of humanity even if we have to suffer ridicule, persecution, loss of life, home, or country. The action of the Dutch physicians during the German occupation of The Netherlands in 1940-1945 is an instructive example of this; they dissented from the medical regulations issued by the Nazis and opposed the formation of a Physician's Bureau.

They said in their official statement of opposition:

> No matter how much the ideas and constitutions of nations may have changed in the course of time, the physician has always remained the undisputed protector of two holy and precious values: the respect for life, and charity toward the sick human being. From time immemorial until the present the vocation of the physician has been a vocation of confidence, indeed a priestly vocation. The physician as a person who realizes the smallness of his knowledge in the face of the magnitude of the mystery of life, suffering and death, can retain the necessary

> spiritual power for his responsible work only as long as he experiences his profession as a calling from God, and his duties as dictated by eternal, supernatural laws.
>
> We are gravely concerned about your forthcoming directive for physicians. We know that you represent a very special philosophy of life. Our knowledge of the German 'physicians' ordinance' concerning the task of the physician in which the care for race and nation take precedence over that of the individual, makes it only too clear to what extent the national-socialistic conception of the medical profession differs from ours.
>
> Although we do not deny that the care of the community and the participation in social hygiene measures constitute part of the task of the physician, we can recognize this duty only insofar as it proceeds from and is not in conflict with the first and holiest precept of the physician, namely, the respect for life and for the physical well-being of the individual who entrusts himself to his care (Conrad W. Baars, 'Dutch Physicians' Protest against Nazi Regulations' in *Child and Family*, Vol.11, No.2, 1972, 171,172).

In May 1974, a number of these Dutch physicians, together with their colleagues from other countries, formed the World Federation of Doctors Who Respect Human Life. Its regular publication, *News Exchange*, issued by the General Secretary of the World Federation, shows how this organization has branched out to many Western countries in Europe, North America, and elsewhere.

Members of the World Federation took part in the drafting of the 'Declaration of the Rights of the Unborn Child' which was adopted in Milan, Italy, on December 3,4, 1977. The President of the World Federation, Dr K.F. Gunning, is the author of *Coming from ... Going Where? A scientific approach to ethics* (1980). In this book he investigates whether there is a scientific basis for a natural ethics; he 'found there was'. For those who are interested in a scientific approach to medical ethics and who are acquainted with scientific theories, this book provides fascinating reading.

If physicians, biotechnologists, bioethicists, and others presently maintain that changes in medical ethics have come about because of public opinion, moral latitude, legislative reform, and other social pressures, they are indeed correct. But that observation constitutes no ethical justification for the doctors themselves. The laws of humanity to which they ought to be committed do not change. A moral commitment to these laws takes precedence over all other medical-moral responsibilities. This means that abortion and other life-destroying operations, treatments, and experiments, should not be accepted as morally-justifiable acts, whether they be performed by physicians or any other scientists. The foundations of medical ethics have not been *made* by medical ethicists, scientists, and physicians; they have been *recognized* by them as the only 'sure' foundations for all medical-moral decision-making.

To sum up, these foundations are not made by the conscience of the individual physician, nor by decisions of medical assemblies, nor by the views of society, nor by human laws. These foundations are made by the 'power' that provided us with 'the laws of humanity'.

Christians will want to speak of the foundations of medical ethics in a more specific manner. We recognize that for them there is a four-in-one foundation of ethics:

Law	—the laws of humanity, natural law, laws of nature, Decalogue, and so on.
Gospel	—the word of God's forgiveness in Christ, the gift of justification.
Apostolic exhortations	—the moral mandates which aid the Christians' life of sanctification (holiness).
Faith	—the body of the Church's teachings based on revelation: the Law, the Gospel, and the Apostolic exhortations and doctrines.

In an empirical sense, this means that Christians live by a pilgrim's ethic: they are justified by grace (Gospel) and live out the mystery of Romans 6 (faith), in a life of sanctification which is not in conflict with the will of God (Law), as they move toward the final reality of the age which is to come (Apostolic exhortations and teachings).

The ethics of Christians are not in conflict with a medical ethics founded on the laws of humanity. Their ethics include the data from the New Testament, particularly the teachings of Christ and his apostles. Christian ethics therefore has a re-enforced foundation and Christ-centred perspectives.

The three questions raised at the beginning of this section can now be answered:

There is an ultimate norm or principle at the centre of medical ethics: the *laws of humanity*.

There are rules or concrete standards of behaviour which ought to be governed by principles which are not in conflict with the *natural law* and the *laws of nature*.

The formation of the character of the physician is indeed a concern of medical ethics because it is in the doctors' decision-making process that their moral commitment to the *universally valid laws* becomes 'visible'.

The integrity of the physician as person, healer, citizen, and creature can be safeguarded only if he or she remains faithful to the medical vow embodied in both the Hippocratic Oath and the Declaration of Geneva (1948). Of these moral principles the President of the Australian Medical Association (SA Branch), Jeanette Linn, recently wrote:

> They are fine sentiments, hopefully to be maintained by us all in the face of the many and various modern-day pressures, and in the face of the disillusionment with these types of principles that is common within our society (*Monthly Bulletin*, SA Branch AMA, April 1981, 2).

The Essence of Medical-Moral Decision-Making

The present authors realize that there is great diversity and complexity in contemporary ethics, including bioethics (see Introduction). A number of important sociomedical and bioethical issues of the day have been dealt with in the previous chapters, and ethical appraisals have been made and suggested.

In this summary chapter we want to reiterate the need for a *rule ethics* rather than an *act ethics* to help us in our understanding of the essence of medical-moral decision-making.

The nature of medical-moral and bioethical decisions is determined by our philosophy of life. If we regard human life as sacred, or as having a unique value, our decisions will be different from those made by people who regard human beings as 'higher' or different forms of animal species. If a human sperm and ovum, a fertilized human egg, an embryo and fetus have no bioethical status, or if they have no meaning in the context of our ethics of life (bioethics), then those who hold such a view do not have a moral objection to their destruction, manipulation, or use for experimentation.

There are scientists and ethicists who believe that the intrinsic value of human life is not objectively higher than that of the animals, but who do not expose this assumption or belief to critical scrutiny. If they were to do so, then their conclusions about abortion and other bioethical issues would be at once more obviously logical, and more obviously unattractive, humanly speaking.

The application of scientific knowledge to human beings often poses ethical problems insofar as it touches upon our human moral values. It is essential then that we evaluate the activities of those working and experimenting in the areas of biotechnology, biomedicine, and health care.

Those who adhere to an **act ethics** evaluate the outcome of a process rather than the process itself. For example, if the IVF process results in a nice and wanted baby, IVF is morally right. If we regard a particular social situation as intolerable for our security, welfare, and survival, we may (if we live, say, in an over-populated area) ask the government to introduce compulsory sterilization, abortion, or infanticide. The promotion of the greatest amount of good for the greatest number of people as a primary moral obligation (utilitarianism) is nevertheless bound by existing situations and foreseeable consequences (situationism).

Such kinds of acts ethics lead to a medical-moral decision-making process in which ethical criteria, norms, principles, and rules are no longer the essence of that process. Human technological goals and their 'merits' are then far more important than the 'means' (including human subjects) used in research and laboratory experiments.

Furthermore, an act ethics may condone a good effect arrived at by bad means. In act ethics the moral law and ethical rules and principles are made subject to the purpose and consequences (outcome) of the act itself. In this kind of 'consequentialist' ethics, the good outcome of a bad process may be acceptable. (The bad outcome of a bad process is not as problematic morally as a bad outcome of a good process.) We ought not to judge the moral good of the outcome in isolation from the moral rightness or wrongness of the process itself.

For instance, the lives of the world's 'test-tube babies' are a good in themselves, but the manner in which the beginning of their lives was manipulated was morally wrong. This constitutes, of course, no moral burden for those children, for the ultimate responsibility for the mode of their conception is not theirs. The moral responsibility rests with the participants in the test-tube fertilization and the initial development of human life *in vitro*.

The essence of medical-moral decision-making ought to be determined by the six fundamental principles or concepts of a **rule ethics** which are particularly relevant to biomedicine, biotechnology, and bioethics.

These concepts are:

the principle of the sanctity or unique value of human life
the principle of double effect
the principle of totality
the principle of distinction between ordinary and extraordinary treatment
the principle of justice
the principle of seeking understanding.

The principle of the **sanctity of life** reminds us that all human life is a sacred gift and has unique value. It is a good in itself. It has dignity and inherent rights derived from the natural law. It demands respect and claims inviolability since life is my *self*.

The principle of **double effect** reminds us that a human action may produce two effects: one good, and the other bad. For example, a therapeutic termination of pregnancy may prevent the death of the mother, but may not save the life of the unborn child (see IV.2 on Abortion). On the basis of this principle, we can never condone an evil act as being permissible, or tolerate the use of bad (evil) means to produce a good effect. A human action must never *intend* to have a bad effect, but it may, unfortunately, have some bad consequences or side-effects. In medical-moral decision-making, we must place the human action in the 'balance of effects and values'; the good effect must outweigh all possible less-than-good side-effects. The moral value in the goals of our action must not lead to the use of immoral means to achieve such goals.

The principle of **totality** reminds us that 'the parts exist for the sake of the whole'. This principle is applied in medical surgery whenever limbs have to be amputated, or diseased organs removed.

The principle of the **distinction between ordinary and extraordinary treatment** reminds us of the need to use life-sustaining means for healing purposes, or for giving the patient a chance of recovery from a serious accident or illness. Life-sustaining technological means should not be used if they frustrate the dying-process after it has reached an irreversible stage. 'Useless' treatment shows disrespect for the patient, and irreverence for life and death.

The principle of **justice** reminds us of our moral obligation to share both social burdens and benefits (distributive justice). Distributive justice is very important in relation to medicine and bioethics (including medical ethics). We recognize 'at least four different norms of distribution': equality, need, effort, and social contribution.

> I will not permit considerations of religion, nationality, race, party politics or social standing to intervene between my duty and my patient (Declaration of Geneva, 1948).

This part of the 'medical vow' is related to the principle of justice in the context of the physician-patient relationship. Only in human society does it make sense to speak of justice. In the doctors' service to humanity, the principle of justice plays a very important role. All physicians, medical specialists, technologists, and biomedical experts should act in accordance with the principle of justice.

The principle of **distributive justice** must operate in such a way that the norm of equality is applied to all human beings from conception to natural death: that the needs of all are recognized, and the efforts in serving are geared toward the well-being of all, including patients and 'human subjects'. All biomedical, biotechnological, and ordinary medical endeavours should be geared toward the enhancement of our 'life-together'. It is an offence against the principle of distributive justice to judge some human beings as too unworthy, too small, too handicapped, too poor, or too racially or socially inferior, to be treated equally with the rest of 'respectable' society. To medically manipulate or destroy some human beings for the social or political advantage of others is to strike at the heart of justice.

Finally, the principle of **seeking understanding** reminds us of the Church's ability, willingness, and calling to give guidance in moral decision-making. This is part of its mission and witness. The Church is not irrelevant. It is the symbol of 'intrusion, continuity and justice' (Martin H. Scharlemann). The Church knows the natural law because its clergy and people are called to live, think, and act under the guidance of the divine Scriptures. Since bioethics is 'everybody's business', the Church also speaks in this area. The Church is unique in being able to bring medical-moral decision-makers to an understanding of themselves and of others because it speaks with the authority of Christ.

It is clear from what we have said about rule ethics that it is a **normative** ethics. This means that it 'asks questions directly related to the criteria and standards of right and wrong action, what things are good and evil, and questions about moral conduct in general' (John Ladd, 'The Task of

Ethics' in the twelve-part entry 'Ethics' in *Encyclopedia of Bioethics*, Vol.1, 400-406).

In some countries there is a great interest in ethics. In the USA, for example, 'at least 11,000-12,000 courses in ethics are currently taught at the undergraduate and professional school levels' (*The Teaching of Ethics in Higher Education*, A Report by The Hastings Center, 1980, 1). But this level of interest is certainly not noticeable in Australia. We doubt very much if bioethics is even part of the formal course of (Christian) Ethics or Morality given in theological seminaries or religious institutions of learning.

The essence of medical-moral decision-making is, as we said, determined by our philosophy of life. It is in a sound rule ethics that the moral principles derived from the natural law can be embodied and objectively applied.

For The Common Good

The common good of all humanity is served only if the socio-moral and bioethical policy-making institutions in our society adhere to fundamental values derived from the laws of humanity. An ethics advantageous to the common good of all can never be a 'value-free' ethics. Such ethics, vigorously promoted by a number of secular ethicists, creates a moral vacuum; biomedical research and biotechnological experiments on human subjects are carried out as if there are no moral problems to be faced or solved.

To whom, or to what, do doctors and scientists appeal if in their scientific work they are faced with socio-moral or medical-moral questions as to whether their endeavours and goals are ethically justified? They themselves may follow a certain method of moral argumentation.

They may appeal to authority.
They may appeal to general agreement (*consensus hominum*).
They may appeal to intuition, self-evidence, or gut feelings.
They may appeal to the outcome of proper argumentation (the dialectical or Socratic method of argumentation).

It is difficult in a pluralistic society to appeal to **general agreement**. Most of the issues which we have discussed in this book are the subjects of continuing discussion, argumentation, and controversy. The old consensus has broken down, and no new consensus has been reached.

An appeal by scientists to **intuition, self-evidence, or gut feelings** is highly dangerous. The philosophies of life held by researchers in the life sciences are often radically different from those held by many members of society.

The **Socratic method of argumentation** is a valid and attractive way of solving moral dilemmas. But the difficulty here is that, in our contemporary moral climate, there is no agreement on basic ethical principles and moral values. And proper argumentation becomes impossible whenever ethics is made subservient to the partisan politics of interest-groups, with their sloganizing and popular appeal to self-interest.

Meddling in matters of human life and death should not be permitted on the basis of intuition or the outcome of an unsatisfactory debate. All this reveals the continuing need for the **appeal to authority**, and therefore for a clear, sound rule ethics.

A proper rule ethics is not ethical egoism (considering only the good of self), or ethical elitism (considering only the good of the elite), or ethical parochialism (considering only the good of one's class, group, or sex); it is ethical universalism (considering the good of mankind). Ethical universalism is not understood here in a 'person-neutral' sense; it implies that the common (universal) good is shared by each and all human beings. Rule ethics should seek to foster the common good of all without sacrificing the rights, values, and well-being of the individual.

Many Western countries spend millions of dollars on health care, medical research, and biotechnological experimentation. During the International Hospitals Federation Congress, held at Sydney, Australia, in October 1981, the Australian Federal Minister for Health remarked that

> the continued existence of hospitals in Australia could be guaranteed only if there was a reduction in demand for the high-cost services they provided. In the long term, one of the best ways of reducing hospital costs will be to keep people out of them.

Australia with a population of 14 million people has 1,100 hospitals and 1,300 nursing homes — a total of 160,000 beds (1 bed for every 90 persons). Costs of the public hospitals (which account for the biggest expenditure) have risen from $400 million in 1969 to almost $3,000 million in 1979.

> The growth and importance of technology means that hospitals will come to demand by far the greatest public investment of any part of health care. Until now achievement was measured in the expansion of resources, turnover and new technological development.
> The last decade set the scene for greater questioning and debate about community needs, health care priorities, the cost and benefits of high technology and the need for more emphasis on prevention, health education, rehabilitation and home care.

The contradictions in policies governing contemporary health care and biomedical research and experimentation are painfully obvious.

> We spend millions on research into the causes of infertility — while promoting contraception and sterilization.
> We spend millions on artificial insemination experiments and embryo transfer techniques — while promoting abortion.
> We spend millions on genetic engineering and research on human subjects — while we neglect the basic requirements for maintaining the socio-moral health of the community.

On the one hand, act ethics encourages people to do their own thing in the manner they like or prefer (mostly for the benefit of themselves); it is not advantageous for the common good. On the other hand, rule ethics, both as a social ethics and bioethics, is derived from natural law and does not violate or assault the laws of nature; it is an ethics advantageous for the common good.

A Christian summary of such ethics can be put thus:

> An ethics which ought to be observed and adhered to by all is a rule ethics derived from the universally valid natural or moral law, enhanced by the wisdom of the Divine Scriptures and the medical-moral tradition, and which does not assault the laws of nature.

Such rule ethics will preserve the moral integrity of those who work in the fields of medicine, biomedicine, and biotechnology. At the same time, those responsible for socio-moral policy-making will be able to formulate proper guidelines and rules governing health care, medical treatment, biomedical research, and biotechnological experimentation, including, where necessary, the prohibition of certain research and experiments on human subjects.

The common good of all involves the common concern and responsibility of all. We should not give political answers to ethical questions by allowing morality to be decided by who shouts loudest or who can apply enough pressure. Nor should we treat serious socio-moral concerns as if they are irrelevant. The common good is related to the right to live, the value of life, and the meaning and purpose of living.

If we respect human life, treasure human values, and foster a proper understanding of the meaning and purpose of living as human beings, we will be freer to do to others as we wish that others would do to us (Luke 6:31).

7

CHAPTER

THE CASE BRIEFLY PUT

The Case Briefly Put

The main ethical issues in this book have been set in the context of health care as understood in Jewish, Christian, and secular traditions.

The Human Person

The human person is not just a physical being; he is a psychological, emotional, and spiritual being as well. We speak of a person as healthy who is healthy in body, mind, and spirit.

There has been, and still is, a tendency to talk about the physical health of a person in isolation from the other aspects of the whole person. But it is a fact that physical symptoms may reflect a psychological or a spiritual sickness rather than some physical malady. Notwithstanding all the talk about ministering to the whole person, many practitioners and technologists practise their arts on the presupposition that human beings can be treated simply as biological organisms.

The understanding of health care in both the Jewish and Christian traditions stands in sharp contrast to the contemporary secular habit of assessing medical treatment in terms of 'success' in the realm of the physical. Yet the successful treatment of a symptom or condition, if it has side-effects to the detriment of the individual, the family, or society, may not be, ethically speaking, the best treatment.

Throughout this book we have appealed to the human consensus as to what is right or wrong. The safe-guarding of human life and the care and protection of marriage and family life are concerns common to humanity. Various United Nations documents and other instruments of International Law hold that killing and attacking the family unit are wrong, and that States have an obligation to protect people's lives and to protect marriage and the family.

The Basic Moral Issue

The issues we have discussed deal with the fundamentals of human procreation and human life. These issues ought to be judged from an ethical point of view within the context of the human person as a physical, spiritual, and psychological being, and in terms of the well-being of the family as the fundamental group unit of society in which we are (or should be) conceived, born, and nurtured.

It is not in the interests of humanity to attack nature, to disobey fundamental human insights as to what is ethically right (the natural law), or to assume that those who wish to 'plan' society are necessarily wiser than nature itself.

This is not to say that all interfering with nature is wrong. On the contrary, medical science, like many other sciences, has brought great benefits to human society. But, as we well know, the application of scientific knowledge to weapons, industry, and agriculture has also brought great dangers to human society. The present ecological awareness of man in terms of the environment and the protection of certain animals is not, unfortunately, yet evident in terms of the well-being of all human beings.

There are people who find the killing of whales morally abhorrent — and yet support the killing of the human fetus (abortion), and the killing of the retarded and the elderly (euthanasia). It is precisely in regard to the respect for human life that the great divide between traditional ethics and contemporary ethics is most evident. Indeed, most of the division of opinion in modern bioethical issues turns on this fundamental point.

Being Human

According to the great religious teachings of Judaism and Christianity, life is a gift from God, a good in itself. Human life is not evaluated in terms of its 'usefulness' to others or society at large; nor is it evaluated in terms of quantity (how old or young is a person) or quality (an assessment based on purely subjective criteria). Human life is seen as the 'crown' of God's creation, made in the image of God. To destroy human life is an attack not only upon persons (the receivers of life from God), but also on God who is the giver of the gift of life.

According to the modern secularist, however, human life, particularly human embryos and fetuses, is not to be regarded as specially sacred. Indeed, in *Test-Tube Babies* (ed. William A.W. Walters and Peter Singer, Melbourne, 1982), Helga Kuhse and Peter Singer argue that

> a human being is a being possessing, at least at a minimal level, the capacities distinctive of our species which include consciousness, the ability to be aware of one's surroundings, to be able to relate to others, perhaps even rationality and self-consciousness (60).

It can readily be seen that the attributes they describe as necessary to being human are, on the one hand, purely subjective notions, arbitrarily chosen, and, on the other hand, could equally apply to rats, dogs, cats, and rabbits.

The conclusions they draw are, to say the very least, frightening:

> To claim that every human being has a right to life solely because it is biologically a member of the species *homo sapiens* is to make species membership the basis of rights. This is as indefensible as making race membership the basis of rights. It is the form of prejudice one of us has elsewhere referred to as 'speciesism', a prejudice in favour of members of one's own species, simply because they are members of one's own species (60).

The conclusions drawn from this argument are that abortion-on-request is valid, and that the destruction of human embryos is ethically possible since neither fetuses nor embryos have the qualities described.

It is typical of secularist thinking that human life is only to be regarded as worthy of respect, as far as the right to life is concerned, if that human life meets certain criteria of 'humanness'. Those criteria are capable of such subjective interpretation that it is difficult to see what human life is ultimately to be regarded as worthy of respect.

Moreover, if humans are not of more significance than rabbits — it being 'speciesist' to assert they are, we must all become vegetarian or else have reason to feel not a little insecure.

According to Kuhse and Singer's definition of a human being quoted above, none of us is human when we are asleep, unconscious, or in a coma. And if we use the definition suggested by Joseph Fletcher (see pages 65 and 66 above), then a newborn baby is certainly not a human person, and all of us would be suspect (if not non-human) at some time in our lives.

The suggestion made by Kuhse and Singer that it is prejudice to regard human persons as being of more significance than members of other species is, of course, nonsense. Even according to their own view that life is valuable only when it is functionally valuable, when it is useful, humanity is to be treated with special respect because it is, by a long way, the most highly developed species.

According to human consensus and awareness, the God who has created everything made man to be 'special'. This 'specialness' is not to be dismissed as arrogant prejudice on our part. Rather, that 'specialness' both in terms of goodness and evil, creativity and destruction, is evident throughout our human history.

Indeed, as we have pointed out, personhood is not an *achievement*; it is an *endowment*. We do not become human from some 'subpersonal human animal'; we are human persons from the moment of our conception. To pick a moment in our growth to maturity as the moment when we become a human person is both arbitrary and dangerous. We are what we are because that is in the nature of things.

Further, nature 'does not revolve around function; function revolves around nature'. Our functions as human persons are geared to our development and survival. We have certain functions as human persons because we are human; we are not human because we can 'perform' certain functions. A person may be king or queen of his/her country but, through circumstances, unable to execute the functions of a monarch. That person is still a king or queen. That same truth applies to us as human persons. Through accident or congenital damage, immaturity or old age, we may not be able to discharge some of our functions as a human person —but we are still human. Our capacity to function may be impaired — but we are still human beings, and not rabbits.

Respect for Human Life

In terms of the ethical debates on abortion, infanticide, and euthanasia, the respect for human life is the fundamental issue. It is not surprising that those who justify the killing of the unborn child are able also to justify the killing of born children, the retarded, the elderly, and all those other 'non-persons' who are not 'useful' to society, whose lives may be inconvenient to others, and who are to be sacrificed on the altar of 'functional usefulness'.

In making ethical decisions, we need to be clear about first principles and about our method of deciding what is right and what is wrong.

According to part of the common wisdom of humanity, life is sacred, and stable marriage and family life are essential for the well-being of adults and for the care and nurture of children. This common wisdom we may call the natural law. Linked with the natural law, there are also the laws of nature with which we have to be in harmony if we are to live happily. These laws of nature are evident everywhere, and include the whole process of human procreation.

We need also to know what method we will use to make our decisions. There are two methods used: rule ethics and act ethics. Those who use the act ethics are the utilitarians and the situationists. This method of ethical decision-making is based upon an assessment of the results or outcome of a particular act or process, rather than an assessment of the process itself.

An act ethics has no need of notions like the natural law or the common wisdom of humanity. Indeed, it rejects such notions as a coming to the problem with the solution already in hand. It argues that we may want to contradict such first principles if the situation 'demands' it.

IVF and AID

In the cases of *in vitro* fertilization and artificial insemination, this is particularly clear. Those who support IVF and AID look at the couple who are childless because of the infertility of either or both husband and wife. IVF or AID will give such a couple a child or children; the couple will be able to experience the thrill and fulfilment of child-bearing. The 'good' result or outcome is pregnancy leading to the birth of the child. But the refusal to look at the processes of AID and IVF from an ethical point of view means that a 'good' result may be used to justify a 'bad' means.

Obviously, results are not unimportant. 'Bad' results flowing from a 'good' or morally-neutral process usually persuade us not to proceed with that process. But does the birth of a child, who is a good in himself, justify the means of conception if those means are adultery, or fornication? In the same way, it does not follow that IVF and AID are justified simply because a child is born to an otherwise infertile couple.

Situation and utilitarian ethics have, then, no objective basis upon which to proceed; it is the situation or the results, as we subjectively evaluate them, which determine the rightness or wrongness of the deeds we do to achieve those results. Inherent in such an approach are all the possibilities for the abuse of human beings, for the rightness of what the community does will depend upon the attitude of the majority of the community to the desirability of the results.

The alternative is the rule ethics that we have described in Chapter VI. Here the principle of the sanctity of human life is the starting-point; the difficult or hard cases are assessed according to five other objective principles. The principle of double effect, for example, means that we never set out to abort or to destroy human life. A therapeutic termination of pregnancy is one in which the doctor sets out to save the life of the mother, but with the unfortunate second effect of not being able to save the life of the child.

A rule ethics commits us to justice as one of the governing principles. Distributive justice means that we do not discriminate against another person because that person is too unworthy, too small, too immature, too handicapped, too poor, or too racially or socially 'inferior'. To manipulate or destroy other human beings for one's own political, economic, or social advantage is unjust. It is only by applying the objective principles of a rule ethics that we can be sure that injustices are not perpetrated in the name of humanity.

Returning to AID, the process itself is open to several objections based on these ruling principles. For example: 1) the men who donate their sperm are being encouraged to sire children for whom they will take no responsibility; and 2) the process involves an intrusion into the marital relationship by a stranger as 'represented' by his sperm.

It is a fact that people like to know their biological origins. Many people search their family trees. Adopted children now have the right to know their real parents. In the case of AID, doctors who destroy the records of donors are imposing their views on the child for all time. Already there is a demand by AID children to know their fathers. The complexity of the relationship of the sperm donor to child, mother, and social father, will no doubt be confusing to the child.

The intrusion of the donor into the marital relationship cannot be justified by the good of the desired pregnancy for the couple. In any case, decisions concerning AID are made only with reference to the desires of the adults involved; the good of the child is entirely overlooked. We cannot be sure that anonymity will prevail. Just as community attitudes to adoption have changed so that an adopted child may know his biological parents, so, too, attitudes to AID are changing. John Morgan in *Test-Tube Babies* acknowledges that there are few studies on AID-conceived children, yet concludes that there are 'so far' no serious difficulties — a case of believing what we want to believe. It is too early to tell just how such children will be affected.

In the case of IVF, we have argued two fundamental objections to that process which cannot be made good by the birth of a child.

IVF involves the foreseen loss of human embryos due to the intervention by human hands. Such embryos have been lost in the development of the process, are being lost in the development of IVF for a surrogate mother by implanting an 'adopted' embryo in the uterus, are continually lost by the process itself in its normal application. In fact, two or three embryos are implanted at a time. Most are lost before a pregnancy is achieved.

It has been argued that embryos are lost naturally anyway at about the same rate; but no such assertion has been proven. No one really knows how many embryos are lost naturally. In any case, death by human hands cannot be justified simply because death occurs naturally; to do that would be to justify homicide in general. Further, such IVF embryos are not being 'sacrificed' to save another person's life; rather, it is the sacrifice of many in the hope of one pregnancy.

Most IVF programs require the woman to have an amniocentesis if she becomes pregnant. They then abort any 'defective' child.

IVF also involves separating the unitive and procreative aspects of intercourse. In the case of artificial contraception, we have seen the rise of the contraception-mentality. Sexual intercourse is viewed as something to be enjoyed, without restraint, and without the complications of pregnancy; any pregnancies that occur can be aborted. This mentality envisages a view of the sexual relationship that excludes its primary purpose: the begetting of children.

IVF supplants natural sexual intercourse with laboratory fertilization. So does AID. Neither method 'cures' infertility. The methods by-pass it. It has been argued that all that the medical technologist is doing is 'aiding' nature; in reality, it is by-passing nature. And since conception may have nothing to do with sexual intercourse between husband and wife, certain consequences follow.

Artificial insemination began by using husband's sperm only. AIH is now virtually abandoned in favour of the more 'effective' method of AID. Likewise, IVF began with husband and wife, but has now been made available to couples who cannot produce their own child by the adoption of someone else's leftover frozen embryo.

Since the frozen embryos are 'parentless', what becomes of those that remain? They are used for human experimentation with the possibility of them being grown artificially so that a scientist may use their organs for other purposes.

To see IVF as aiding and abetting nature is to fail to see it in its total context. Once the complete separation of the unitive and generative aspects of intercourse is accepted, once conception is seen as distinct from sexual intercourse, and the wastage of human embryos seen as ethically acceptable, there is no final objection to surrogate motherhood, cloning, or the complete gestation of the fetus in an artificial womb.

This ought to be clearly understood. The IVF process, like the AI process, begun by using sperm and eggs of a married couple, is now being developed so that unwanted frozen embryos can be implanted in the womb of an 'adopting' parent. Once the process is accepted, what basis is there for objecting to these 'adoptions'? And if the human embryo and fetus are not to be regarded as human persons, what objection can there be to using them for experimental purposes? Indeed, how can an objection be raised to the complete gestation of a child outside of the womb if conception has nothing necessarily to do with the sexual relationship between husband and wife?

If it is suggested that the interests of these children might deter such technological advancements, then we can only point out that such considerations have not so far deterred the medical technologists. Nor indeed have they been deterred by socio-legal complications as to which parents IVF and AID children really belong, and what claim such children might have on their real parents.

There is an alternative to IVF, and that is to further develop micro-surgery techniques to mend damaged Fallopian tubes. This would be entirely acceptable ethically.

One wonders why this technique is not more vigorously pursued.

We have not argued our case because we have no sympathy for infertile couples. It is out of concern for them, for any children they might have from using IVF and AID, and for the good of society as a whole, that these processes have to be carefully evaluated from an ethical point of view.

Once we begin to accept that human life can be destroyed and experimented with, it is difficult to place restraints on those involved. It also means that justice will be increasingly violated as the horizons of the new biomedical technology are expanded.

The natural law, the fund of common human wisdom, is reflected in the great religions of Judaism and Christianity and in the great medical codes. As these religious and natural insights are increasingly abandoned, so too are the great medical codes being modified to allow what was previously disallowed.

A Final Word

When we tamper with human procreation, we tamper with something so precious and essential that we dehumanize that intensely-human experience of love, marriage, a loving sexual relationship, and the begetting of children. Such manipulations are not without consequences. The IVF and AID children are immediate good consequences since human life is a good in itself. But the immediate bad consequences are the unnecessary attack on nature involving the destruction of human persons and the violation of the ethical integrity of natural marriage.

The Jewish and Christian religions warn us that we are not just physical beings. Sex and procreation are not just bodily functions, but have a deep spiritual, sacramental, and psychological significance. A fully healthy person is one who is physically, spiritually, and psychologically healthy. An attack on any one facet of what it means to be human is an attack on the other parts as well, an attack on the whole human person, and ultimately an attack on the family and human society at large.

APPENDIX

ETHICAL CODES*

* The texts of the three Codes, including the introductory remarks, are taken from the 'Appendix — Codes and Statements Related to Medical Ethics' in *Encyclopedia of Bioethics*, Vol.4, 1749; 1764,1765; 1788, 1789.

Declaration of Geneva

World Medical Association
1948

Adopted by the General Assembly of the World Medical Association at Geneva in 1948 and amended by the 22nd World Medical Assembly at Sydney in 1968, the Declaration of Geneva was one of the first and most important actions of the Association. It is a declaration of physicians' dedication to the humanitarian goals of medicine, a declaration that was especially important in view of the medical crimes which had just been committed in Nazi Germany. The Declaration of Geneva was intended to update the Oath of Hippocrates, which was no longer suited to modern conditions. Of interest is the fact that the World Medical Association considered this short declaration to be a more significant statement of medical ethics than the succeeding International Code of Medical Ethics. The words in italics were added to the Declaration in 1968.

At the time of being admitted as a member of the medical profession:

I solemnly pledge myself to consecrate my life to the service of humanity;

I will give to my teachers the respect and gratitude which is their due;

I will practise my profession with conscience and dignity;

The health of my patient will be my first consideration;

I will respect the secrets which are confided in me, *even after the patient has died*;

I will maintain by all the means in my power, the honour and the noble traditions of the medical profession;

My colleagues will be my brothers;

I will not permit considerations of religion, nationality, race, party politics or social standing to intervene between my duty and my patient;

I will maintain the utmost respect for human life from the time of conception; even under threat, I will not use my medical knowledge contrary to the laws of humanity.

I make these promises solemnly, freely and upon my honour.

Nuremberg Code

1946

The Nuremberg Military Tribunal's decision in the case of the United States v. Karl Brandt et al *includes what is now called the Nuremberg Code, a ten-point statement delimiting permissible medical experimentation on human subjects. According to this statement, humane experimentation is justified only if its results benefit society, and it is carried out in accord with basic principles that 'satisfy moral, ethical, and legal concepts'. To some extent, the Nuremberg Code has been superseded by the Declaration of Helsinki as a guide for human experimentation.*

1. The voluntary consent of the human subject is absolutely essential.
This means that the person involved should have legal capacity to give consent; should be so situated as to be able to exercise free power of choice, without the intervention of any element of force, fraud, deceit, duress, over-reaching, or other ulterior form of constraint or coercion; and should have sufficient knowledge and comprehension of the elements of the subject matter involved as to enable him to make an understanding and enlightened decision. This latter element requires that before the acceptance of an affirmative decision by the experimental subject there should be made known to him the nature, duration, and purpose of the experiment; the method and means by which it is to be conducted; all inconveniences and hazards

reasonably to be expected; and the effects upon his health or person which may possibly come from his participation in the experiment.

The duty and responsibility for ascertaining the quality of the consent rests upon each individual who initiates, directs or engages in the experiment. It is a personal duty and responsibility which may not be delegated to another with impunity.

2. The experiment should be such as to yield fruitful results for the good of society, unprocurable by other methods or means of study, and not random and unnecessary in nature.

3. The experiment should be so designed and based on the results of animal experimentation and a knowledge of the natural history of the disease or other problem under study that the anticipated results will justify the performance of the experiment.

4. The experiment should be so conducted as to avoid all unnecessary physical and mental suffering and injury.

5. No experiment should be conducted where there is an *a priori* reason to believe that death or disabling injury will occur; except, perhaps, in those experiments where the experimental physicians also serve as subjects.

6. The degree of risk to be taken should never exceed that determined by the humanitarian importance of the problem to be solved by the experiment.

7. Proper preparations should be made and adequate facilities provided to protect the experimental subject against even remote possibilities of injury, disability, or death.

8. The experiment should be conducted only by scientifically qualified persons. The highest degree of skill and care should be required through all stages of the experiment of those who conduct or engage in the experiment.

9. During the course of the experiment the human subject should be at liberty to bring the experiment to an end if he has reached the physical or mental state where continuation of the experiment seems to him to be impossible.

10. During the course of the experiment the scientist in charge must be prepared to terminate the experiment at any stage, if he has probable cause to believe, in the exercise of the good faith, superior skill and careful judgment required of him that a continuation of the experiment is likely to result in injury, disability, or death to the experimental subject.

International Council of Nurses

Code for Nurses 1973

The International Council of Nurses approved an international code of ethics in 1973, which includes several notable changes over its earlier 1965 code. (1) The 1973 code makes explicit the nurse's responsibility and accountability for nursing care. It deletes the statement found in the 1965 code: 'The nurse is under an obligation to carry out the physician's orders intelligently and loyally', which tended to abrogate the nurse's judgment and personal responsibility. (2) The 1965 code stated that 'the nurse believes in the ... preservation of human life', and added: 'The fundamental responsibility of the nurse is threefold: to conserve life, to alleviate suffering and to promote health'. In its place, the 1973 code points to a fourfold responsibility: 'to promote health, to prevent illness, to restore health and to alleviate suffering', adding that 'respect for life, dignity and rights of man are inherent in nursing'. (3) The traditional concept of the virtuous nurse was expressed in the 1965 code: 'In personal conduct nurses should not knowingly disregard the accepted pattern of behaviour of the community in which they live and work'. In its place, the 1973 code incorporates a statement that places emphasis on the profession: 'The nurse when acting in a professional capacity should at all times maintain standards of personal conduct that would reflect credit upon the profession'.

The fundamental responsibility of the nurse is fourfold: to promote health, to prevent illness, to restore health and to alleviate suffering.

The need for nursing is universal. Inherent in nursing is respect for life, dignity and rights of man. It is unrestricted by considerations of nationality, race, creed, colour, age, sex, politics or social status.

Nurses render health services to the individual, the family and the community, and coordinate their services with those of related groups.

Nurses and People

The nurse's primary responsibility is to those people who require nursing care.

The nurse, in providing care, respects the beliefs, values and customs of the individual.

The nurse holds in confidence personal information and uses judgment in sharing this information.

Nurses and Practice

The nurse carries personal responsibility for nursing practice and for maintaining competence by continual learning.

The nurse maintains the highest standards of nursing care possible within the reality of a specific situation.

The nurse uses judgment in relation to individual competence when accepting and delegating responsibilities.

The nurse when acting in a professional capacity should at all times maintain standards of personal conduct that would reflect credit upon the profession.

Nurses and Society

The nurse shares with other citizens the responsibility for initiating and supporting action to meet the health and social needs of the public.

Nurses and Co-Workers

The nurse sustains a cooperative relationship with co-workers in nursing and other fields.

The nurse takes appropriate action to safeguard the individual when his care is endangered by a co-worker or any other person.

Nurses and the Profession

The nurse plays the major role in determining and implementing desirable standards of nursing practice and nursing education.

The nurse is active in developing a core of professional knowledge.

The nurse, acting through the professional organization, participates in establishing and maintaining equitable social and economic working conditions in nursing.

INDEX